Business Economics in a Rapidly-Changing World

The Evaluation of the Impact of Natural Monopolies on the National Economy and Competitiveness

Business Economics in a Rapidly-Changing World

Additional books in this series can be found on Nova's website under the Series tab.

Additional e-books in this series can be found on Nova's website under the e-book tab.

BUSINESS ECONOMICS IN A RAPIDLY-CHANGING WORLD

THE EVALUATION OF THE IMPACT OF NATURAL MONOPOLIES ON THE NATIONAL ECONOMY AND COMPETITIVENESS

DALIA STREIMIKIENE
AND
AKVILE CIBINSKIENE

nova publishers
New York

NOTICE TO THE READER

Library of Congress Cataloging-in-Publication Data

ISBN: 978-1-63483-790-3

Published by Nova Science Publishers, Inc. † New York

Contents

ABSTRACT

Under conditions of global competitiveness, the impact of natural monopolies to the countries economy and competitiveness became very important. Natural monopolies are essential for existence of industry, business and society as a whole in a country. They mostly represent the energy sector. In recent times such sectors as electricity supply, water supply, natural gas supply and district heating are still representatives of natural monopolies. What can be done to avoid negative impact of natural monopolies to a country‘s competitivenes? What kind of reforms in the energy sector can have a positive impact to a country‘s competitivenes? What kind of changes in natural monopolies are not necessary? This monograph is commitet to try to find the answers to these questions.

The authors of the monograph have studied the issues of natural monopolies impact on the national economy and competitiveness for many years. Dalia Streimikiene has conducted many research in energy sector and owns great knowledge and experience. Akvile Cibinskiene has analyzed natural monopolies price impact to contry‘s competitiveness in her doctoral dissertation. For this monograph these two scientists have joined their experience, knowledge and efforts.

The attempts to reveal accumulated knowledge, insights, calculations and conclusions of the monograph were driven by the long-term institutional economic science research programme “Long-term Competitiveness Challenges of Lithuanian Economy” implemented together with the Research Council of Lithuania, Kaunas University of Technology and other universities of Lithuania.

INTRODUCTION

Professional management, transparency, free competition with private companies, and openness to foreign capital and technology can help state-owned energy companies maximize their potential and deliver optimal long-term dividends for their nations.
(Roger F. Noriega and Felipe Trigos, American Enterprise Institute, 2013)

Relevance of the topic (problem). Under the conditions of the today's globalization, competitiveness is becoming more important aiming to reach a country's economic development or attracting foreign investment. Production factors can be transferred from one country to the other more easily, that is why the importance of higher evaluation of a country's competitiveness arises. This problem is an issue for such a small country as Lithuania.

Natural monopolies represent a country's energy sector; being infrastructure resources of the country, they are important for its economic development, growth and competitiveness. The economic theory and international practice shows, that natural monopolies play an important role in economic development, create a background for the survival and development of a country's' economic subjects.

Scientific problem and level of research done. It is generally recognized that a country's public infrastructure is a set of economic activities, which consists of services provided by natural monopolies. Much empirical research carried out in different countries proves that public infrastructure positively affects a country's economic potential [1, 2, 3].

Concept and features of natural monopolies were analysed by Ely [4, 5], Farrer [6], Baumol [7], Schmalensee [8], Sharkey [9], Berg and Tshirhart [10], Foster [11], Wilson, Capelic [12], Depoorter [13], Joskow [14, 15], Robins [16], Mosca [17], Samuelson [18], Gary, Wolff, Palaniappan [19]. As natural monopolies most often form in the sectors providing public goods and services, regulation of their activities and prices of the products and services they provide, is becoming especially important. In order to protect the public from misuse of this market form, economically reasonable and effective state regulation is needed, which would ensure the provision of their services and economically fairly price them. Features of natural monopolies determine need for it's regulation. In order to avoid monopolistic exploitation of consumers and to institute some kind of competitive conditions there should be regulation of natural monopolies applied. The main reason for regulation of natural monopolies is to ensure a balance of consumers and natural monopolies interests. The regulation must encourage natural monopolies to reduce costs, improve product and service quality, increase the efficiency of investments and to create conditions for competition.

However, the regulation can not be limited to the cost and price, as these goods and services have a feature of mass consumption. Regulation of natural monopolies has to secure the qualitative provision of their services for its customers as well as the provision for new customers. Issues of natural monopoly's regulation where studied by Posner [20, 21], Panzar, Willig [22], Schmalensee [8], Joskow, [23, 14, 15], Berg and Tschirhart [10], Kahn [24], Aktan [25, 26], Samuel [27], Auriol, Picard [28, 29], Chang, Marshruwala [30], Filho [31], Mizutani [32]. Goals for natural monopolies regulation were analysed by Demsetz [33], Comanor, Mitchell [34], Jankauskas [35, 36], Simanaviciene [37], Moreau [38], Menezes [39]. Empirical studies of natural monopolies privatization were undertaken by Vicers, Yarrow [40], Bishop, Kay, Mayer [41].

Many competitiveness assessment models [42, 43] identify factors affecting the country's competitiveness. The competitiveness of the country's natural monopolies may operate through the prices of its goods and services, which affect the factors of competitiveness. Such effects can be treated as indirect. But competitiveness can be affected not only because of the price of natural monopolies services, but also by the existence of natural monopolies goods or services provided in the country, security or their provision and their quality.

There are a lot of studies conducted all over the world dealing with energy markets liberalization especially in electric power sector [44, 45, 46, 47] however all these studies investigated the impact of energy market liberalization on energy prices and didn't take into account other important issues of competitiveness such as environmental sustainability, energy supply security and affordability, job creation etc. Therefore it is important to create a broader conceptual model for investigating the energy market liberalization impacts on competiveness of the country.

Problem of the monograph – how to assess the impact of natural monopolies on countries competitiveness.

Object of the monograph – the impact of natural monopolies on competitiveness.

Aim of the monograph – to develop a model for assessment of impact of natural monopolies on a contry's competitiveness and apply this model in energy sector in order to define the best measures for mitigating negative impacts of monopolies.

To achieve the aim of the monograph following tasks are set:

1. To analyse the concept, features, of natural monopolies monopolies and reasons, goals and means for its regulation.
2. To define the impact of natural monopolies' for the economy through its relation with countries economic subjects.
3. To study the relationship between natural monopolies and country's competitiveness.
4. To review natural monopolies of Lithuanian energy sector and their liberalization processes.
5. To review literature dealing with the impact of energy market reforms on energy prices and competitiveness'.
6. To develop a model for assessment of impact of energy market liberalization on competitiveness of the country.
7. To apply the developed model for assessment of electric power market opening impact on competitiveness of Lithuanian energy sector.
8. To develop policy recommendations based on conducted research.

The ***structure*** of the monograph is determined by its aim and tasks which are dealt with in four chapters. *Chapter 1* is dedicated to set the theoretical background explaining the relationship between natural monopolies and countries competitiveness, analysing concept, features of natural monopolies and reasons for their regulation, as well as it's relation with economic subjects in the country. *Chapter 2* presents the broad review of Lithuanian energy sector natural monopolies in electric power, natural gas and district heat sectors and their liberalization processes and stages of market opening. *Chapter 3* analyses and systematizes results of studies dealing with the impacts of energy market opening on energy prices and competiveness. *Chapter 4* presents the model for multi-criteria assessment of impact of energy market liberalization on competitiveness of the country.

Research methods. The systematic and comparative analysis of scientific literature. Multi-criteria analysis, econometric modelling and statistical data analysis using the software package Microsoft Excel and SPSS.

LIST OF ABBREVIATIONS

CAEM	Center for the Advancement of Energy Markets
CBEM	Common Baltic Electricity Market
CBP	Cost Based Pools
CHP	Combined Heat and Power Production
DH	District Heating
DSO	Distribution System Operator
EAPI	Energy Architecture Performance Index
EC	European Commission
EPPI	Energy Policy Performance Index
EU	European Union
EUETS	European Union Emission Trading Scheme
FSRU	Floating Storage and Regasification Unit
GDP	Gross Domestic Product
GEA	Global Energy Assessment
HFO	Heavy Fuel Oil
HHI	Hirschman-Herfindahl Index
HPP	Hydro Power Plant
HPPS	Hydro Power Pump Storage
IPP	Independent Power Producers
ISO	Independent System Operator
JSC	Joint Stock Company
LCP	Large Combustion Plant
LNG	Liquefied Natural Gas
LMP	Locational Marginal Pricing
MO	Market Operator
NCCPE	National Control Commission for Prices and Energy
NPP	Nuclear Power Plants
OSP	One-sided Pool
OTC	Over the Counter
OXERA	Oxford Economic Research Associates
PBP	Price Based Pools
PP	Power Plant
PPA	Power Purchasing Agreements
PPP	Power Purchasing Parity

PX	Power Exchange
RAB	Regulatory Asset Base
RES	Renewable Energy Sources
RTO	Regional Transmission Organizations
rTPA	Regulated Third Party Access
SB	Single Buyer
SET	Strategic Energy Technology Plan
SOE	State-owned Enterprise
TEN-E	Trans-European Energy Networks
TIC	Technological Innovation Center
TPA	Third Party Access
TPP	Thermal Power Plants
TSO	Transmission System Operator
TSP	Two-sided Pools
VAT	Value Added Tax
WACC	Weighted Average Costs of Capital
WEF	World Economic Forum

Chapter 1

NATURAL MONOPOLIES AND THEIR IMPACT ON COUNTRY'S COMPETITIVENESS

"Is not there a monopoly in the heating sector at the moment? Natural monopoly by itself means that competition here is practically impossible. There are no intentions to lay an alternative heat trail next to the existing one. No one builds alternative pipelines or high voltage electricity lines. This is natural monopoly"
Sekmokas, A. (Minister of Energetics of the Republic of Lithuania, 08.11.2012)

1.1. NATURAL MONOPOLIES

The notion of natural monopoly describes the monopoly, which has some specific features, which exclude it from regular monopolies. The notion of natural monopoly is also a complex dilemma in public politics. To simplify, natural monopoly exists in such field where one company is capable to produce or provide such amount of production that would satisfy all market's demand cheaper than if the same amount was provided by two or more companies.

1.1.1. Consept and Features of Natural Monopolies

Mosca [17] states that even American and Italian marginalists - Cournot [48], Mill [49], Walras [50] and Edgeworth [51] realized that specific companies turn into monopolies due to the sole reason of not having any competition in the given sector. Smith [52] had never used the expression of "natural monopoly," though he provides an explicit description of features of what later was named as natural monopoly: "Some natural productions require such a singularity of soil and situation, that all the land in a great country ... may not be sufficient to supply the effectual demand'; the consequent 'enhancements of the market price are evidently the effect of natural causes which may hinder the effectual demand from being fully supplied, and which may continue therefore, to operate forever' [52].

The earliest clear definition of natural monopoly can be found in the literature, in the outline of Malthus [53] "The Nature of Rent," where natural monopoly is distinguished from artificial (created by regulations) monopoly. For Malthus [53] there are 'peculiar products of the earth… which may be called natural and necessary monopolies‘ [53]. The expression again appears in the work of Bastiat, who writes: “People who class together artificial monopoly and what they call natural monopoly … or quite blind or quite superficial” [54]. Therefore Mosca [17] states that the reason why the adjective was used was to purposefully distinguish natural monopoly from artificial.

It is confirmed by Mill [49], who explains that natural monopolies are created by circumstances and not by regulations [49]. However he does not include examples where the monopoly exists due to the technology, such as supply of gas or water. Thus we can say that Mill [49] was the first one to apply the expression of monopoly arising from the production process itself. Expression of natural monopoly which can be found in France was more precisely applied by Walras, where he states that transportation networks, such as railways, roads and canals form the natural monopoly [55]. Lowry [56] and Sharkey [9] claim that Mill [49] was the first one to use the expression of natural monopoly in 1848.

In the first edition of Samuelson’s book [18] and until the end of 1970 it was considered that natural monopoly emerges in cases when economy of scales exists for the whole demand of the population. There the economy of scales is defined as having high fixed costs and low or none variable costs. Excessive capabilities is an indicator of a natural monopoly mentioned in this book, as the company is producing less than its optimal level of production. Mosca [17] claims that if the demand of market could take more production, variable costs of the company would increase, while the fixed costs would remain unchanged, thus the difference between long term and short term average cost curves would be insignificant. Economy of scale is also considered as an obstacle for entering the market: due to the power of the monopoly, which results from the economy of scale, natural monopoly is viewed as a problem for the market and intervention from the government is needed (in a form of nationalization, regulations or anti-competition).

Kahn [24, 57] defines natural monopoly in this way: natural monopoly is an industry branch which possesses economies of scale in production, i.e., decline in average costs when the volume is increased and which lasts up to the point when one company satisfies the whole demand of the market. Later Baumol [7] expanded the definition of natural monopoly more accurately - by taking into account the nature of production function he distinguished firms into strong and weak monopolies. A company can be called natural monopoly if it can satisfy the whole market’s demand with lower average costs than the costs that two or more companies would incur had they had to produce the same quantity of production. Baumol [7] provided a modern approach on defining the natural monopoly. In a sector where one company can satisfy market’s demand with lower unit costs than of two or more companies (cost function sub additive) or in a sector where new companies are not “naturally” attracted and would not be able to survive even without rough measures of existing monopoly (sustainability of the monopoly), the company can be defined as natural monopoly.

It is generally approved that country’s public infrastructure as a whole (e.g., roads and waterways) is the basis for economic activities. The majority of infrastructure’s elements are natural monopolies. Empirical studies performed internationally suggest that public infrastructure positively affects country’s production potential [1, 2, 3]. Filho [31] states, that economic history, both in developing and developed countries, shows that the effects of monopoly power are much more pervasive than just the consumer-producer relationship, affecting development patterns and even distribution patterns in society, so it can also be attributed to natural monopolies.

Baumol [7] formulated the basis for the definition of natural monopoly for most of regulative politics and for the majority of economic research in infrastructure sectors. Jamison [58] notes that current examples of political decisions, which are based on the analysis of Baumol [7], include the Ministry of Commerce of New Zealand in its research on utility services' market structure and the bureau of Production economics of Australia in its analysis on infrastructure pricing cariied out in the year 1995. Economic research in which the definition of Baumol [7] was applied directly can be found in the works of Evans and Heckman [59, 60], Shin and Ying [61], Armstrong and Leppel [62], Tschirhart [63], Newbery [64] and others.

The features of natural monopoly are discussed in the economic studies since 1848, started by Mill [49]. In general, some of these features are interconnected with each other. Here the features of natural monopoly and their evolution will be discussed.

If we analyze the features of natural monopoly, it is obvious, that natural monopoly should be characterized by the features of regular monopoly as well. Usually monopoly is characterized by:

- one seller and large number of buyers;
- no close substitutes;
- strong barriers to the entry into the industry.

This list of monopoly features can be expanded by other features, which more deeply describe monopoly and explain above listed characteristics: nature of demand curve (demand for monopoly production is the whole markets demand); specialized information; abnormal profit; the seller's control over the prices; consumers don't have perfect information, etc.

Most of the economists define natural monopolies in the same way, stressing low average and marginal costs, high fixed costs and low variable costs, high initial investments and production with economies of scale. Schmalensee [8] claims that if distribution center has declining average distribution costs, such distribution system is a natural monopoly. The existence of networks, their importance and association with natural monopolies were mentioned by Farrer [6], De Viti de Marco [65], Mosca [17]. American economists Lowry [56], Sharkey [9] claim that the activities of natural monopolies had been discussed hundred years ago. Ely [4] distinguishes natural monopoly due to some specific characteristics that it has. Marshal [66] notes specific monopolistic industries that cannot be separated. The fact that the main characteristics which define natural monopoly had been developing over time is noted by Kahn [24, 67, 68], Schmalensee [8], Baumol, Panzar and Willig [69], Laffont and Tirole [70, 71], Armstrong, Cowan and Vickers [72]. These authors together with Samuelson [18] associated natural monopoly with declining average costs. Natural monopoly's ability to apply different tariffs for provided services (e.g., day and night) was analyzed by Baumol [7], Baumol, Bailey and Willig [73], and Panzar ir Willig [22]. Baumol [7] stressed the cost function sub additive of economies of scale. Becker [74] claimed that natural monopoly is just a temporary form of the market, while Wilson, Capelic [12] note that the number of natural monopolies decreased due to technological innovations.

Samuelson [18] theory regarding production economies of scale, which is related to high fixed costs and low variable costs that are related to natural monopoly, had been criticized. The most of relevant critique appeared in the articles released after 1977, dealing with natural monopoly in multiple output production – and from the theory of contestable markets. It caused a significant change in the definition of natural monopoly. Later on natural monopoly was used to describe sub aditivity of a cost function (productions costs are lower if one company produces everything) and sustainability (entry to market is unprofitable). Mosca [17] claims that this theory not only demonstrates that economies of scale do not help in defining natural monopoly, but also that by itself it is not an entry barrier: to block the entry, economy of scale has to be associated with high initial costs (sunk cost).

Ely [4] defines natural monopoly as a company which is a monopoly due to the specific characteristics associated with these monopolies and proceeds by listing them: railways, telegraph, telephones, channels, reclamation facilities, ports, gas supply, vehicle roads' network and others. According to Mosca [17] it is interesting that the Marshal suggested a different definition for companies from this "class," which are often called monopolies, but which rather can be better described as indivisible industries [66].

The expression of sub additivity is the exact mathematical explanation of natural monopoly, which was explicitly described by Baumol [7]. Depoorter [13] stressed that there is a close relation between the production economies of scale and sub additivity. A one-product companies' economy of scale is sufficient, though not an obligatory condition for natural monopoly. Baumol [7] suggests that from scientific disputes it seems that the monopoly is "natural" when it can achieve the result with lower social costs and this can be done when economy of scale occurs. Economy of scale is neither obligatory nor sufficient for monopoly to make it the cheapest production organization form.

Baumol [7] defines strict and general cost function subadditivity in the following way. Cost function C(y) is strict and generally sub additive, if

$$C(y1 + \cdots + ym) < C(y1) + \cdots + C(ym) \tag{1}$$

Product N=1,....N if any m production vector y1...ym , for any product N is equal.

It is a clearly mandatory and sufficient condition for natural monopoly for any combination of goods in industry, when producing all products N. Sub additive means that it is always cheaper to have one company for production rather than few firms providing this combination of goods and vice versa [7].

When the average production costs for the company decline when the production volume is increasing, its production technology is considered as having characteristics of production of economy of scale. Natural monopoly cannot be created, but rather the company becomes into it due to its specific business process, with sufficient level of technology, due to special technical conditions for business organization. As a result of the improvement in technology, one day natural monopoly can become into a competitive industry sector. The best example in this case is the telephone network providers. Becker [74] considers monopoly to be a temporary state of the market. Research shows that in the future, due to improving technology, natural monopolies can become into a competitive sector, however as long as there is at least one natural monopoly, there is a need to perform an analysis on its economic activity.

Farrer [6], mentioned in the work of Sharkey [9] describes the provided services of natural monopolies as necessary, it means that the services are provided for a high number of users. He also claims that the production process of natural monopoly requires high capital costs. Farrer [6] says that in a natural monopoly the goods and services have to be produced and provided in places that are very favorable for the specific activity. This aspect can be applied for goods and services that are related to natural resources, however nowadays especially due to the improvement in technology, this aspect is no longer exceptional to describe a natural monopoly. Moreover, Farrer [6] believes that goods and services coming from natural monopolies should have a direct connection with the customers. This indicator is typical when distributing the services of natural monopolies through particular networks (electric power, water, etc.) Together with the improvement in technology this aspect also became less exceptional, as some services of natural monopolies can be supplied for new technologies indirectly, remotely (e.g., wireless phone connection). Ely [5] mentioned Sharkey [9] while analyzing natural monopolies always emphasizes that the relation between fixed and variable costs has to be large. It means that fixed costs are significantly higher than the variable costs.

Mosca [17] claims that natural monopolies usually appear in two production types: the first is defined by its necessity for a large infrastructure to be able to launch its activity, for instance transportation networks and some specific utility services; the second due to the network existence effect.

Telecommunications industry, supply of electric power and water are often provided as examples of natural monopolies. These sectors encounter relatively high fixed costs. Costs to produce even a marginal volume are high. On the other hand if the initial investment is already done, the average cost decreases with every additional unit of output. Depoorter [13] claims that competition in these industry sectors can be described as socially unwanted, as high number of companies would duplicate the capital equipment. Classical example would be two identical companies which provide water and each of them separately setting an own underground pipeline. It is publicly known for all economists that water and wastewater systems are natural monopolies and they cannot compete in a regular way. The users, who are provided with underground pipelines, which required high capital investments, which are connected with equipment that can be characterized as having an economy of scale (e.g., dams and reservoirs, water and wastewater cleaning equipment) cannot stop buying from ineffective or low-quality service provider. Gary, Wolff, Palaniappan [19] note that natural monopolies cannot compete for the users in a regular way, as the users are incapable of easily churning from the supplier.

Smith [52] even in those times used the term on natural monopoly to associate the water supply to a big city. After him, Mill explained in which sectors production in scale is more beneficial than in low volumes by providing post, water and gas supply examples [49]. Mill a contemporary of French origin [49], Dupuit [75, 76] distinguishes another situation of natural monopoly, i.e., transportation networks, which he calls "de facto" monopolies. According to him, it is impossible for a new company to enter the market of transportation networks, as the requirement for high capital cannot be applied for a higher number of businessman than it is provided; the new company attracts customers from the monopolist and the revenue will not cover the fixed expenses for both of the companies. And the first business exploits better conditions by leaving worse ones for new entrants. Briefly: instead of one good business we will have two bad ones [75]. According to Walras [50], the competition cannot exist as the nationalization of land required for communication networks can be decided only by the government. Walras [50] writes: "implementation of second water or gas system in a city which already has one of these, which can satisfy the demand or building second roads network in a country which already has one sufficient for communication would be an absurd way of achieving economy" [50]. For De Viti de Marco [65] Telephones industry looks like monopoly not only because of the cost aspects but also due to the network effect. Classical examples of natural monopolies on a federal level are the supply of electric power, oil, gas, also railroads and separate telecommunication sub-sectors. On a regional level these are utility services, including the heating, drainage and water supply systems, etc.). Wilson, Capelic [12] mentioned that recently in most of the countries the level of state regulative sphere became significantly lower due to technological innovations and due to a new approach to the way how markets form and are regulated.

After analyzing the works of Farrer [6], Ely [4, 5], Sharkey [9], Berg and Tshirhart [77], Train [78], Schmalensee [18], Foster [11], Joskow [14, 15], Robins [16], Baumol [7], Depoorter [13], Mosca [17], Samuelson [18], Gary et al. [19], Wilson, Capelic [12], who analyzed the activities of natural monopolies, the following features that describe natural monopolies can be concluded:

1. one supplier of good or service;
2. goods or services are provided for a high number of users;
3. company's goods or services have no close substitutes;
4. high sunk costs;
5. cost function subaditivity;
6. declining average costs (economy of scale in production).

By combining the first two features of natural monopoly we can claim that demand for its goods and services is inelastic, as the amount of consumption will not change significantly after a change in the price due to the lack of close substitutes.

When comparing these characteristics of natural monopoly with the characteristics of monopoly it is worth noticing that the characteristics of natural monopoly do not include market entry and exit obstacles. Theoretically, they should not exist in the case of natural monopoly, as the extra-ordinance of natural monopoly is created by conditions, in which competition is economically unbeneficial and legal obstacles are unnecessary.

It is possible that after reaching a monopolistic position, a company would use its dominating conditions in the market to achieve higher profit. Natural monopolies which work in this way create market imperfections.

We start with Mill who claims that "When… actually a business of public importance can be favorably developed in a scale which would make… the competition… unreal… it is better to consider it as a public function [49]. As it is mentioned by Ekelund and Herber, he offers: "decentralized supply of services on municipalities' level on country's property and managed by locally elected Council. It is widely known that Dupuit was a supporter of a free market and despite that he proved that as the transportation network is a monopoly, a private owner of the monopoly can abuse his position; hence Dupuit was for public intervention: "National control of any sector" as he says "is an exception which has to be always considered with special conditions. Now here (transportation network, water supply, lighting, heating) we have monopoly conditions [75].

The principle of "Competition for the Field," proposed by an English reformat Edvin Chadwick [79], is widely recognized: the government can regulate the entry to natural monopoly's market with competitive negotiations for the price; this principle means that natural monopolies are nationalized and owned by private capital, though some level of regulations is always needed. Walras [50] also wanted the government to intervene in to railways either by directly controlling or regulating them. The importance of nationalization of railways is highly expressed by Ely [80, 81], while Hadley finds a necessity for governmental regulations in a complex controlling objective "abusing the power of monopoly without destroying the industry" [82] and Adams [83] observe restored social harmony while expanding the responsibilities for the state in the "industries of increasing revenues."

To the desire to incite productive and allocative efficiency, there may be non-economic reasons to impose regulation on a network industry. Attention should be paid to public safety, continuity of supply, public service obligations, environmental externalities and information disclosure.

Agrell and Bogetoft [84] indicate that Friedman [85] clearly states that a natural monopoly per se does not necessitate a legal monopoly; it is merely a transient phase in the technological development.

Gary et al. [19] underlines, that in spite of everything, competition is still possible, e.g., in Great Britain the limited competition system is being tested, where big water consumers can purchase the bigger part of the consumer water from different bulk suppliers, who supply water through regulated monopoly's supply companies. Though successful, the system is only partly competitive as the customers cannot individually control the quality of water they purchase – they are restricted by the quality of water which is supplied for their neighbors via the pipeline by the general supplier.

1.1.2. Reasons, Goals and Means for Regulation of Natural Monopolies

Uekusa [86, 87] states that regulation is defined as legally justified actions by governments to limit or control the behaviors of individuals and firms. Mizutani [32] underlines that Economic theory of regulation has the idea that regulation is subject to economic laws. In the economic terms vocabulary, the definition of state regulation is presented as: "state regulation – the sum of state's means, by which it is pursued to satisfy the interests of different groups and to protect the interest of specific society's members, correct so called market imperfections and achieve new objectives. State regulations means include price regulations, market monitoring, anti-monopolistic regulations, taxation and a number of other interventions into the market. "It is a general definition of regulations. Konig and Taylor [88] claim that in wider terms, regulating can be defined as laws of all forms. Simanaviciene [37] states that by using regulative means the state tries to create stable economic and social conditions for the development of the economy, which would allow to ensure business conditions, diminish negative impact for the environment and society that comes from the production. By using them it is possible to regulate collection of taxes, property protection, provide information for economic subjects. Regulation can help to provide aid, enhance the development of science and technics, and support economic freedom and initiatives. This is general business regulation, applied for all economic subjects, which regulates the organization of companies' activities, tax payments and others.

Noll [89] proposes that regulation was justified by particular conditions of scale and scope for what were called "infrastructure" or "public utilities" and later "network" industries. They were considered as natural monopolies, a case of market failure. Berg [90] notices that infrastructure sectors are too visible and politically sensitive to be relegated to or left alone by legislative and executive branches of government. Most of the natural monopolies provide infrastructure goods or services. Kerf, David Gray, Taylor [91] also emphasize that regulation has always been closely tied to natural monopolies. When such services are provided by public entities, many regulatory issues become immaterial. Effective regulation is most important for the creation of a competitive and incentive-based climate for the private provision of infrastructure services. Regulatory improvements provide a better operating regime for existing facilities or components and emerge in response to technological developments that provide new options and structures for the provision of infrastructure services. Regulation of a natural monopoly is intended to eliminate, stamp or allocate economic rents. Mizutani [32] emphasizes as well, that regulation is also justified for reasons related to value judgment, especially with basic public utility services, which affect many economic activities. Because these services are essential to daily life, regulation is generally justified as necessary to achieve the following goals: economic stability, income redistribution, provision of merit goods, civil minimum, promotion of regional balance, and so on. Mizutani [32] also emphasizes, that the reason for government involvement in the market is related to the phenomenon of natural monopoly. In essence, under the monopoly provision, socially optimal marginal cost pricing must be practiced. Without this regulation, the quantity of services provided is less and the price is higher than in the optimal case. Waterson [55] also emphasizes that a government can influence private company plans in a variety of ways, and thus achieve objectives which are essentially the same as those that could be reached by private company itself. Next argument for state control is that it facilitates income redistributional means. It may be considered desirable to have universal access to basic utilities and essential services.

One of government‘s roles is to help solve problems due to shortcomings in the market mechanism. Mizutani [32] proposes, that such problems can in general be classified into two groups. The first group contains concerns to market failure issues, for example market failure due to natural monopoly, public goods, externalities, imperfect information and so on. These are the cases, where the market cannot secure efficient resource allocation and then government involvement is justified. The second group contains problems, related to value judgment. As example it could be fairness of redistribution, economic stability, provision of merit goods, civil minimum, regional balance, etc. It is assumed justifiable that government be involved in the market to solve these problems.

Government‘s involvement in the market system is justified as necessary to improve problems that the market cannot solve (matters related to market failures and value judgments). Among several reasons for the government to play a role in the market, the following are seen important and excluded by Mizutani [32]:

1. to provide public goods;
2. to ameliorate the problem of natural monopolies;
3. to protect public interests.

Conducted research shows that in foreign and Lithuanian scientific literature which analyzes the regulation of natural monopolies, the definition of regulation itself is defined similarly, however foreign authors call it as just “regulation” or “governmental regulation,” while in the works of Lithuanian authors it is defined as “state regulation.” The state does not execute the regulation function, as this function is performed by state management institutions, with a more accurate definition of this regulation – governmental regulation.

The activity of regulation systems is economically imperative, therefore it has to be effective. Network (natural monopoly) services constitute a large fraction of the final sum for the users and more competitive segments of energy market depend on the activities of these networks, as stressed by Joskow [92]. One strong argument for state control raised by Waterson [55] is that it facilitates economic planning of key sectors of the economy, such as state ownership of coal, gas and electric power industries may facilitate the planning of the energy sector. Bergara, Henisz, Spiller [93] stress electric power companies and identify three features of electric power sector that make the activities of this sector so considerable. First, economies of scale limit the number of suppliers in each region. Second, technology requires huge sunk costs. And finally, production is consumed massively. Each of these features provides implications for the government to behave opportunistically. According to Haney, Pollitt [131], due to that it is highly important to determine the effectiveness of electric power regulation. Waterson [55] also stresses that the government is in a position to regulate, if ministers gain utility in proportion to the size of resources they have to control, by emphasizing that effective regulation also requires sufficient amount of resources. Inappropriate regulation carries considerable costs for the governments, for the firms and for the economy as a whole.

Mizutani [32] stresses that political interference might be a reason for inefficiency. While politics is necessary to signal citizens' wishes, too much political interference in a public corporation can hinder its healthy management. Posner [94] expanded the theory of regulation by claiming that politicians also use regulation to achieve support from other affected groups, specifically consumer groups and some production factors (e.g., workforce). It is executed through a regulated pricing structure, through cross-subsidies. Waterson [55] also noted that regulation is often a political question. Fama [95] excludes another strand to the Economic theory of regulation, which is that once the agency has an objective, those charged with carrying out the policies do so to the best of their ability. He states that this is not because they wish to act in the public interest as exemplified in the values of their political masters, but rather because they wish to succeed in their careers and the way to do so is to appear efficient. This is rather strict version of the managerial labor market theory. Stigler [96] claims that politicians can apply regulation for votes and money. Companies also need regulation to enhance their profits. It can be done in few different ways. For instance by assigning the taxes to others and applying processes to provide companies with subsidies; increasing market entry costs; controlling the producers of close substitute goods; regulating prices; eliminating the competition in prices in a specific sector. Stigler [96] explained that this process is viable as the benefits are huge and concentrated in few firms and politicians, the costs are low bus widely diversified across consumers/voters. Though regulation costs are bigger than the benefit, the regulation can still be viewed as a result of incapability or high costs for users/voters, to organize a resistance for it. Mizutani [32] points that while regulation and public involvement can be justified as necessary from the point of view of value judgments, in reality there are many individuals with different values. He stresses that because it is often difficult to find common ground, unfortunately policy making is often hindered by political conflict.

Stigler's [96] article deeply analyzed "Economic Theory of Regulation." Stigler treated regulation as an instrument by incumbent firms to prevent entry by newcomers. In his paper, regulation is analyzed as the result of demand for regulation by firms lobbying Government to protect their existing rents, and of supply of regulation by Politicians interested in maximizing their utility function through votes and campaign contributions [97].

It is well known that public property is inefficient, as it motivates governments to preserve or subsidize unprofitable companies. Kornai [98] was the first person to call such ineffectiveness as "soft budget constraint." This definition explains plenty of ineffectivenesses that emerge in social economics, such as shortages or low price response. As less effective companies can apply for governmental subsidies, they lack financial discipline for effective management. Mizutani [32] underlines that availability of subsidies creates cost inefficiency by lowering managerial incentive to improve performance. Subsidized public corporations tend to incur higher costs than non-subsidized corporations. He also underlines that public corporations were criticized because of their inefficient management, which led to enormous deficits. For similar reasons, soft budget constraints also create inefficiency in organizations. The transition from a public to a private property is therefore often called a measure of poor performing public companies [99, 100].

Mizutani [32] states, that public goods are provided, in general, by the public sector, because these goods and services are considered to be difficult for the market to provide due to their "non-rivalry in consumption" and "non-excludability" nature. He also underlines, that a public provision of services is in general recognized as less efficient than a provision of the same services by private company under the same conditions. It means that a public corporation incurs higher costs than a private company when the same level of output service is produced. However, it is not necessarily true that a public corporation is always inefficient. Kagami, Tsuji [101] also underline, that state owned enterprises generally are run by the public sector because of market failures related to economies of scale, externalities and public goods. Depoorter [13] proposes, that half a century ago it was believed that public ownership of companies is the best solution for such market imperfections as monopoly. According to Mizutani [32] public corporation's inefficiency is due to its ambiguous goal, so the purpose of a public corporation is not to pursue profits, but to address social interests, which are not always equivalent to social benefits. A public corporation continues providing services, even when its goals are unclear. On the other hand, as a private company's existence depends on the generation of profits, efficient management of the public corporation is required. Public corporations do not face a pressure from the capital market. Even if the management of a public corporation is not well organized, its citizen owners are so widely dispersed as to have little influence on management, a situation which exacerbates the public corporation's lack of efficiency. Another matter of public ownership is the lack of governmental economic orientation. Kornai and Weibull [102], Shleifer and Vishny [103] demonstrate "paternalistic" or political behavior in the way they seek to protect the labor force; Shapiro and Willig [104] portray the government as malicious. Their main conclusion is that privatization improves company's internal effectiveness. Overview of an empirical study of 65 companies by Megginson and Netter [105] confirms that private companies generally operate more productively and profitably than state agents. However in sectors with increasing revenues, the benefits of effectiveness are not automatically transposed for the customers. The change in property structure does not resolve the lack of competitive pressure. There are reasons in favor of public provision. One of them is that the public sector is presumably pursuing the public interest, according to OECD [128]. In general, private companies are considered as pursuing profits, an activity not always beneficial to the public, whose interests are broader than simply seeking profit, assumes Mizutani [32].

Economic efficiency is achieved when the resources are allocated in a way for the company to achieve the highest possible net benefits by using them. In competitive market it is possible to achieve Pareto optimum, when it becomes impossible to increase the benefit received by any party without decreasing the benefits received by any other party. In order to allocate the resources effectively it is necessary to create conditions for competition to exist. When the market is competitive, uninterrupted allocation of resources in the market can create higher economic wellbeing than the one which would be achieved if the government planned the allocation, however there are specific circumstances under which the competition is not always possible and thus natural monopolies emerge. In this case, regulation is undertaken in order to achieve effective economic activities. Monopolies are inefficient relative to competitive firms since it is more difficult for the owners of monopolies to identify and reward good performance versus good luck, states Williamson, Mumssen [107]. The absence of a competitive benchmark makes it more difficult to motivate efficiency via performance incentives for monopolies. Depoorter [13] proposes, that generally in a competitive market companies are interested in lowering their costs to obtain higher profits by maintaining the same selling price or for the price between the old price and the new costs. An objective to survive in such market motivates the company to lower its costs.

Waterson [55] also underlines, that it is commonly predicted, that perfect competition leads to efficiency. In case of perfect competition, the price for goods is equal to marginal costs, as companies participate in the game of competitive prices. In case of monopoly, the profit-seeking behavior of the existing company will raise the price for consumers and reduce production volumes. Therefore, monopolistic price setting leads to transition of benefit from the customer to the producer. In case the price is set high enough, pursuant to obtain higher profits for the monopoly, a part of potential customers will be undermined, as they will not be able to afford themselves to purchase the product for the higher (wisely set) price. Thus, as underlined by Depoorter [13], monopoly leads to dead weight losses: a part of additional benefit for the user, which the monopolist cannot obtain, and which is lost by the users. As a result of the monopoly price setting, these customers might be forced to consume more expensive substitutes or less relevant products, though public resources would be better used for producing more of the monopolistic product. Therefore Depoorter [13] stresses that the argument of negative monopoly's impact for the wellbeing of the economy was widely discussed in many debates. According to Pajarskas [108], the state has to create the best possible conditions for private initiatives to function, maintain the system under competitive condition, and control the activity which is not in favor of fair competition. In its anti-monopolistic policy, the state has to weaken detrimental monopoly's impact for the competition and also has to seek for wise competition. Private monopolists can set high prices that are higher than the costs with a reason to earn higher profits.

Depoorter [13] raises a question whether the condition of natural monopoly raises a question: if internal efficiency, cost optimization can be achieved with the presence of natural monopoly? Does the monopolistic company use its resources in the best possible way with current technology? Contemporary anti-monopolistic economists used a term "X inefficiency" to describe internal losses that prevail when the company obtains monopolistic power and is not forced by the competitors to maintain their costs competitively low. Often cited examples are US Steel, General Motors, Sears, IBM and American Airlines. These huge companies, which dominated in their sectors, were accused for becoming the victims of their own inefficiency [109]. Empirical data shows that the sum earned by enhancing the X-inefficiency of is significant [110].

In case of natural monopoly, when the company, which is busy with some specific "universal service" requirements, is unprotected from price competition and free market entry for competitors, it might not be able to protect its position in the market, as potential competitors will enter these segments of the market with prices which would be lower than the costs. The collection of yield happens when the supplier concentrates in those market segments, where the costs of supply are the lowest, e.g., due to geographical reasons, as noted by Zupan [111]. Market's segment can be so unprofitable that no private company would not want or would not be able to seize it. This situation is portrayed in the best way in secondary roads or electrification projects in low-density territories. Public entity is then a natural opportunity, with a condition that the opportunity costs of public funds are not too high. In other case the service is not provided. Empirical studies confirm these results.

Waterson [55] emphasizes that a very common view on regulation is the theory of public interest. The government responds to market imperfections according with the extent of imperfection. Industries, which only occasionally are problematic, would not be subject to continual regulation. Industries which, because of the extent of their natural monopolies and their size, would make a significant influence on everyday life, would be controlled more directly. In the public interest view, regulators perform their allotted tasks and this, presumably, maximizes their utility. From the societal point of view, the public interest theory presents a perfection. The only question left is the extent to which corrective means should be carried out, and this can be solved by equating marginal benefits with marginal costs.

According to the theory of economic regulation, the existence of so-called "natural monopolies" (or market failures) is the central justification of choice for regulation itself. Such a justification for regulation is unsustainable, both for the reasons it evokes and the elements that constitute it, states Filho [31]. These are the sectors in which for various reasons of public order, entry and permanence are controlled. The government, in order to ensure the security as well as the physical and economic integrity of its individuals (users, future users or consumers) establishes conditions to entry and permanence in the market, setting rules of behavior. Network industries, which often owe the features of natural monopolies, are characterized by long-lived investments and increasing returns to scale. This raises two related concerns – protection of consumers from monopoly abuse and protection of investors from opportunistic behavior by governments. Williamson, Mumssen [107] exclude following concerns which arise in relation to network industries:

1. high costs due to inefficiency (productive inefficiency);
2. reduced supply and excessive prices (allocative inefficiency);
3. impacts on other producers (allocative & dynamic efficiency);
4. inappropriate service quality (though this concern primarily relates to a price constrained monopolist who may provide service quality below customers' willingness to pay, and not to monopoly per se); and
5. distributional concerns (concern over the distribution of rents between customers and owners, and/or between prices charged to different groups of customers).

Monopolies decrease supply and increase prices not just for the final consumers, but also to other firms. By pricing above the level required for cost recovery a network industry reduces demand, and leaves customers who would be willing to purchase their output at cost reflective prices with unmet demand, explains Williamson, Mumssen [107]. Overall economic welfare is therefore reduced.

If the lowest possible production costs is a social goal, then it should be one company from that specific sector. In this way, the exploitation of limited public resources would be minimized. But if there is only one company there cannot be competition, which otherwise would facilitate effective distribution of resources for the society. Thus a company, which is natural monopoly, is a candidate for regulation of prices and entry to the market, which can substitute competition, as underlined by Berg, Tshirhart [77]. They claim that if the natural monopoly is not sustainable, then prices which hinder entry to the market do not exist. Despite its cost advantage over potential new participants in the market, the monopolist cannot find a compilation of prices, which would hinder the entry for producers with higher costs. Since natural monopoly cannot protect itself, it needs regulative protection against new market entrants, which would ensure that the products reach the society with the lowest possible costs. If natural monopoly is protected, then the customers have to be protected from high prices, which have to be set by the regulator. However, in order to make the market more competitive, Depoorter [13] emphasizes that different conditions are necessary. The most important of them is absence of market entry obstacles. Perfect competition markets are based on free market entry.

Incentives to skimp on quality arise when prices are held below monopoly levels since a reduction in quality of service is tantamount to an increase in price. This is underlined by Williamson, Mumssen [107]. The problem of under-provision of service quality is therefore something that must be addressed under regulation, but arises principally because regulation seeks to constrain prices, rather than as a consequence of monopoly per se.

Governmental intervention into the market is caused by the fact that markets do have failures, which are related to imperfect market's structure or social and political reasons. Parker [112] distinguishes these main circumstances, under which it is impossible to achieve economic benefits:

- **External effect:** when activity related to consumption or production causes indirect effect on other activity spheres, which cannot be directly seen in market prices (e.g., production process can soile the environment, which is a negative impact for the society).
- **Public goods:** goods and services, which are consumed by the user without reducing the opportunities for another user to consume the very same goods and services and none of the users have obstacles to consume this product or service. It means that marginal supply enhancement costs are equal to zero or insignificant, and there is no reason to restrict the supply of the good or service. Public goods are associated with non-exclusivity (if the public good is produced, everyone has equal opportunities to consume it) and uncompetitive consumption (consumption of one user does not restrict the consumption of other users) conditions.
- **Merit and demerit goods:** there are few types of goods or services which should not be restricted from those who wish and can afford to obtain them. Merit goods include

education, utility services and healthcare. Demerit goods – drugs, tobacco and alcohol, which should be prohibited or limited by regulation or taxation.

- **Inexplicit information:** resources in the market are distributed inefficiently when there is not enough information. The best functioning market can be achieved when customers and producers have sufficient amount of information.
- **Monopoly:** markets cannot compete. Competition and anti-monopolistic laws and economic regulation of natural monopolies are applied to protect customers from monopolistic prices, bad quality services and cartel agreements.

However when it comes to defining whether regulation is justifiable, additional information is needed: first, are there any obstacles to enter the market of regulating company, and second, is natural monopoly sustainable, as suggested by Berg, Tshirhart [10]. If there are market entry barriers, which can be a result of high sink cost that are needed for the company to start the production, then regulation can be justified. In this case there are clearly no competing powers and natural monopolist could increase its prices and produce lower amounts without regulation than what are the social needs for price and quantity. To avoid this situation, the regulator can set the prices which would maximize social utility with an assumption that the company would reach the break-even point. Berg, Tshirhart [10] also underlines that if there are no market entry barriers, there is no need for regulation if the natural monopoly market is contestable. The market is contestable if the entry to the market and exit from the market for other companies is free of charge. If the market of natural monopolist is contestable, the danger of new market entrants outweighs the competition, hence regulation is not needed.

Whether the regulation is necessary in contestable markets depends on, as proposed by Berg, Tshirhart [10], whether natural monopoly is sustainable. A sustainable natural monopoly will be able to set prices which will hinder new market entrants. When setting sustainable prices, natural monopolist uses its low cost structure in order to repel potential new market entrants, whose costs are higher or at least the same. At the same time, natural monopolist cannot increase his prices to the point where he would earn economic profit, as in this way new market entrants would be attracted to set lower prices in one or more markets and resell them in these markets from natural monopolist. Regulation is not necessary, as natural monopolist is regulated by the market powers. According to Depoorter [13], market contestability would be a total loss for the regulation, as without regulation monopoly would achieve price efficiency. In other words, regulators should motivate, not repel new entrants to the market of the monopoly.

Regulation does not aim at eliminating market failure, but rather at establishing a multitude of choices and vast access to economic knowledge, which will never occur in a free market. Filho [31] states that regulatory guarantee of alternative networks is then a paramount. If the regulation is at the origin of economic dominance (as a result of specific political decisions taken at the moment of privatization, for example) it must be the source of the structural order of monopolistic activity. This structural order, of monopoly according to Filho [66] is also hereby demanded for social reasons. As elsewhere demonstrated, the monopolization by private individuals or essential services, such as most utilities sectors, is one of the main factors, especially in developing countries, of the escalation of the triple draining phenomenon, emphasizes Filho [31].

In 1970s the reasons to regulate natural monopolies' prices and joining the networks were actively researched by Winston [113]. Regulation of some industry sectors was completely cancelled. Other regulated sectors had been restructured by facilitating competition in potentially competitive segments and new regulative mechanisms were applied for the main segments of the sectors, which maintained the features of natural monopolies [113, 114]. Theoretical and practical questions of regulating natural monopolies were discussed in the works of Berg and Tschirhart [10], Joskow [14, 15, 23], Panzar and Willig [22], Posner [20, 21], Kahn [24, 57], Schmalensee [8], Aktan [25, 26], Chang, Mashruwala [30], Auriol, Picard [28, 29], Samuel [27]. Reasons for the application of regulation was the study object of Demsetz [33], Comanor, Mitchell [34]. The activities of regulated companies had been analyzed by Averch and Johnson [115], Tamonis, Kveselis, Tutlyte [116]. Williamson, Mumssen [107] state that the objectives and practice of regulation around the world suggest that distributional concerns may dominate in terms of the underlying motivation for and conduct of, economic regulation. They propose, that pressure for regulation may therefore prove irresistible, whether or not net economic gains are anticipated. Regulations are often classified into two groups: economic regulation and social regulation. There are three goals of economic regulation: control companies 'behavior by limiting price, service quantity and the number of firms in the market; to correct inefficiency due to resource allocation in the market; and protect consumers from unfairness. The goals of social regulation are: to control firm's behavior seeking to protect employees from harmful working conditions; to maintain a good environment; to protect against natural disasters. Regulations and their relation with market failures is studied by Uekusa [87] and it shows that purpose of economic regulation is mainly to resolve problems stemming from natural monopoly and imperfect information and the purpose of social regulation is to resolve issues related to external diseconomies and demerit goods. Because public utility industries have characteristics of natural monopolies, entry into and exit from the market have been strictly regulated emphasizes Mizutani [133]. The entry regulation limits the number of firms in the market to maintain socially desirable results or to protect against destructive competition. Exit regulation makes existing firms to provide services to users continuously, who would be adversely affected if service providers were freely allowed to exit the market.

According to Wilson, Capelic [12], economic regulation is necessary, to:

- ensure the interests' balance between the users (justifiable price) and regulated companies (financial results that are attractive for the creditors and new investors);
- ensure that the price structure is based on fair and effective allocation of costs for different types of users;
- motivate companies to lower their costs and excessive amount of employees, enhance the service quality, enhance the effectiveness of investments, etc.;
- create competitive conditions.

An analysis conducted by Berg, Tshirhart [77] reveals that technological changes can transform potentially competitive industry into natural monopoly and vice versa. Whether is an industry natural monopoly or not, is in commutable fact. Technology and demand are the most important influencers and if they change, industry organization can also be changed. Industries, which used to be natural monopolies can become competitive and some new industries may become natural monopolies, proposes Waterson [55] as well. A. Marshall [66] in his book "The Principles of Economics" analyzes the impact of "increasing revenues" wen regulating monopolies and oligopolies, however he skeptically looks at the fact that pure monopolies can survive for a long period of time or set profit-generating prices, which are higher than the market prices.

After analyzing the assumptions for natural monopoles' regulation it is obvious that they emerge from the features of natural monopolies. As there is only one supplier of the good or service and these goods or services are provided (maybe even necessary) for a big number of users and they do not have close substitutes, a need arises to regulate the activities of natural monopoly to ensure its provided goods or services supply and/or its continuity. It is related with the protection of both, producers and customers. From one side, ensuring conditions for the producer so that he would be able to provide goods and services, and from the other side protecting the consumer from too high prices set by the monopolist, cancellation of supply of goods or services and quality. Therefore, when summarizing, we can say that the main reason for natural monopolies' regulation is: to ensure business conditions for natural monopolies and regulate them at the same time, so that they would not abuse their monopolistic power on customers.

Regulation is used pursuant to diminish disproportions caused by monopolistic or competitive market powers, confrontations in economic and social spheres. It dominates not only in the regulation of private businesses' activities, by providing them with some behavioral norms, but also in indirect control of state entities. Regulation is needed and necessary, as markets have failures, which are caused by economic reasons. For example, imperfect market structure (natural monopoly, oligopoly, monopolistic competition). With regulative means, the government seeks to create stable economic and social development conditions, which would ensure conditions for businesses, decrease negative impact of production for the environment and society.

Regulation affects many life aspects in nowadays economy and has quite a few economic, social and political goals. Regulation of infrastructure – mainly energy, gas, water, telecommunications and transport – seeks to avoid possible ineffectiveness and other factors that cause low effectiveness, arising from many natural monopoly features from these sectors. The main and the most disputable goal of regulation – control of prices and profits in monopolistic markets. Another important goal of regulating – determination and maintenance of discounts or other agreements, including conformity to strict service control requirements, investment levels and technical standards.

The objectives of regulation in developed countries, such as the US and Canada, the UK and other EU countries are broadly as follows [117]:

1. increase efficiency and quality of service;
2. reduce costs – both operating costs and the costs of investment;
3. reduce prices to final consumers so that prices correspond to the economic costs of supply;
4. allow companies and investors to have the expectation of a normal rate of return (for regulated, monopoly elements);
5. enforce competition policy goals and prevent market abuse in potentially competitive elements;
6. reduce excess capacity margins;
7. maintain universal service obligation.

It may be said, therefore that the basic objective of regulation in this hypothesis is the creation of a regulatory environment in an economic context where alternatives to the consumer do not exist and where strong deterrents to its establishment are present. Filho [31] states, that this definition shall influence the entire construction of principles of the regulation and shall help demonstrate the need for clear differentiation between function and content of the regulation of dominated sectors.

The main objective of regulation is protection of users' interests. Basing on analyzed literature on natural monopolies' regulation analyses [35, 58, 37, 33, 34, 38, 39], it is possible to distinguish the following main natural monopoly regulation goals:

1. Protection of users' interests, in order to ensure quality consumption:
   a) ensure the supply of services by satisfying the interests of the whole society and both, business subjects and citizens;
   b) ensure appropriate quality of provided services;
   c) ensure "reasonable" price for the provided services.
2. Ensuring companies' financial stability.
3. Facilitating the competition between producers, service providers and with some exceptions between the users.
4. Gathering and distribution of reliable information.

The analysis of reasons and goals for natural monopolies' regulation allows to claim that their activity and the extent of their products' consumption creates reasons to regulate their activity, therefore possible regulative ways have to be reviewed.

Mizutani [133] excludes in general, three methods of government involvement: taxation, subsidization and regulation. Regulation aims to control behavior of firms and individuals by law.

Depoorter [13] names state ownership of companies that provide natural monopoly services as a possible regulation alternative. There are reasons why the state may prefer to own rather than just to regulate. The most obvious reason for state ownership is to ensure social ownership of production, in the sense of "for the people," as noticed by Waterson [55]. Thus, state ownership of natural monopolies can be considered as some form of regulation.

Privatization was undertaken in the 1980s in the UK and has been studied both theoretically and empirically [118, 41]. Many countries have had various experiences with privatization over the years. Donahue [119], Gomez-Ibanez, Mayer [120], Ramamurti [121], Parker [122], Mizutani [32] propose, that the government's financial difficulties led to the privatization of public corporations. By privatizing public corporations, government was relieved of the financial burden of providing all the subsidies on which those public corporations had grown dependent. He affirms, that privatization was adopted as a mean of achieving fair competition with other private companies. He excludes reasons for privatization: one reason why public corporations had been inefficient was that they had experienced little competition and one more reason for privatization was to reduce political interference. According to Mizutani [32] the privatization of public corporations was seen as a way to mend the management-union relationship. There were other reasons for privatization as well, among them the private sector's willingness and desire to use new technology. The 1980s and 1990 can be characterized by the crusade of market forces against large governments and a notion of “small government“ has been introduced under UK and US neo-conservative administrations backed by such international organizations as the World Bank and the International Monetary Fund. Major state-owned enterprises (SOEs) have been privatized and thousands of regulations have been eased and/or abolished. Auriol, Picard [28] emphasizes that in many cases governments allowed to privatize public property due to critical budget situation. During the 1980’s debt crisis, international financial institutions such as the World Bank and International Monetary Fund made privatization one of economic aid conditions. Governments kept using income from privatization to lighten the austerity means undertaken in their budgets.

Waterson [55] stresses that the terms such as privatization, liberalization and deregulation are often mixed up, or are not clearly defined. For example, Redwood and Hatch [123] note that “The word privatization has become a portmanteau word covering a wide variety of different policies currently being pursued toward the nationalized industries….” Waterson [55] defines that privatization or denationalization means a change in form of ownership from public to private. Some activities of the former company may be hived off, the company may be forced to contract out some of its previous activities, some or even the whole of the company‘s equity may be sold. Mizutani [32] defines that privatization means transferring ownership of an enterprise or public services from the public to the private sector. This can be done either on a complete or partial basis. He says, that in a broad sense, privatization refers to the transfer of any government function to the private sector, reflecting the role and purpose of each country‘s government‘s role. Privatization may be partial or full.

Waterson [55] underlines, that liberalization means relaxing or abolishing restraints on entry into some of the areas previously been monopolistic. According to him deregulation means the removal or substantial diminution of the regulations by which the firm or firms in an industry are governed. This might mean the removal of price controls on a natural monopoly, which could nevertheless remain a natural monopoly. If the regulations prelate to entry or the qualities required of entrants, then deregulation is in some ways akin to liberalization.

Privatization includes well known economic costs related to sectors’ economies of scale [28]. Owners of infrastructure and public utilities receive benefits for their power in the market. By giving direct control of companies’ actions, state loses the control of prices – a disadvantage for the customers. Theoretically it could be avoided by calling auctions to purchase the company with a selling criteria being the lowest offered price for the customers [124]. However a study [125] on 600 concession contracts signed around the world suggests that in practice the contracts are drawn in public competition for the highest purchase price or for the highest annual payment.

Dominance of privatization over benevolent regulation is not clear. Auriol, Picard [28] state that actually deadweight losses, resulting from monopolistic pricing are the main reason to put public property to the first place. They propose that by having full information the government can imitate the results of private monopolies, so that privatization would never be optimal. However in case of asymmetric information between the governments and the companies, privatization can prevail over public property, as shortage of information enhances social costs of subsidies.

The results of the research, made by Auriol, Picard [28] show that market segments can be sufficiently profitable to attract companies to enter them. Then privatization and price liberalization prevail over regulation, if alternative public fund costs are sufficiently high. At the end, the supply of public utilities and their infrastructure are more market-oriented in developing, rather than in already developed countries. It is proved by empirical tests. The results of the same research Auriol, Picard [28] indicate that when market segments are more profitable, the decision upon privatization is limited by transitory opportunity costs of public funds. The state actually thinks that it is optimal to establish a state owned company with relatively high opportunity costs of public funds. Extremely poor countries are suffering from financial problems and waiting for potential income, which can be obtained from state-owned company. Privatization of profitable publicutilities, e.g., fixed telephone lines or international communication services are thus not effective. The market segment can be so profitable that a second company could enter the market. Then privatization together with price liberalization are no longer optimal, as competition is possible.

In the research made by Auriol, Picard [28], the discussion emphasizes the viability of resource redistribution and macroeconomic financial restrictions. Empirical literature in expansion studies provide evidence for the relation between these two questions in natural monopoly and oligopolistic markets in developing countries. Also, improvements for the effectiveness of productivity, related with privatization had been emphasized in theoretical as well as empirical literature.

Waterson [55] points, that governments should understand that privatization of itself may do little to help the consumer, in the absence of means to increase competition whenever such means are possible. Competition can be introduced either at the point of privatization, or indeed in its absence, or through antitrust means designed to ensure that the dominant firm does not succeed in any attempts to stifle potential opposition.

It is interesting to note that even before Demsetz [33], De Viti de Marco [65] again revealed the principle of "Competition for the field": he thought that the government could provide franchise rights for the most effective company and deny to renew it if the company behaves as monopolistic.

Kerf et al. [91] states that in sectors where duplication in the provision of services is not possible, various modes of bidding for concessional arrangements have introduced competition that promotes efficiency and raises the quality of the service. Where natural monopolies are unavoidable, awarding concessions through repeated franchise bidding subjects the monopolies to competition. Auctioning monopoly franchises to the lowest-cost providers also results in lower prices for consumers. To ensure efficient service for users, several other factors must also be taken into account: technical merit, experience of the bidder, operations expertise, and financial capacity. According to Depoorter [13] competition for franchise is associated with open right to provide for society, where regulator declares that he will accept proposals from all companies that want to supply the product. Each proposal for the competition could constitute the price, which the company would be willing to set for the users, had it received the franchise rights. In such competition process, the price is ultimately decreased to a price, when the company which wins the competitions gets profit equal to zero. Kerf et al. [91] also underlines, that concessions should be used in areas where they are most likely to help development, though they can be used in any industry. They are most likely to help development when they are used to regulate natural monopolies. They are not necessarily the wrong option. In the potentially competitive industries governments should think carefully about whether ordinary competition can be made to work by reforming market structure before turning to a concession. It is Demsetz [33] who underlined that formal regulation is unjustifiable, where the government can allow to compete for exclusive rights to provide goods or services in the given franchise time period. There is no monopoly-price determination, as it was already determined during the competitive competition. In other words, competition on a franchise level will be sufficient to lower the price to a level, at which it would be lower than if it was pursuant for monopoly profit maximization, emphasizes Depoorter [13]. They also note that the winner of a monopolistic franchise does not always fulfil the service contract conditions. Also, if one company once got the franchise rights for some period of time and for exclusive information about the costs, production processes and their control, future's franchise competitions will only happen between equal competitors.

Since one infrastructure sector may contain potentially competitive and naturally monopolistic segments, it is sometimes useful to unbundle these segments. Before awarding concessions in an infrastructure sector, governments should consider what is the best structure for that industry in the sense of vertical or horizontal separation, underlines Kerf et al. [91] Mizutani [133], Kerf et al. [91] stress that vertical separation is a method to dividing different activities according to the process of service production. Separating vertically i.e., upstream segment, such as generation is separated from a downstream segment, such transmission. Vertical restructuration, including ultimate vertical separation is an imperative political choice for the creation of competition, as infrastructure sectors in the world are liberalized, as noted by Pittman [117]. According to Mizutani [32] Geradin, Kerf [127] horizontal separation divides similar services into several organizations.

Mizutani [32] excludes also functional separation, which refers to dividing different services into disparate organizations. This is similar to horizontal separation but with more focus on the scope of service activities.

Pittman [126] underlines that there are plenty of models which offer how to restructure and manage infrastructure sectors. Proponents of various vertical separations provide the benefits of cancelation of competition and regulation, while defendants of vertical integration stress the economy and incentives to organize into the network. Pittman [126] distinguishes the following three cases, though there also are transitory choices, which can be applied in practice:

- **Vertically integrated monopolist.** It is a traditional model, when one fully integrated company operates as monopoly on P (production) and N (network) levels in respective sectors. The real market power of such monopolist might sometimes be restricted by intermodal competition or by integrated monopolistic competitions operating nearby; e.g., when two roads or two long distance electric power transitory lines serve the same city through opposite sides.
- **Vertical separation.** Company operates as the owner of monopolistic network N. There is competition in production P, but network company N is not allowed to enter the market.
- **Vertical integration and competition.** Company operates as monopoly in the network and as one of the competitors in production. This case will include the necessity of regulation, as the integrated company maintains separate accounts for its transition (network) and production operations and direct regulation of internal prices for an integrated company.

Wilson, Capelic [12] take traditional natural monopoly example and claim that electric power, gas, telecommunications and railway industries require reforms, which would make the problem solving easier:

- Regulated and unregulated activities should be maximally separated one from another. Similarly it is necessary to reform companies into social infrastructure, so that they would become municipality's property or to privatize them.
- Regulated activities should be defined by transparency and availability of information for regulator's agencies, also when assisting to determine sufficiently high prices, which would ensure normal profitability and thus attract new investments.
- Potentially competitive activities should be identified and reorganized with an interest to create a really competitive environment.
- Competition in these sectors can only develop if the regulators create respective conditions. The regulators have to ensure that potential market participants would have free access to the market.
- Collective management mechanism in natural monopolies has to be restored.
- Investment projects have to be aligned with the demand of economies of scale.
- Pricing mechanisms have to be reformed in all sectors of natural monopolies.
- Controlling firms, which execute administrative supervision on federal level, redistribute profit and revenues, have to be abolished.
- Costs have to be reduced and economic efficiency as to be enhanced in all spheres of national monopoly, which will need additional incentives to curb redundant employment and eliminate rarely used and ineffective production equipment.

A regulated environment is marked by several unique conditions, which are different to those in a deregulated environment, note Delmas in Menard, Ghertman [97]. They create a need for firms to adapt to the new conditions. Deregulation is defined as the complete or partial elimination of regulation in a sector with the intent of improving economic performance [128]. While deregulation eliminates or reduces restrictions imposed on firm strategies, it also brings some uncertainty regarding agency controls since the intermediary role of regulators between principal and agents diminishes [97]. Deregulation can take many forms, such as deregulation of market entry or exit; or deregulation of price control. It can be partial or complete, slow or fast. Kim and Prescott argued that both the form and speed of deregulation impact the speed of governance adaption [97]. Both partial forms of deregulation may have an impact on firm efficiency. Some firms that made capital investments during the regulatory period when the rate of return was regulated may not be able to recover these costs in a deregulated environment because the power rates necessary to pay for these plants may be too high to attract buyers in a competitive market. The "stranded costs" produced by this phenomenon would be more difficult to recover with the advent of competition than under the previous regime of regulated monopoly [129]. Kerf et al. notes, that deregulation can also stimulate competition, providing substitutable services [91].

As Joskow noted: "electric power sector reforms have significant potential benefits but also carry the risk of significant potential costs if the reforms are implemented incompletely or incorrectly" [130]. Joskow holds that most of the deregulation experiences of the electric utility sector around the world have not followed the textbook liberalization model and show the problems associated with incomplete or incorrect deregulation [130]. Competition is harder to foster in the electric utility sector than in most other sectors of the economy. Electric power generation is marked by high capital costs and constraints on building power plants that limit the number of players. These constraints on power plant construction limit competition as well as the flexibility of supply to respond to changes in demand [131].

Kagami, Tsuji [101] propose, that market mechanisms, with less intervention from state or government, have been pursued in every corner of the globe during the 1990s. They state that privatization of state owned enterprises and deregulation of economic activity bring about:

1. free entry and competition;
2. cost and price reduction;
3. improved services;
4. increased efficiency and efficient resource allocation;
5. temporary asset sales income to the government.

Most of the countries considered sustainability as one of the most important principles for good regulation. Sustainability is also as always needed for regulated businesses. Menezes [39] underlines that even though there is no universal definition for regulation sustainability, predicted meaning of this term is that one should expect similar decisions from the regulator given that the circumstances are similar. Even when different regulation models are applied, consistency needs the results to be justified according to the conditions in each industry and any residual differences should not be materialistic enough to implement false initiatives of companies or investors. Menezes [39] states that consistency of regulation can diminish the maintenance costs for companies which operate in different jurisdictions or industries, by eliminating the duplication of efforts. It is almost not doubted that consisted regulation could provide significant benefits. However consistency by itself cannot be the goal, as it has its own price.

According to Haney, Pollitt [132], though at the moment the incentivized energy networks' regulation is widespread, it cannot be said about the best practice of related comparative analysis methods. Research of Haney, Pollitt [132] shows that there are a number of methods used internationally; very few countries follow the principles of good practice defined by Lovell and there are interesting regional effects, which reveal that regulators are affected by their neighbors' paths. We use the best practice index to analyze which sectors and institutional characteristics have the biggest impact for the execution of advanced regulative methods. Incentivized energy network regulating expansion was inseparable part of reforms in most of the countries. Transmission (high-voltage) and distribution (low voltage) networks and in electric power, gas sectors do have natural monopoly features. Therefore they require regulation in order to facilitate effectiveness. Incentivized regulation came as a bonus for traditional price or costs regulation. By imitating market's pressure, the goal of incentivized regulation was to provide more lectures for the companies about ways how to reduce costs, apply innovations, enhance service quality and transfer the benefits of effectiveness for the customers [133, 134, 135].

Kopsakangas-Savolainan, Svento [136] suggest that moral problem can be solved with a specific form of incentive regulation (Price Cap regulation, Rate of return regulation or

Yardstick Competition), however then you have costs of adverse selection. Price cap regulation is extremely weak for extraction of taxes for the benefit of the user or the society and possibly leaves a large fraction of financial rent for the company. Then the goal of the regulator is to find such regulative mechanism, which assesses social costs of adverse selection and moral loses. One of such methods is so called Menu of Contracts regulation, where each company receives a cost-contingent and the company can choose a contract from the list, for which it would give priority [137].

Principal problem here is to draw such Menu of Contracts, which would minimize expected payments for the agent, applied restrivition that all types of agents accept contracts and produce the good [136]. Rogerson [138] uses the expression of fixed cost covering for the simplified Menu of Contracts. The deterministic procedure of this Menu is such: at first the responsible (regulator) people provide the agent with a Menu of Contracts, where the price is set as a function of costs and then the agent decides which contract to choose.

Price regulation of natural monopolies is also important in attaining efficient resource allocation, maintaining a reasonable price level, and protecting users from unfair treatment. Mizutani [32] states that to solve problem of monopoly pricing, there are three possible solutions. First, the government can give subsidies for the monopoly. Second, government can have a direct provision of the monopoly. Third possibility is to switch from marginal cost pricing to average cost pricing, where the price of the utility service becomes the average cost. Figure 1 shows the characteristics of public goods and gives typical examples.

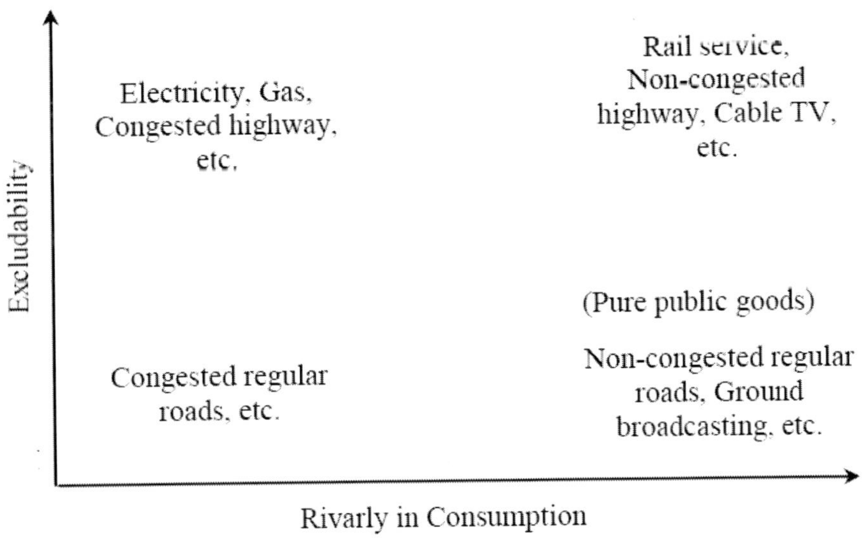

Source: author.

Figure 1. Characteristics of Public Goods and Examples.

Argell, Bogetoft [84] distinguish four types of regulatory mechanisms:

- cost-recovery regimes (cost of service, cost-plus, rate of return);
- fixed price (revenue) regimes (price-cap, RPI-X);
- yardstick regimes;
- franchise auctions.

Rate of Return Regulation or Service Cost Regulation are traditional regulation methods for natural monopolies. The purest form of this regulation – profit norm – is fixed by the costs. Benefits of profit norm regulation are relatively easy practical application, possibility to use the second best (e.g., Ramsey – Boiteux) or untypical prices, use of conscious cross-subsidies and rate hearings provide a possibility for the users to express their opinion. Moreover, a benefit of this method is also a bigger long-term investment definition. The biggest disadvantages of this regulation method are that it does not motivate to produce efficiently and if the allowed capital profit norm is higher than capital costs, so called Averch-Johnson effect (cost deviation) prevails. Also, profit norm regulation is associated with high administrative costs [136].

Price Cap Regulation is probably the most significant alternative for profit norm regulation, as discussed by Kopsakangas-Savolainan, Svento [28]. This method of regulation was proposed by Littlechild [139] for the first time and since then is applied in regulation of most companies (telecommunications, gas supply, water supply, airlines, railways, electric power etc.) in the United Kingdom and also in other countries. In the purest form of this regulation either the price or the price limits are fixed. It means that the company faces a risk related to the price and demand for the materials. On the other hand, the company is motivated to lower its costs as it can achieve benefits out of it. It was viewed as the main advantage of tis regulating method. Disadvantages include undefined service quality, the fact that possible benefits are rejected (e.g., Ramsey-Boiteux prices), applying price cap regulation can be complex and can be a good chance to get capturing the regulatory processes by the company. Price Cap regulation essentially separates profit and costs of the regulated company, by establishing price cap. This method is also used as "RPI-X" model. In this model, the price cap each year is set with respect to the price index and effectiveness factor X. Potential problems, related to practical application of price cap regulation method, are: price review procedure, obligation for the quality by regulator's management and rules how to define the parameter of X [140, 133].

It was discussed [92, 137, 70], that probably the optimal regulation mechanism is somewhere between two extremes, i.e., between the pure regulation of service costs (profit norm) and pure price regulation Then the regulation model will either have profit-sharing contractor or moving scale's mechanism (price, which regulated company can set is partly responsible for the real changes in costs and partly fixed ex ante). It was also discussed that generally, when offering the price it depends on cost contracts, regulation Menu of Contracts with different cost distribution provisions, the regulator can act better than to simply offer the only profit distribution contract [70]. Kospakangas-Savolainan, Svento [136] claim that the wellbeing can be improved by changing the pure, cost based regulation to regulation of Menu of Contracts.

Generally it is known that in reality fully informed regulators cannot exist. In most of the cases regulated company has more information about its costs and other factors. Respectively, the regulated company can use this information as a strategic advantage in the regulation process in order to enhance its profit or to reach other management goals for the disadvantage of other customers. Many regulatory agencies had put a lot of efforts to decrease this information asymmetry. Theoretical regulation's (especially incentives) studies developed and they provided new information for the regulators [140, 62, 137, 70]. There can be pointed out that there are two general types of regulatory bodies – independent agencies and government bureau – and that performance is likely to differ between them.

Capture theory relates to the critique of agencies. Waterson [55] states that, whatever the original guidelines given them, goes the argument, the agents get drawn into doing what is in the best interest of those they are regulating – they are, wittingly or unwittingly, captured by the people they are supposed to be policing. Menard, Ghertman [97] point out another refinement to Stigler is provided by Becker [142, 143]. He analyzed the importance of deadweight loss from regulation. Marginal gains by winners require the use of increasing political resources to offset those raised by losers to limit their losses.

Stigler and Friedland [144] were among the first to seriously challenge, through an empirical study, the Pigovian view that regulation contributes to welfare. They compared the influence on price and quantities of electric power consumption of a series of independent variables including regulation. They found a very small difference in price between regulated and unregulated States, with weak statistical significance. The welfare view was shown as wrong empirically. With the publication of 1971 paper by Stigler, the "welfare approach" lost most of its former credit. The conclusions of both papers reinforced each other. It took 31 years to find that results of the article published in the Journal of Law and Economics of 1962 included major errors, due to the coding and the use of common rather than natural logarithms [145]. Correct results showed a price reduction of about 25 percent and a quantity increase of 50 percent in regulated versus unregulated States [145]. Academic endorsement of Stigler's theory might have been much weaker if proper results would have been available. The empirical recognition of some success of regulation in reaching welfare objectives came too late, once regulation was either abandoned or discredited.

Peltzman, Levine, Noll [146] made a non-statistical evaluation of the validity of the welfare-Pigovian approach versus the one developed by Stigler et al., on railroads, trucking, airlines, long-distance telecommunications, stock brokerage, bank deposits and oil. He found five out of seven industries amenable to Stiglerian explanations and two (trucking and long-distance telecom) contradicting its predictions [139].

One of the most important empirical contribution to confirm the role of formal institutions on investment and welfare from Levy and Spiller [147]. They analyzed the role of the credibility of Government commitments for foreign telecommunication firms purchasing previous State-owned operators after deregulation introduced privatization and competition [139]. The credibility of Government commitments is nearly correlated with uncertainty, one of the attributes of transactions. Deregulation per se does not provide sufficient incentives for investors under conditions of high Government uncertainty.

Joskow [148] used the behavioral theory of the firm [149, 150, 151] to explain the behavior of the electric utility regulator. The period starting in 1969 witnessed increasing costs, including those of inputs for electric power production, because of wide spread inflation as well as the end of economies of scale in that industry. The result was lower profits and rates of return of firms below the level allowed by the regulator. Operators initiated numerous requests for reviews to obtain increased electric power and gas rates. Beside pressures from utilities, environment protection groups started to influence the regulator at the time [97].

Reregulation could be motivated by a set of complementary forces. Menard, Ghertman [97] states that the relevance of the dominating policy paradigm is likely to differ amongst countries, or between states in the US, and may not resist overtime when its legitimacy is weak. Deregulation may not be totally accepted as a dominating paradigm in several political instances. The efficiency of deregulation could become questionable in selected industries when temporary or long lasting failures affect a large body or customers-voters, especially if it creates a political opportunity for electoral competition. Reregulation is now on the policy agenda. For electric utilities the International Herald Tribune likely pointed to an important issue when it posted as headline: “Power deregulation creates US backlash: many states restore regulated systems“ [152]. Reregulation is now part of the research and policy agenda in social sciences and among policy makters [97].

Lovell distinguished the indicators of a good practice for the efficiency analysis [153]. It is important to mention that application of the good practice methods is not a guarantee for the best business results [154]. Haney, Pollitt [132] state that institutional rules resulting from this game also create opportunities for the ones in the government to enhance their income by the expense of others. Political powers determine economic institutions, which on their own determine economic results [155]. This relation between a political power and economic institutions explain why ineffective institutions can appear and survive for a long period of time, even though they have a negative impact on general country’s economy [155].

Haney, Pollitt [132] point out that in case of electric power networks, a form of political parties can cause a big impact on the existing type of regulation environment. e.g., in case there is no opposition for selfish actions of the government (allegedly, due to corruption or due to lack of clear separation between permissible, executive and court law) the reliability of regulation regime is affected negatively. It can cause the regulator to choose an advanced incentive regulation method, partly because of the challenge to collect data from regulated companies. If the regulator is not reliable, companies’ incentives to provide information are weakened and it causes possibilities for limitations. Reliability of regulatory agency can be enhanced by its independence from the government.

During the period studied, states Delmas et al. in Menard, Ghertman [97] deregulation has a negative impact on efficiency and a positive impact on the provision of renewables, even after accounting for the effect of a dozen control variables. The negative effect of deregulation on efficiency provides an interesting result as it illustrates the costs of partial deregulation (without, however, proving that full regulation would produce greater efficiency).

Kagami, Tsuji [101] exclude these demerits of privatization and deregulation:

- unemployment and reduced labor union power;
- reduces service in remote areas;
- declined supply stability or reliability;
- foreign capital dominance;
- bad debt problems;
- survival of the fittest;
- disorder or crises in certain sectors.

Kagami, Tsuji [101] point out, that privatized concerns often ignore unprofitable areas which were previously subsidized by state-owned monopolies. Services to remote areas tend to be shut down or cut back. Price competition sometimes produces negative effects such as supply instability. Privatization and liberalization invite foreign capital.

Kagami, Tsuji [101] point out that regulatory reform has two aspects: deregulation or loosening regulations, and controls improvements in the quality of existing regulations or sometimes making new regulations. Haney, Pollitt [132] underline that political institutions cause direct and indirect impact on economic institutions [155] and by themselves for the regulation results.

Kagami, Tsuji [101] point out that on-going privatization of state owned enterprises and deregulation have been generating fundamental changes in society in the following areas:

- The role of government and markets,
- Ownership (domestic as well as foreign participation by foreign direct investment),
- Performance and services (prices, quality, varieties, etc.),
- Industrial structure (production and employment),
- Institutional and contract arrangements (leasing, concession, out-sourcing, etc.),
- Financial arrangements (such as private financial initiative),
- Legal frameworks,
- Regulatory or monitoring bodies,
- Consumer attitude and lifestyle,
- Income distribution.

Merits of privatization and deregulation include cost and price reduction, increased efficiency with better business performance, improved services, increased customer satisfaction, and augmented government revenues. Demerits include increased unempoyment, reduced labor union power, the appearance of oligopoly or monopoly, foreign capital dominance, the treatment of universal service, and bad debt problems [101].

Agrell, Bogetoft [84] claim, that regulatory reform is a positive sign of economic dynamics. Dynamic regulation is all about how to transform and adapt industry structure, rather than replacing it. Depoorter [13] states, that in some cases the government might think it is acceptable, especially in the case of natural monopoly, to limit the number of companies operating in the respective market.

1.1.3. Transformations of Natural Monopolies

Technological innovation is very important factor, which cannot be ignored, analyzing natural monopolies. Technological advance was an impulse to transform some specific natural monopoly markets into competitive markets. The most significant is the case of changes in telecommunication industry, where the increase in value of microwaves and their development and satellite technologies became technological alternatives for traditional satellites. Depoorter [13] underlines that the value of technical expansion should not be under-stated. They claim that during the last 29 years renewed believing in market processes proved the governments in countries with market economies to private most of their public sector companies, including the strategic ones: steel, energy and telecommunications.

Berg and Tshirhart [77] and Smith [52] noticed that competition between the sectors of communication industry could have emerged from the economy of scope, which goes beyond industry boundaries. Zakem [156] and Stevenson and Penn [157] described how energy companies meet the competition from non-energy firms. The competition between different companies is called multilateral competition [58]. An example of multilateral competition exists in telecommunications, where local phone station companies face competition with such firms (long-distance phone connection and cable TV companies), which operate beyond the boundaries of company's station. Jamison [58] stresses that few factors create multilateral competition. Globalization and cost structure changes increase the number of opportunities for the company as well as raises its motivation to enter non-traditional markets. Technologic changes allow companies to use their new capabilities and overcome the boundaries of traditional industry and market without leaving the existing market. Surpassing the barriers of traditional market can empower companies to use economies of scale. Elimination of regulation can abolish arbitrary differences in regulation between markets and companies [77, 159, 160]. Table 1 shows systemized examples of natural monopolies analyzed by different authors.

Table 1. Examples of natural monopolies analyzed by different authors

Author	Date	Postal services	Telecom Munica-tions	Transport	Water supply and sewage	Energy sector (electric power, gas supply and heating)
Smith	1776				X	
Mill	1849	X			X	X
Dupuit	1852				X	X
Ely	1886		X	X	X	X
De Viti de Marco	1890		X			
Walras	1936			X	X	X
Waterson	1988	X			X	X
Zakem	1991					X
Ohmae	1991		X			
Canning, Fay	1993			X		
Bradley, Nauman, Nolar	1993		X			
Thierer [161]	1994		X			
Berg, Tshirhart	1995		X			
Stevenson, Penn	1995					X
Wilson, Capelic	1997		X	X	X	X
Jamison	1997		X			X
Kerf	1998			X	X	X
Depoorter	1999		X		X	X
Jankauskas	2000		X	X	X	X
Kagami, Tsuji	2000		X	X		X
Rioja [162]	2003		X	X	X	X
Menard, Ghertman	2009	X	X			X

Source: author.

Overview of the literature (Table 1), analyzing natural monopolies shows that the range of analyzed natural monopolies sectors has changed. Earlier research of natural monopolies focused on such sectors as: postal service, telecommunications, cable TV, energy, water supply and sewage disposal, gas supply, railways, transport, heating. As we now can see, the technological progress has eliminated such sectors as telecommunications, cable TV and partly postal service from the range of natural monopolies. Most attention in the recent years is paid to the research which focuses on energetic sector and such natural monopolies as electric power supply, gas supply and heating. Water supply and sewage disposal is still treated as natural monopoly, but studies on these natural monopolies are more relevant for less developed countries.

1.2. Natural Monopolies' Impact on Countries Economy and Competitiveness

1.2.1. Natural Monopolies' Relation with Economic Subjects

Natural monopolies provide services for industry enterprises, as well as for households. Some of these services are essential for almost all businesses or hauseholds, while other – less essential. Generally there can be stated, that such services as energy (electric power, heating, oil) supply, water supply and sewage disposal are very important for every countries industry and citizens. This fact can be proved analyzing the statistics of energy consumption (Table 2).

As we may see in the Table 2, number of active economy subjects changes not significant, as well as the number of households and the final consumption of energy either shows no significant changes. It leads us to the conclusion, that energy demand is no price elastic. Kuodis [167] suggests that households' demand for energy is rather inelastic – we cannot proportionally reduce our consumption of heating, electric power or petrol with respect to the extent of changes in the price. He stresses that that is the main reason why the increase of energy prices might be so dangerous for the economy of Lithuania: citizens are forced to spend more money on it, while leaving less of disposable cash for other purchases. It reduces the growth of the economy, as producers of other goods receive less income, hire less employees, etc. Total energy consumption in percent terms show that the industry during the selected period used between 64.70 and 70.79 percent of energy, and households respectively between 29.21 and 35.30 percent of energy. Producers of the final goods or services include incurred expenses for energy to the cost of the good or service, while households pay not only for the directly consumed energy, but also for the energy which was used to produce goods or services and which therefore was included into the costs of the goods or services. Energy consumption in separate Lithuania's industry sectors is provided in Table 3.

As we can see in the Table 3, production of chemicals and chemistry products, food products, beverages and tobacco, wood, wood and cork products, other non-metal mineral products, rubber and plastic products and furniture requires the most energy. The lowest amount of energy was consumed by the main pharmaceutical products and pharmaceutical preparations, vehicles with engines, trailers and semi-trailers, leather and leather products.

Table 2. Final energy consumption in Lithuanian industry and households, 2002-2013

	2002	2003	2004	2005	2006	2007	2008	2009	2010	2011	2012	2013
Total consumption in industry, constructions, transportation, agriculture, fishing, services and other activities, in thousand tons oil equivalent	2642,80	2746,10	2918,70	3089,70	3316,00	3647,30	3515,00	3022,90	3163,40	3180,20	3300,00	3257,20
Total consumption in industry, constructions, transportation, agriculture, fishing, services and other activities in percent	64,70	65,18	66,35	67,19	67,86	70,79	69,36	65,81	66,47	67,44	68,22	68.94
Number of active economic subjects, units	68429	68356	69861	72330	73344	76516	81376	84574	83202	86987	83624	90790
Consumption of active economic subject, in thousand tons oil equivalent	0,04	0,04	0,04	0,04	0,05	0,05	0,04	0,04	0,04	0,04	0,04	0.04
Total consumption in households, in thousand tons oil equivalent	1441,80	1467,00	1480,20	1508,80	1570,80	1504,90	1553,10	1570,30	1595,80	1535,30	1537,10	1467,80
Total consumption in households, in percent	35,30	34,82	33,65	32,81	32,14	29,21	30,64	34,19	33,53	32,56	31,78	31.06
Number of households, in thousand units	1357	1362	1380	1440	1425	1425	1413	1393	1389	1392	1327	1309
Consumption of one household, in ton of oil equivalent	1,06	1,08	1,07	1,05	1,10	1,06	1,10	1,13	1,15	1,10	1,16	1.12

Source: [163, 164, 165, 166].

Table 3. Total Energy consumption in Lithuania's industry in 2008 – 2014, in thousand tons oil equivalent

	2008	2009	2010	2011	2012	2013	2014
Total Energy Consumption in Industry	**393**	**365**	**398**	**434**	**452**	**452,3**	**483,7**
Chemicals and chemical products	204,4	199,3	213,2	249,7	251,5	236	259,7
Food products, beverages and tobacco	57,2	56,3	59	62,3	62,8	69,5	69,8
Wood, wood and cork products, except furniture; goods from straws and plaiting	25,3	20,6	22,4	19,7	31,7	32,5	35,2
Other non-metal mineral products	22,7	13,9	16,3	17,4	19,3	21,3	22,3
Rubber and plastic products	16,3	16,1	15,5	18,4	17,1	18,8	20,3
Furniture	14,1	8,3	10,8	12,5	16,9	19,4	22,9
Textile products	10,7	14,8	10,9	9,3	9,9	10	9,8
Paper and paper products	7	8,1	20,7	14	8	10	10,7
Clothing sewing	5,5	4,9	5,3	5,2	5,4	5,1	4,5
metal products, except from vehicles and equipment	5,5	4	5	5,9	7,8	6,7	7,5
Other mining and exploitation of quarries	3,6	2	2	2,5	2,1	2,3	2,2
Printing and reproduction of data	2,9	2,2	1,9	2,9	3,2	3,1	2,9
Other transportation means and equipment	2,8	2,7	2,2	1,5	1	0,9	1,1
Not associated vehicles and equipment	2,8	2,7	2,8	3,1	4,4	4,5	2,7
Other production	2,5	2,4	2	2,1	2,6	2,9	2,8
Electric power equipment	2,3	1,4	1,6	1,6	2,6	3	3,6
Computers, electronic and optical goods	2,3	1,2	1,5	1,4	1,5	1,9	1,9
Core metals	1,6	2	1,8	1,9	2,2	1,8	1,7
Main pharmaceutical products and pharmaceutical preparations	1,2	1	1,2	1,3	0,8	1	0,4
Vehicles with engines, trailers and semi-trailers	1,1	0,6	1,1	0,9	0,8	1,1	1,3
Leather and Leather products	0,5	0,3	0,8	0,4	0,5	0,5	0,4

Source: [168].

Analysis of energy consumption dynamics in 2008 – 2014 reveal that the consumption in paper and paper products production substantially increased in 2010, while we can see the decline in energy consumption in textile products manufacturing, while growth tendencies can be observed in chemical and chemistry products and furniture production.

Consumption of services provided by natural monopolies creates a closed circle. It becomes obvious when we analyze the increase in prices of these services. As it was already mentioned, the services of natural monopolies are more or less necessary for all economic subjects: for households – final product consumption, for production and other business subjects, as transitory consumption good. Kuodis [167] underlines that heating and electric power is an intermediate consumption good practically in the production of all produced goods and services. In a long run, producers transfer the increased energy costs to the price of their products, therefore the price of the goods and services increase. Filho [31] also note that since energy prices are increasing not only for the producers but also for the final consumers, i.e., households, their demand for non-natural monopoly goods and services decrease (the increase of households' income is not related to the increase in natural monopoly's service prices). Thus, internal demand declines due to two reasons: increase of households' expenses for natural monopoly's services and increase in prices for goods and services.

1.2.2. Natural Monopolies' Impact to the Economy

Existence of natural monopoly services affects the growth of economy by increasing the productivity of production factors and by providing services which ensure country's economic activity. Natural monopoly services help to enhance the production volume in two ways:

- Natural monopoly services (water, energy) are intermediate production costs and any decrease of these costs would increase the production profitability, thus creating opportunities to raise production volumes, revenue and occupancy.
- Natural monopoly services enhance the productivity of other production factors (labor, etc.) – e.g., by providing the opportunity to move from manual to automatized work, shortening workers' commute time and improving information sources which are transferred on electronic platforms.

In literature, these characteristics are associated with infrastructure, and a part of infrastructural fields are natural monopolies. Thus, positive impact of natural monopolies for the economy can be defined by, first, existence of natural monopolies by itself. Their existence in the country nowadays imply that the country is sufficiently developed and its citizens and businesses can be provided with such resources as energy, water, etc. It can be proved by previously discussed characteristics of natural monopolies.

Filho [31] states, that dead-weight loss refers to the loss of use for such consumers owing to their failure to use the subject product, plus the opportunity cost to those consumers who continue to use the product and who pay uncompetitive high prices charged by the monopolist and who thus reduce or eliminate their use of other products. This can be attributed to the negative impact of natural monopoly for economics.

One more harmful consequence of a monopoly is the lack of motivation on the part of the monopolist to innovate and improve efficiency [31]. This question is often discussed by economists and has no satisfactory solution. The principal argument, proposed by neoclassic theoreticians in favor of monopolies: the efficiency gained with economies of scale. In the case of natural monopoly this lack of motivation can be reflected by the price of services and makes a negative impact to the economy if it is increasing or not decreasing (if it is possible by improving efficiency of applying innovations).

One more point to be highlighted is the harmful effect of monopolies on the distribution of social income. A monopoly that allows for uncompetitive price increases implies the transfer of income from consumers to the stakeholders of the monopolist [31]. The same was already discussed earlier in the context for natural monopoly, so the consequence is the same. Neoclassic theoreticians, who believe in the invisible hand of market, criticize this opinion. They say that it is no possible to maintain a monopoly unless a portion of the profits earned is shared with consumers through a reduction in prices.

Summarizing there can be stated that natural monopolies have both positive and negative impact to the economy of the state. As positive it is emphasized the existence of natural monopolies as such. It means that the state is endowed with the main infrastructure and its services for citizens and industry. The negative consequences of the natural monopoly cover topics, related to the price of services: dead-weight loss, lack of motivation to innovate and improve efficiency and distribution of social income.

1.2.3. Relationship between Natural Monopolies and Country's Competitiveness

Countries also compete, but instead of international trade they compete for attracting the capital. In other words, countries compete by setting economic environment conditions (e.g., taxes, economic activity regulation norms), which could attract foreign investments (some analysts call that kind of locational competition). Vilpisauskas [118] claims that there are not many studies which analyze that kind of competition and moreover, it is not agreed when does it cause tax reduction and softening of regulation norms.

In terms of the analyzed problem, companies which operate in the same country should pay the same price for the goods or services of natural monopoly. In this way, when competing against each other they might seek for competitiveness:

1. by changing the consumption volumes of natural monopolies' goods and services;
2. by changing the consumption volumes of other resources;
3. by installing new technologies or applying innovations to reduce the cost for natural monopolies goods and services;
4. by substituting the resources with cheaper ones.

Cibinskiene [169] claims that in terms of infrastructural natural monopolies' goods and services price effect on country's competitiveness, Porter's [170] "National Diamond" model can be applied without considering the critiques from other authors, but appreciating its universality and determined relationships between separated factor groups, which are maintained and applied in the models of the authors who criticized him (Cho [42] "Nine Factors," Rugman, D'Cruz [43] "Double Diamond"). Here was analyzed the price change effect of natural monopolies' services for the competitiveness, however if assessing the competitiveness, it is possible to consider not only the prices of natural monopolies' services. In many models for country's or region's competitiveness assessment, some factors, according to which the general competitiveness is assessed, are distinguished. Porter [170] "National Diamond" and Rugman, D'Cruz [43] "Double Diamond" models, which assess factor conditions, separate the follow factors: human resources, physical and knowledge factors, capital and infrastructure. Hence, existence of natural monopolies and provided services are associated with infrastructure and affect country's competitiveness through the factor conditions of this model. In Lengyel [171] regional competitiveness pyramid, the existence of natural monopolies and provided services are associated with infrastructure and human capital factor. In De Vet, Baker, Dalgleish, Pollock, Healy [172] Regional competitiveness tree model, the existence of natural monopolies and services is associated with infrastructure, internet accessibility, and industrial services accessibility. In the by

Gardiner, Martin, Tyler [173], Atkociuniene [174] complemented regional competitiveness pyramid model, such factors as infrastructure and human resources are also distinguished, as they can be associated with the services of natural monopolies.

Currently, to indicate a countries international expansion in mass information media or scientific articles, usually there are results of Global economics competitiveness index and World competitiveness index presented. According to Jatuliavicience and Kucinskiene [175], the global competitiveness index is an integrated assessment tool of macro environment due to its explicitness is often used to determine country's or region's competitiveness. Global competitiveness index includes 12 pillars. The second pillar is infrastructure and it underlines that extensive and efficient infrastructure is critical for ensuring the effective functioning of the economy, as it is an important factor in determining the location of economic activity and the kinds of activities or sectors that can develop in a particular instance [176].

Countries' competitiveness scores are assessed by international organizations. Often mentioned are World Economic Forum's (WEF) competitiveness report and International Institute of Management Development's competitiveness yearbook.

When assessing infrastructure that we associate with the services of natural monopolies, some factors, as determined in Table 4, are distinguished according to the World competitiveness index. Here we have results for Lithuania in 2012 – 2013, 2013 - 2014 and 2014-2015.

Table 4. Results of Lithuania Infrastructure's assessment with the World's competitiveness index

Criteria	Lithuania's Ranking 2012-2013	Lithuania's Ranking 2013-2014	Lithuania's Ranking 2014-2015
Quality of overal infrastructure	42	44	43
Quality of roads	32	34	36
Quality of railroad infrastructure	20	21	22
Quality of port infrastructure	35	35	47
Quality of air transportation infrastructure	86	75	75
Available airline seat km/week, millions	97	97	97
Quality of electricity supply	41	46	41
Mobile telephone subscriptions/ 100 pop.	13	19	22
Fixed telephone lines/100 pop.	56	61	55

Source: [176, 177, 178].

From this assessment it can be seen that not only the existence of natural monopolies is important, but also the quality.

IMD word competitiveness yearbook [179] also states countries' competitiveness rankings. The methodology of this index computation includes 4 major criterions:

1. Economic activity (79 criterions assessed).
2. Effectiveness of governmental activities (70 criterions).

3. Business effectiveness (71 criterions).
4. Infrastructure (113 criterions).

Assessment of infrastructure gets the most attention, its assessment criterions are separated into 5 sub-sections, which are further divided and later assessed using separate criterions, amongst which are services provided by natural monopolies.

Conducted research shows that the impact of natural monopolies on country's competitiveness is definitely significant and they are included to most of the assessment models and to the factors of competitiveness assessment indices. It can be assessed by considering not only the prices of these goods or services, but by emphasizing the existence of their service supply, stability and other aspects, which according to different competitiveness assessment methods can also be considered as factors of competitiveness, which affect the competitiveness of the country and its economic subjects.

Chapter 2

REVIEW OF LITHUANIAN ENERGY SECTOR NATURAL MONOPOLIES

The theory of natural monopoly is an economic fiction. No such thing as a "natural" monopoly has ever existed. The history of the so-called public utility concept is that the late-nineteenth- and early-twentieth- century "utilities" competed vigorously and, like all other industries, they did not like competition. They first secured government-sanctioned monopolies, and then, with the help of a few influential economists, constructed an ex post rationalization for their monopoly power.
(Thomas J. Dilorenzo "The Myth of Natural Monopoly," The Review of Austrian Economics, vol. 9, No2 (1996), Liudwig von Mises Institute.

2.1. ELECTRIC POWER SECTOR

The Lithuanian electric power sector since 1997 has undergone a reform process away from the regulated system towards a market based system. There are 3 periods of electric power sector reform in Lithuania: 1997-2002; 2003-2009 and since 2010. The main reasons for electric power reform during these two periods were corporatization and commercialization.

2.1.1. Stages of Electric Power Market Opening

Lithuania is EU member state since 2004. The Lithuanian energy policy and legislative framework for the electric power sector are harmonised with the policies and legislation of the European Union (EU). In January 2002 a new electricity law, which provides the basic principles for electric power sector regulation according the EU law came into effect. It formulates the relationship between electric power and service suppliers and their customers, and sets out the conditions for the development of competition in the electric power sector. The law sets out the stages for electric power market liberalization and for the recognition of consumers who are eligible to conclude direct electric power purchase contracts with power producers or independent suppliers.

Lithuanian National Energy Strategy was adopted by the parliament (Seimas) in October 2002.

The aims of the strategy include the following:

- Liberalization of the electric power and natural gas sectors by opening the market pursuant to the requirements of EU directives.
- Privatization of specific electric power and natural gas enterprises.
- Preparation for the decommissioning of the Ignalina Nuclear Power Plant and the disposal of radioactive waste and long-term storage of spent fuel.
- Integration of energy systems into EU energy systems within the next 10 years.
- Development of regional cooperation and collaboration with a view to create a common Baltic electricity market (CBEM) within the next five years.
- Reform of the electric power market in Lithuania is divided into several periods: 1997-2002; 2002-2009; after 2010.

First Reform Period 1997-2002

The Lithuanian electric power sector since 1997 has undergone a reform process away from the regulated system towards a market based system which fulfills the requirements of the EU directives regarding electric power markets. The first step in the reform process was corporatisation and commercialisation. Corporatisation was introduced according to the Energy Law when the Lithuanian state power system was reorganised into a special joint-stock company "Lithuanian power." The second step was separation of the heat activities from JSC "Lithuanian power." It started with the issuing of the law on restructuring of Lithuanian power in April 1997. The shareholders' meeting in July 1997 approved a plan for separation of heat activities from Lithuanian power by creating independent companies, with municipalities as main shareholders. In some cases, several municipalities created regional heat companies. The third step was separation of non-core activities. The independent regulator was established in 1997.

Second Reform Period 2002-2010

The Law on Electricity was passed in 2002. The Law sets the main objectives of the Lithuanian electric power sector policy, including one requiring development of a legal framework for the functioning of a competitive electric power market. The Law defined the structure of the electric power market and determined the pace and level of the market opening. Electric power generation and supply were determined as competitive activities, prices of generation and supply were not regulated and set by the market, except if some generators or suppliers dominate in the market – in the current case some price regulation mechanism was to be developed and applied by the Regulator – National Control Commission. The Commission is also responsible for supervision of the non-discriminatory access to the grid, it sets the transmission and distribution tariffs using the incentive price regulation - price cap formulas.

JSC "Lithuanian power" was split into several independent companies: "Lithuanian power" (exporting electric power) with Transmission system operator (TSO) and Market operator (MO) functions (Kruonis hydro power plant (HPP), Kaunas HPP), two Distribution system operators (DSO) and several electric power generation companies. One distribution company was privatized. Competition in generation and supply. Licenses were granted for several independent suppliers and 2 public suppliers.

In 2004 – Law on electricity was amended according EU Second energy package. Full market opening was envisaged for the commercial consumers since 2004 and for all consumers since 2007. However because of Ignalina nuclear power plant (NPP) dominating on the market and significant share of supported generation (CHP, renewables) the eligible consumers didn't change their supplier.

In 2008 the holding company LEO.LT (61,7% shares of Lithuanian Republic and the rest JSC NDX Energija) was created for the new NPP construction. The subsidiaries of this company were "Lithuanian power" (TSO, MO, Kaunas HPP, Kruonis HPP) and two DSO companies.

In 2009 holding company LEO.LT was restructured again. The private DSO was bought by the Lithuanian Government back. The structure of electric power sector remain like before 2008.

Third Reform Period from 2010

From 2010 - The Electricity law was amended to address EU Third energy package and Lithuanian power company was restructured by separating TSO (LITGRID) and Market Operator (BALTPOOL) activities into separate companies and also establishing JSC Energy Supply as independent energy supplier. Kruonis HPPS (hydro power pump storage) and Kaunas HPP were also separated. Start up of Power Exchange (PX) from January 1, 2010. The NordPool model was applied.

The main objectives of electric power sector reform are generalized in Table 5. They are: to create competitive electric power market and to ensure fair competition; to ensure and promote the effective electric power generation; to ensure the constancy and reliability of electric power generation, transmission and distribution; to promote the development of internal electric power arket and electric power export, modernization of infrastructure of market implementation, energy pricing clarity and transparency; to impose public service obligations which may relate to security of society, environmental protection and generating installations using local, renewable and secondary energy; to create favourable conditions for investments in the electric power sector; to promote environment friendly technology.

2.1.2 Market Structure

First Reform Period 1997-2002

Before restructuring of the electric power sector in 2002, the Special Purpose JSC Lithuanian power operated as a vertically integrated natural monopoly carrying out production, supply, transmission and distribution of the electric power in Lithuania.

Second Reform Period 2002-2010

From January 1, 2002 the former Special Purpose JSC "Lithuanian power" was split into several independent companies, including the transmission company, two distribution companies and several generation companies. New market players - the transmission system operator, the market operator, two distribution system operators, two public suppliers and several independent suppliers were granted licenses and started their operation in a new market.

Table 5. Rationale for Electric Power Sector Reform in Lithuania

Rationale for Electric Power Sector Reform in Lithuania	
Efficiency, Costs and Prices	
Improve Productivity of ESI	+
Lower electric power prices	+
Improve labour productivity	+
Increase competition	+
Provide customer choice	+
Privatisation	+
Sustainability and Reliability	
Promote demand-side management	+
Reduce environment impacts	+
Improve electric power supply reliability	+
Remove pricing anomalies	-
Investment and Capital Market	
Enhance investor confidence	+
Reduce government debt	-
Free government scarce resources	+
Encourage foreign investment	+
Develop capital market	-
Social Welfare	
Enhance affordability	-
Accelerate electrification	-
Future Challenges: An Overview	
Investment	+
Climate Change	+
Reliability	+
Further Reform	-
System Losses	-
Electrification	-

Source: author.

The Law on the Reorganisation of Special Purpose Company Lithuanian power was adopted and the following types of undertakings were established in electric power sector of Lithuania:

- electric power producers (i.e., undertakings generating electric energy);
- suppliers (i.e., those that carry out delivery and/or sale of purchased or produced electric power to customers);
- transmission undertakings (i.e., those that carry out the transportation of electric power through the transmission network);
- distribution undertakings (i.e., those that carry out the transportation of electric power through the distribution network with a view to its delivery to customers);

- market operator (i.e., the undertaking responsible for the organisation and administration of trade in electric power and payment settlements between producers, suppliers and customers);
- operators of the transmission networks (i.e., the undertakings that carry out the management of the transmission system and balancing and reserving of generation and consumption of the electric energy);
- operators of the distribution networks (i.e., the undertakings that carry out the management of the distribution system within the territory of their services).

Separation of the activities of the generation, transmission, distribution and supply of electric power provides for the possibility to implement the principle of transparency in the electric power sector.

The electric power market structure and the main institutions in electric power sector of Lithuania from 01 January 2002 are presented in Figure 2.

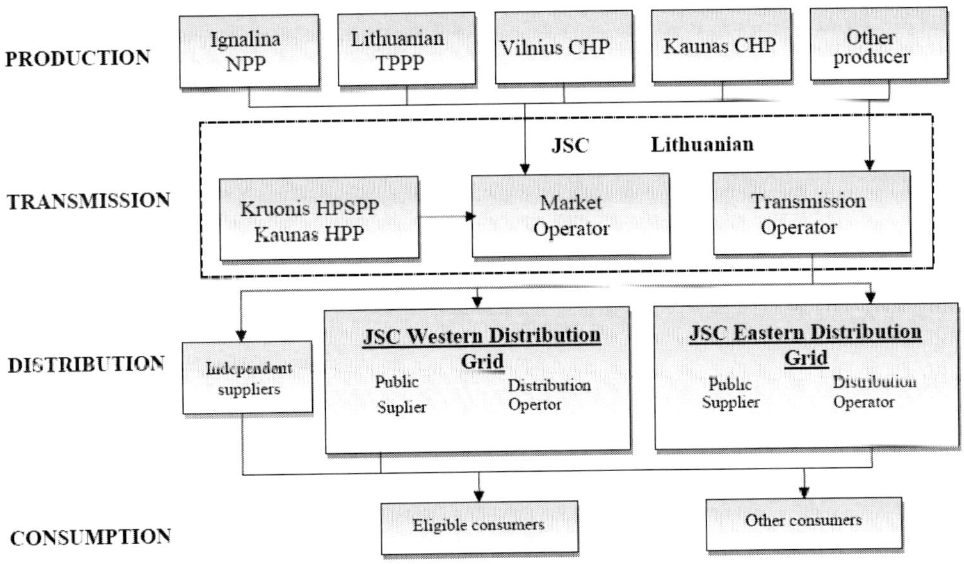

Source: author.

Figure 2. Electric Power Market model in Lithuania, from 01 January 2002.

In 2004 the Law on Electricity was amended in order to adjust it to the latest EC Electricity Directive: full market opening was envisaged for the commercial consumers since July 2004 and for the residential consumers – 3 years later, from July 2007 (Figure 3). At the same time the Regulator was obliged to monitor and supervise market ensuring fair, non-discriminatory access to the grid and transparent use of the grid capacities.

Despite of the full market opening for all commercial consumers, number of the customers changing their supplier did not increase as only the largest consumers have done it.

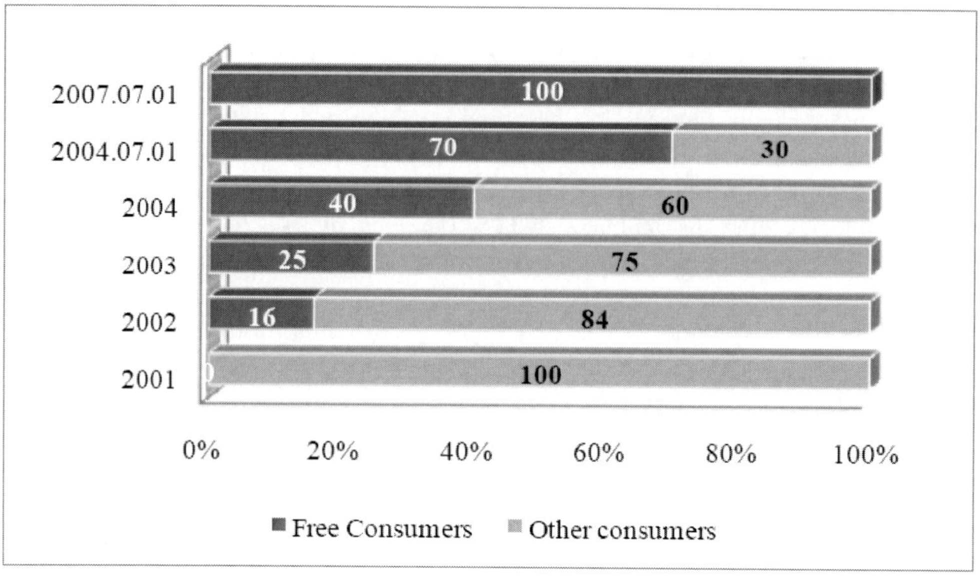

Source: author.

Figure 3. Market opening in Lithuania, %.

Third Reform Period from 2010

From 1 January 2010 the Lithuanian market is based on the same principles as the Nordic power market (for wholesale trade organization), where price and flow are calculated at the same time to increase market efficiency (implicit auction). Electric power market structure and new players in electric power market are presented in Figure 4 and described bellow.

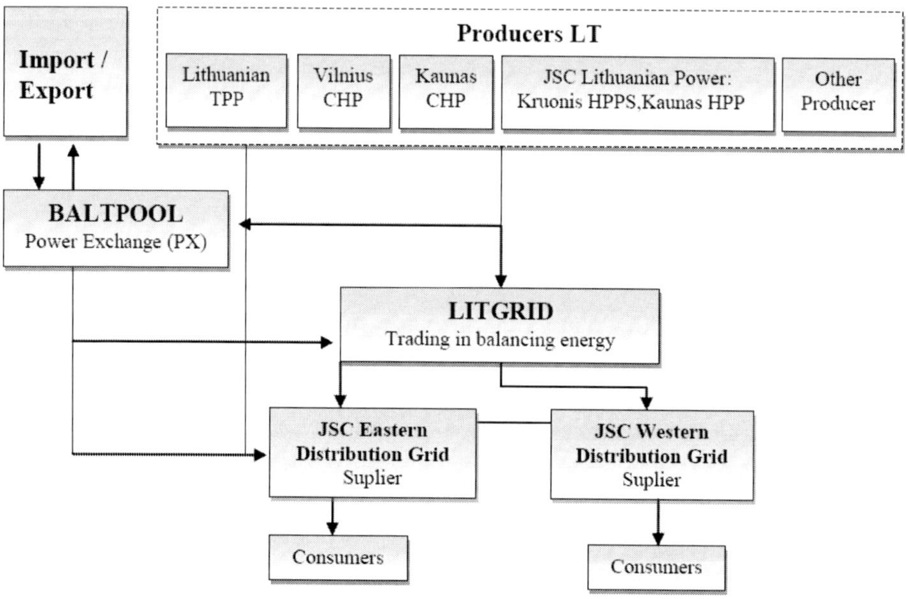

Source: author.

Figure 4. Electric Power Market model in Lithuania, from 01 January 2010.

JSC Litgrid, a daughter of JSC "Lithuanian power" to function as the electric power transmission system operator, was established. The company performs electric power planning, dispatch control and operational planning. The company was established while implementing EU legal acts, stipulating the separation of control of transmission system from generation and supply.

JSC Baltpool, a daughter company of JSC Litgrid was established to function as the electric power market operator. JSC Baltpool organizes wholesale electric power trade in Lithuania. Legal acts to regulate the activities of the electric power exchange were enforced and the NPS trading platform was sucessfully adapted to the Lithuanian electric power exchange. The company was established in compliance with the Electricity Market Development Plan approved by the Government of the Republic of Lithuania on July 8, 2009, with the aim to implement measures for the creation of a common electric power market of the Baltic States following the principles and experience of the electric power market (Nord Pool) of the Nordic countries.

The market participants roles in electric power market are presented in Figure 5.

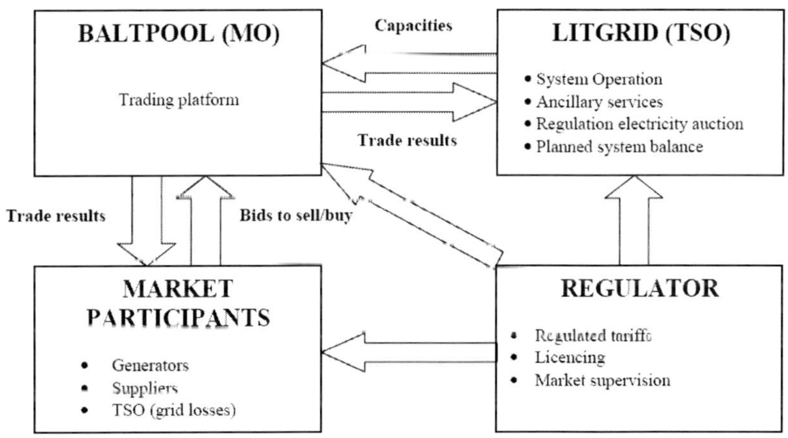

Source: author.

Figure 5. Market participant roles in Lithuania, from 01 January 2010.

From 1 January 2010 price formation principle - marginal price setting. Hourly trading and balancing responsibility applied for all market participants.

Product: hourly electric power quantity.

Period: 24 hours day-ahead.

Trading arrangements: intersection of supply and demand curves, which is represented by the last supply bid matching demand bid

Cross-border capacity allocation: implicit auction – capacity and energy is traded simultaneously.

Trading days: all year days.

Bidding arrangements: specialized electronic trading platform provided by NordPool is in operation, where participants place their bids.

Currency: Litas.

Price settlement: announcement until 14:30 LT time.

2.1.3. The Ownership

The ownership in electric power sector of Lithuania has undergone significant changes since 1997.

First Reform Period 1997-2002

Before 2002 the Lithuanian electric power sector could be described as a single vertically integrated monopoly JSC *"Lithuanian power"* and *the State Enterprise Ignalina Nuclear Power Plant* as the largest electric power producer, both owned by the state.

Second Reform Period 2002-2010

On the 1st of January 2002 vertically integrated state owned monopoly was split up into five enterprises, thereby unbundling electric power generation, transmission and distribution and allowing private investors to obtain shares and some control. The "Lithuanian power" was reorganized and divided into two companies producing electric power: JSC Lithuanian TPP and JSC *Mazeikiai Thermal Power Plant*, one transmission system operator also acting as a market operator JSC *Lthuanian Power and* two distribution network companies JSC *Rytu Skirstomieji Tinklai AB* and JSC *VST AB.*

The controlling shareholder in JSC "Lithuanian Power" was the State of Lithuania holding 96.59 percent of shares in the company, represented by the Ministry of Economy. The remaining 3.41 percent of shares were owned by small shareholders.

The majority shareholders in JSC *Rytu Skirstomieji Tinklai* were the State holding 71.35 percent of shares, E.ON Energie AG held 20.28 percent of shares. Minority shareholders held 8.37 percent of shares. The main manager of state-owned shares was the Ministry of Economy.

JSC VST was privatized on the 23rd of December 2003. The major shareholder in this company was a private Lithuanian capital company JSC *NDX Energija*. It owned 97.1 percent of shares in *VST AB* and small shareholders owned 2.9 percent of shares.

On the 20th of May 2008 national investor *LEO LT AB* was established. The legal form of the national investor is a public limited liability company. The Republic of Lithuania owns 61.7 percent of shares in the national investor, other part of *LEO LT AB* shares is owned by Lithuanian private company JSC *NDX Energija* (Establishment agreement).

JSC LEO LT was a parent company of JSC "Lithuanian Power, JSC VS, JSC Rytu Skirstomieji Tinklai, JSC Visagino Atomine Elektrine, JSC InterLinks.

LEO LT AB owned:

1. 96.4 percent shares of JSC "Lithuanian power," a transmission system operator. The company is not engaged in activity of supply of electric power, it performs the function of market operator, which is responsible for the organization of electric power trade, including auction. Two generation companies operate as subsidiaries of JSC "Lithuanian Power, i.e., *Kruonis Hydro Pumped Storage Plant* and *Kaunas Hydro Power Plant*. These plants ensure the balance of the electric power system, as well as constant electric power supply.
2. 96.4 percent shares of JSC *VST. JSC VST* is a distribution system operator and public supplier of the western part of Lithuania (Establishment agreement).

3. 71.3 percent shares of JSC *Rytu Skirstomieji Tinklai*. JSC *Rytu Skirstomieji Tinklai* is a distribution system operator and public supplier of the eastern part of Lithuania (Establishment agreement).
4. 100 percent shares of JSC *InterLinks*, company responsible for the construction of interconnections with other energy systems (Establishment agreement).
5. 100 percent shares of JSC *Visagino Atomine Elektrine*, company which is responsible for preinvestment activities of new nuclear power plant (Establishment agreement).

Therefore, as a result of vertical integration, *LEO LT AB* is engaged in electric power generation, transmission, distribution and supply.

In 2009 JSC LEO.LT was restructured. The private DSO JSC VST was bought by the Government back. The structure of electric power sector remains like before 2008.

Third Reform Period from 2010

In 2010 the Electricity law was amended to address EU Third energy package and JSC "Lithuanian power" was restructured by separating TSO (LITGRID) and Market Operator (BALTPOOL) activities into separate companies and also establishing JSC Energy Supply as independent energy supplier. Kruonis HPPS and Kaunas HPP are also separated. Start up of Power Exchange from January 1, 2010.

As of December 31, 2009, the JSC "Lithuanian Power" has six wholly owned subsidiaries: Energetikos Pajegos UAB, Kauno Energetikos Remontas UAB, Kruonio Investicijos UAB, Litgrid UAB, Energijos Tiekimas UAB, InterLinks UAB and VsI Respublikinis energetiku mokymo centras. Indirectly, through Kauno Energetikos Remontas UAB, the Company has majority of votes in Gotlitas UAB, and through Litgrid UAB, it has a majority holding in Baltpool UAB.

97.5 per cent of the JSC "LITGRID are owned by JSC Visagino Atomine Elektrine and 2.5 per cent – to small shareholders.

The structure and ownership of electric power industry in Lithuania and other countries are presented in Table 6.

The Management Board of Visagino Atomine Elektrine UAB (VAE) has approved the main guidelines for reorganization of the electric power sector in the short-term future, defining the establishment of four functional blocks. The Reorganization is performed in order to ensure that the model of the Lithuanian energy sector activity complies with the National energy strategy, requirements of the Third Energy Package of the EU, aimed at liberalization of electric power and gas markets and creates conditions for integration of the Lithuanian electric energy system into the European Union market and ensures financing of the commenced strategic energy projects. A structure for the implementation of the sector's reorganization has been created in the Lithuanian electric power sector. In the pursuit of the reorganization, important system changes have been carried out – the formation of block of electric power generation companies has been finished, transmission grid has been separated, distribution networks are being merged. Also, maintenance companies will be established, the Technologies and Innovation Center has already been established. The formation of the transmission block, which will consist of transmission system infrastructure and system operator LITGRID AB, is aimed to separate and purify its activity, to comply with requirements of the Third Energy Package of the EU, to form a strong company, capable of interconnecting the Lithuanian electric power grid with ENTSO-E/ECN (European Network of Transmission System Operators/European Continental Network) grid, beginning with the links to Poland and Sweden, to implement measures, meant to facilitate the liberalization of the electric power market, to transfer auxiliary functions to maintenance companies.

Table 6. Electric Power Industry: Structure and Ownership, 2010

PRIVATIZATION					
	Private ownership			Argentina Singapore	Chile, Japan, Australia (VIC), UK, USA
	Public/Private Corporatisation		Philippines	Brazil, Columbia, China	New Zealand, Canada Australia (except VIC), Germany Denmark, Sweden, **Lithuania**
	Public Corporatisation	Mozambique	India, Thailand, Ghana, Indonesia, Malaysia, Pakistan, Korea, South Africa, Kenya, Sri Lanka		
	Government ownership	Nepal			
		Vertical Integrated Monopoly	**Single Buyer**	**Wholesale Competition**	**Retail Competition**
	RESTRUCTURING				

Notes: Vertical Integrate Monopoly Model offers no competition and no consumer choice. Single Buyer (SB) Model allows for competition in generation, with a single buyer purchasing wholesale electric power. Wholesale Competition Model allows the distribution (that also retails electric power) to choose their supplier. This introduces competition in generation and wholesale supply, but distributors retain monopoly over their franchised customers. Retail Competition Model allows for competition at all levels, from wholesaling to individual customers.
Source: author.

The formation of the generation block, the basis of which will consist JSC "Lithuanian Power" and generation capacities, concentrated in this company, is aimed to purify and concentrate the activity of generation, to reorganize and centralize generation capacities, necessary to ensure the energy independence of Lithuania, to transfer auxiliary functions to maintenance companies.

The formation of the distribution block, which will consist of the merged distribution network companies, is aimed to establish a customer-oriented and effectively functioning company, to obtain all possible benefits while merging the JSC VST and joint-stock company Rytu Skirstomieji Tinklai, to prepare the company, which is currently under merging, for possible attraction of funds, to transfer auxiliary functions to maintenance companies.

The formation of the maintenance block, which will consist of activities separated from other enterprises in electric power sector, is aimed to purify and optimize activities of maintenance, by establishing two companies of network maintenance, by implementing promotion measures of free market and, if it is economically feasible, by allowing entrance of a strategic investor. It is also aimed to establish a generation maintenance company and assets management company, which would manage the non-technological real estate and transport under ownership and sell redundant assets at most favorable conditions. To establish a commercial information technologies enterprise which would perform the sales of data transmission and data center services at the market.

In the course of the reorganization the Technological Innovation Center UAB (TIC) was also established, aimed to concentrate competence of innovations implementation and necessary resources for preparation of strategies and development guidelines and coordination of strategies and functions of main blocks. It is also planned that TIC will provide IT services to LITGRID AB, Visagino Atomine Elektrine UAB and its daughter companies. TIC will also seek a synergy of the merged IT infrastructure while centralizing and cohesively developing IT systems and will provide services of competence improvement by using the National Center for Training of Energy Professionals.

The reorganization of electric power sector, by which it is aimed to improve effectiveness of the system activity, separate and purify activities, increase energy independence and organize electric power infrastructure in accordance with the EU requirements, by ensuring the implementation of the key energy projects, commenced in November 2009, when resolutions were taken regarding the liquidation of LEO LT and possible changing the sector‘s structure. On May 4, 2010 the Government adopted resolution No. 517 “Regarding Approval of the Concept of Amendment Law on Electricity Law of the Republic of Lithuania,” by which the concept of Amendment Law on Electricity Law of the Republic of Lithuania was approved

Reorganization changes in electric power market in 2011 were the following:

On 1 January, 2011 VST AB and Rytų Skirstomieji Tinklai AB merged into a new legal entity LESTO AB, the distribution grid operator, which continues activities of the two predecessors.

On 1 March, 2011 the Transmission System Operator LITGRID AB and the company LITGRID Turtas AB were reorganized by incorporating LITGRID AB into LITGRID Turtas AB. After the reorganization all the rights, obligations and assets of LITGRID AB were transferred to LITGRID Turtas AB. On 4 March, 2011 the company name LITGRID Turtas AB was replaced by the name LITGRID AB. LITGRID AB keeps operating as the Transmission System Operator.

In Quarter III of 2011 Lietuvos Energija AB and Lietuvos Elektrine AB were merged. On 20 July, 2011 the companies were merged into a new legal successor entity Lietuvos Energija AB, which keeps operating the hugest national generation capacities (Kruonis PSHP, Kaunas Hydro Power Plant, and Lithuanian Power Plant in Elektrenai).

The wind farm of 30 MW held by Vejų Spektras UAB was sold to INTER RAO Lietuva UAB.

2.1.4. Electric Power Production and Demand

When Lithuania restored its independence, it inherited from the former USSR an advanced electric power sector – a well-developed transmission system and big power plants. The Lithuanian electric power system consisted of nuclear, thermal and hydro energy generation until the end of 2009 then Ignalina NPP was finally closed. The main institutions in electric power sector are presented in Table 7.

Table 7. Electric power market institutions in the Lithuanian electric power sector

The Ministry of Economy (from 2009 Ministry of Energy)	is responsible for energy policy and for the supervision of the main regulatory agencies in the energy field.
National Control Commission for Prices and Energy (NCCPE)	regulator of the energy sector.
Ignalina Nuclear Power Plant (installed capacity Table 8.)	is owned and controlled directly by the government.
JSC Lithuanian Power	2002-2009 JSC Lithuanian power acted as the market operator and since January 1, 2010 delegated these functions to the newly established JSC Baltpool. It also owns a hydro stations Kaunas and Kruonis.
Lithuanian TPP (installed capacity Table 8.)	is the largest non-nuclear generator and is in separate state ownership.
Vilnius CHP (installed capacity Table 8.)	is owned by Vilnius DH Company, a municipal enterprise, is being operated lease-concession arrangement by a local subsidiary of the French company, Dalkia.
Kaunas CHP (installed capacity Table 8.)	the Russian gas concern GAZPROM is the main owner of the Kaunas CHP and has 99.5% of Kaunas CHP shares.
JSC Eastern Distribution Grid	public supplier, distribution operator. Is in state ownership.
JSC Western Distribution Grid	public supplier, distribution operator. Has been privatized (2003).

Source: author.

Lithuanian electric power market is too small; generators are too big, with different market power, especially because of the prevailing artificially low cost nuclear power plant covering 70% and more of the domestic electric power demand, so liquid electric power market is hardly possible. Even with the closure of the Ignalina NPP national electric power market in Lithuania will be hardly competitive. Concentration in the Lithuanian electric power market until 2005 was very high, and measured by the Hirschman-Herfindahl index (HHI) reached 5572.

Lithuania possesses the Lithuanian condensing power plant fired by oil, gas or orimulsion, several oil and gas fired combined heat and power plants and rather big hydro pumped storage power plant. Electric power generation capacities in Lithuania are presented in Table 8.

Table 8. Electric Power Capacities in Lithuania, (MW)

		1990	Share, %	2001	Share, %	2006	Share, %	2010	Share, %	2015*	Share, %
NUCLEAR	**Nuclear**	**3000**	**51,19**	**3000**	**45,70**	**1300**	**27,72**	**-**	**-**	**-**	**-**
	Ignalina NPP	3000	51,19	3000	45,70	1300	**27,72**	**-**	**-**	**-**	**-**
THERMAL	**Thermal**	**2656**	**45,32**	**2649**	**40,36**	**2330**	**49,68**	**2380**	**65,56**	**2460**	**64,23**
	Lithuanian PP (n.gas HFO)	1800	30,72	1800	27,42	1500	31,98	1500	41,32	1500	39,17
	Vilnius CHP (n.gas, HFO)	384	6,55	384	5,85	380	8,10	370	10,19	370	9,66
	Kaunas CHP (n.gas, HFO)	190	3,24	180	2,74	180	3,84	170	4,68	170	4,44
	Mazeikiai CHP (HFO)	210	3,58	200	3,05	160	3,41	160	4,41	160	4,18
	Other CHP (n. gas)	72	1,23	85	1,29	110	2,35	180	4,96	260	6,79
HYDRO	**Hydro**	**106,1**	**1,81**	**1105,8**	**16,85**	**1020**	**21,75**	**1030**	**28,38**	**1030**	**26,89**
	Kruonis HPPS	-	-	900	13,71	900	19,19	900	24,79	900	23,50
	Kaunas HPP	100	1,71	100	1,52	100	2,13	100	2,76	100	2,61
	Other small HP	6,1	0,1	15	0,2	20	0,43	30	0,83	30	0,78
,RENEWABLES	**Other renewables**	**-**	**-**	**-**	**-**	**40**	**0,85**	**220**	**6,06**	**340**	**8,88**
	Other renewable (biomass)	-	-	-	-	10	0,21	20	0,55	40	1,04
	Wind PP	-	-	-	-	30	0,64	200	5,51	300	7,83
TOTAL		**5861**	**100**	**6564**	**100**	**4690**	**100**	**3630**	**100**	**3830**	**100**
DAILY DEMAND		**4400**		**2000**		**1800**		**2370**		**2750**	

Source: [180].

* Prognosis.

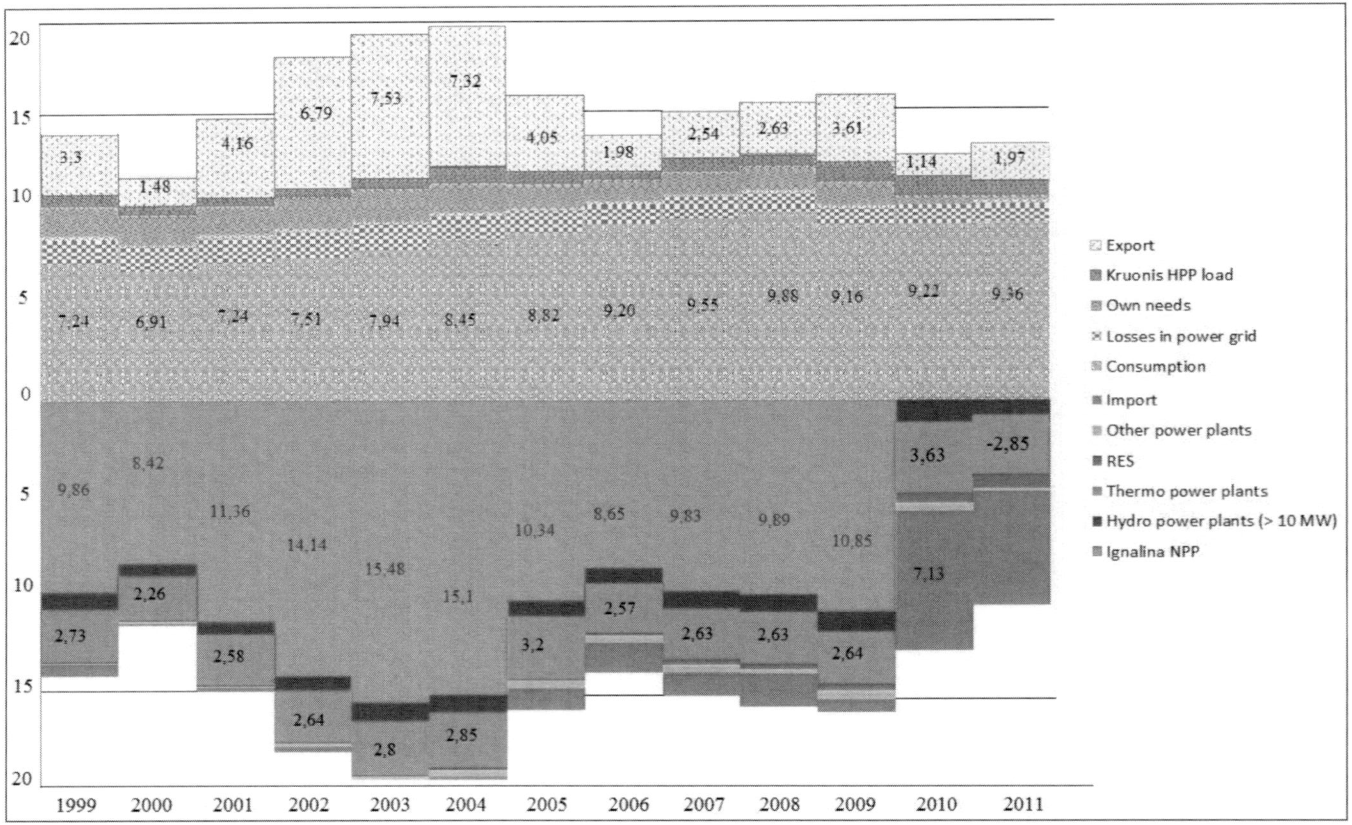

Source: author.

Figure 6. Electric power balance in 1999 - 2011, TWh.

On 31 December 2010, the total installed capacity of power plants in Lithuania reached 3,872 MW. Thermal power stations comprise 68.2%, hydro power plants comprise 26.5% (also including an evaluation of the capacity of the Kruonis Pumped Storage Plant) and renewable sources (wind power plants and power plants using biofuel) comprised 5.3%.

Upon the decommissioning of the last Unit II of Ignalina Nuclear Power Plant thus having lost the generation capacity meeting approximately 80% of total national electric power demand at the end of 2009, the previous exporter of electric power in Lithuania started importing electric power from the third country (the Russian Federation) and became dependent on it. In 2011 the electric power import grew by 22% and represented 59% of the national consumption (Figure 6).

The total installed power plant capacity increased by 4% within one year, reaching 4 021 MW, in thermal power plants (TPP) – by 4%, in power plants using renewable energy sources (hereinafter – RES) – by 14%. In 2011 the installed capacity of company power plants saw the most significant growth in terms of units in kind, from 96 MW to 164 MW. This demonstrates aspirations of industrial companies to have their own electric power supply. The development of electric power generation balance in Lithuania is presented in Table 9.

In 2010, electric power trade activities with other countries were carried out by AB Lietuvos energija, UAB Inter RAO Lietuva, UAB Baltic Energy Partners, UAB Enefit, UAB Energijos kodas, UAB EFT Lithuania and UAB Latvenergo prekyba. Electric power importing and exporting were carried out with Russia, Belarus, Latvia, Estonia and Finland. The majority of electric power imports came from Russia (72%). The majority of electric power exports went to Latvia (79%).

Table 9. Electric Power Generation balance in Lithuania, (TWh)

	1999	2000	2001	2002	2003	2004	2005	2006	2007	2008	2009	2010	2011
Import	0,62	0,14	0,20	0,30	0	0,13	1,09	1,54	1,17	1,68	0,68	7,13	8,71
Other PP	0,06	0,10	0,07	0,15	0,18	0,37	0,42	0,39	0,41	0,27	0,43	0,4	0,07
Ignalina NPP	9,86	8,42	11,36	14,14	15,48	15,1	10,34	8,65	9,83	9,89	10,85	0	0
Hydro PP (> 10 MW)	0,84	0,61	0,66	0,75	0,94	0,88	0,75	0,75	0,86	0,91	1,06	1,21	0,96
Thermal PPP (Power purchasing parity)	2,73	2,26	2,58	2,64	2,8	2,85	3,2	2,57	2,63	2,63	2,64	3,63	2,85
Renewables	0,02	0,03	0,04	0,04	0,05	0,07	0,07	0,10	0,27	0,26	0,34	0,46	0,8
Consumption	7,24	6,91	7,24	7,51	7,94	8,45	8,82	9,20	9,55	9,88	9,16	9,22	9,36
Lossess in network	1,33	1,28	1,42	1,43	1,41	1,27	1,23	1,09	1,12	1,02	0,97	0,99	0,97
Own needs	1,62	1,44	1,55	1,67	1,66	1,61	1,23	1,15	1,20	1,21	1,25	0,44	0,29
Kruonis HPPS	0,68	0,64	0,45	0,55	0,61	0,92	0,75	0,54	0,76	0,82	1,01	1,04	0,80
Eksport	3,30	1,48	4,16	6,79	7,53	7,32	4,05	1,98	2,54	2,63	3,61	1,14	1,97

Source: author.

Development of electric power consumption in Lithuania in 1999-2011 is presented in Table 10.

Table 10. Development of electric power demand structure in Lithuania during 1999 – 2011

Sector	1999	2000	2001	2002	2003	2004	2005	2006	2007	2008	2009	2010	2011
Househols, TWh	1,89	1,77	1,82	1,84	1,97	2,15	2,18	2,39	2,5	2,75	2,75	2,59	2,62
Households, %	26,1	25,6	25,1	24,5	24,8	25,4	24,7	26,0	26,2	27,8	30,0	28,1	28,0
Industry, TWh	3,3	3,27	2,85	2,96	3,02	3,08	3,25	3,14	3,13	3,09	2,65	3,07	3,55
Industry, %	45,5	47,3	39,3	39,4	38,0	36,4	36,8	34,1	32,8	31,3	28,9	33,3	37,9
Transport, TWh	0,08	0,07	0,07	0,06	0,02	0,02	0,02	0,09	0,09	0,06	0,07	0,08	0,09
Transport, %	1,1	1,0	1,0	0,8	0,3	0,2	0,2	1,0	0,9	0,6	0,8	0,9	1,0
Agriculture, TWh	0,3	0,23	0,15	0,15	0,15	0,16	0,15	0,16	0,16	0,16	0,16	0,17	0,2
Agriculture, %	4,1	3,3	2,1	2,0	1,9	1,9	1,7	1,7	1,7	1,6	1,7	1,8	2,1
Services, TWh	1,68	1,57	2,36	2,5	2,78	3,04	3,22	3,42	3,67	3,82	3,53	3,31	2,9
Services, %	23,2	22,7	32,6	33,3	35,0	36,0	36,5	37,2	38,4	38,7	38,5	35,9	
Total	**7,25**	**6,91**	**7,25**	**7,51**	**7,94**	**8,45**	**8,82**	**9,2**	**9,55**	**9,88**	**9,16**	**9,22**	**9,36**

Source: author.

The Lithuanian transmission network has strong interconnections with neighbouring energy systems:

- interconnection with the Latvian energy system by four 330 kV and three 110 kV lines;
- interconnection with the Belarus energy system by five 330 kV and seven 110 kV lines;
- interconnection with the Kaliningrad energy system by three 330 kV and three 110 kV lines.

There is still no interconnection with the neighbouring Polish energy system. There are planned electric power interconnections (it is planned to build two – LitPol Link 1 and LitPol Link 2 – power links with Poland).

2.1.5. Regulatory Arrangements in Electric Power Sector

In the process of the electric power market liberalization in Lithuania the Government has gradually withdrawn from electric power sector regulation by transferring these functions to independent institution. The price setting principles and the prices themselves, entry to the market (licensing), promotion and supervision of competition, defence of customer rights - these and other functions were passed over to the newly established institution - National Control Commission for Prices and Energy - which is not subordinate to the Government.

The NCCPE shall be responsible for securing effective competition in the electric power market, non-discrimination of suppliers and customers and provision of all customers with services of required quality. The Commission shall ensure:

1) the compliance with all rules for the regulation of interconnection capacity and management of interconnectors;
2) the time taken by distribution and transmission undertakings to provide connections of customers' equipment to the system and to restore electric power supply;
3) the provision by transmission and distribution system operators of appropriate information concerning interconnectors and capacity allocation to interested parties;
4) the effective unbundling of accounts with a view to avoiding cross-subsidies between transmission, distribution and generation and supply activities;
5) the terms, conditions and tariffs for connecting new electric power producers to secure that these are transparent and non-discriminatory, in particular taking into account of the costs and benefits of the various renewable energy sources technologies, distributed generation and CHP;
6) the adequate level of competition and transparency;
7) the effective electric power market operation and avoidance of dominating position of energy undertakings in the market;
8) the compliance of Electric power trading rules and other appropriate regulations [181].

Table 11 summarises the main features of energy regulatory framework in Lithuania.

Table 11. Regulatory Framework

Independence of regulator	Monitoring & Compliance	Market Regulation	Network Regulation	Generation Tariff Regulation	T&D Tariff Regulation	End-user Tariff Regulation	Dispute Resolution	Licensing
High	+	+	+	-	+	-	+	+

Source: author.

The newest version of Law on Electricity with amendments was adopted on 2012 and provides that the NCCPE shall monitor the electric power market and publish annual and quarterly electric power market monitoring reports according to the requirements of Description of the Procedure of the Electricity Market Supervision which was approved by the NCCPE in September 2010. The Transmission System Operator and the Power Exchange Operator inform the NCCPE on potential violations of activity terms established for license holders.

Under provision of the new version of the Law on Electricity adopted on 2012 the NCCPE shall create relevant conditions and to ensure effective competition in electric power sector and to prevent the abuse of the market influence. In order to achieve this aim the NCCPE shall undertake market studies related to electric power production and independent supply market. It is necessary to ensure that the procedure of the studies is compliant with the terms and procedure provided for by regulations of the Electricity Market Study Rules approved in June 2012 by the NCCPE.

According Law on Electricity the NCCPE shall combat with major market influence on the electric power market.

Therefore NCCPE establishes obligations:

1) to provide services for cost-based prices, with return on investment according to the reasonability criterion;
2) to provide the cost accounting systems aimed for provision of specific service types;
3) to modify applied service prices or establish a price cap for regulated prices.

When establishing obligations the NCCPE takes into account the right to get return on investment of the entity having major market influence on the electric power market, and providers of transmission, distribution services and/or the public supplier. The Law on Electric power requires that obligations established by the NCCPE must be clearly defined, transparent, non-discriminating, verifiable and ensuring equal opportunities to provide services to customers.

Network Regulation

According to Article 40 of the Law on Electricity of the Republic of Lithuania national electric power market shall be established gradually providing third party access (TPA) to eligible customers and the right to conclude direct power supply contracts with freely selected independent suppliers. Under the Regulated Third Party Access (rTPA) market structure, the transmission company publishes transmission tariff and access requirements so that generators may enter into agreement with the eligible customers. The eligible customers can directly negotiate with the generators. Under this alternative, the remaining customers are charged a cost-based rate by the regulator based on presumably optimal operation. Under the rTPA, the regulator observes the merits of the resources, such as hydro, thermal, and IPPs under very tight regulation. In addition to the regulated market, a spot market may also be created for real-time operation with marginal cost pricing. With this model, competition is created to some extent at the generation level (despite tight regulation) and at the retail level. The rTPA does not offer a level playing field due to lack of a central market, with transparent rules and a single price for all.

The NCCPE shall prepare and approve the methodologies for setting the State-regulated prices, adjusts the price ceilings of the regulated activities and publicly announces electric power tariffs established.

According to the newest version of the Law on Electricity, the NCCPE sets the price ceilings for electric power transmission and distribution services for a five-year time period. The NCCPE also verifies whether the specific prices of the regulated services set by the electric power companies do not discriminate various groups of customers.

The price ceilings of the electric power transportation have been set for the 3 years period (regulated period of 2011–2013) etc. However every year, the price ceilings of the electric power transportation are revised by taking into account the impact of quantity, unpredicted changes, indexation, adjustment ratios etc.

Wholesale Pool

In Lithuania, electric power is traded by bilateral contracts (local contracts) or via Power Exchange. A bilateral contract is an agreement between an energy consumer and an energy supplier to buy and sell a specified quantity of energy at a specific price. All imported or exported energy is traded via Power Exchange. The average daily (or monthly) wholesale price of electric power at the Lithuanian power exchange is usually lower than the regulated price of electric power, but the price of electric power traded at peak times is more expensive.

After closure of Ignalina NPP there is no dominating national electric power producer since 2010, the electric power market has been implemented according to the Resolution No. 740 on Lithuanian Power Market Development Plan adopted on 8 July, 2009 of the Government of the Republic of Lithuania. The newest version of the Law on Electricity adopted in 2012 has provided that since 2013 the public supplier shall establish agreements on electric power supply based on regulated public prices only with households, which had not selected an independent electric power supplier. All commercial users shall buy electric power on the electric power market based Power Exchange prices or bilaterally agreed contractual prices.

There were no significant changes in the electric power sales market in Lithuania during 2010-2011. The market share of Lietuvos Energija AB reduced by 5% and the one of Vilniaus Energija UAB – by 1%, the one of Kaunas Hydro Power Plant UAB – by 2% and the one of INTER RAO Lietuva UAB increased by 1%. The main changes in the sales market there the following: Lietuvos Energija AB lost 37% of the market and because of this the market share of Latvenergo Prekyba UAB grew from 5 to 18%, and that of INTER RAO Lietuva UAB increased up to 19%.

Therefore the biggest structural parts of the electric power trade market in 2010 were taken by AB Lietuvos energija and Lithuanian Power Plant (AB Lietuvos elektrine) – about 40% and UAB Inter RAO Lietuva - 40% (Figure 7).

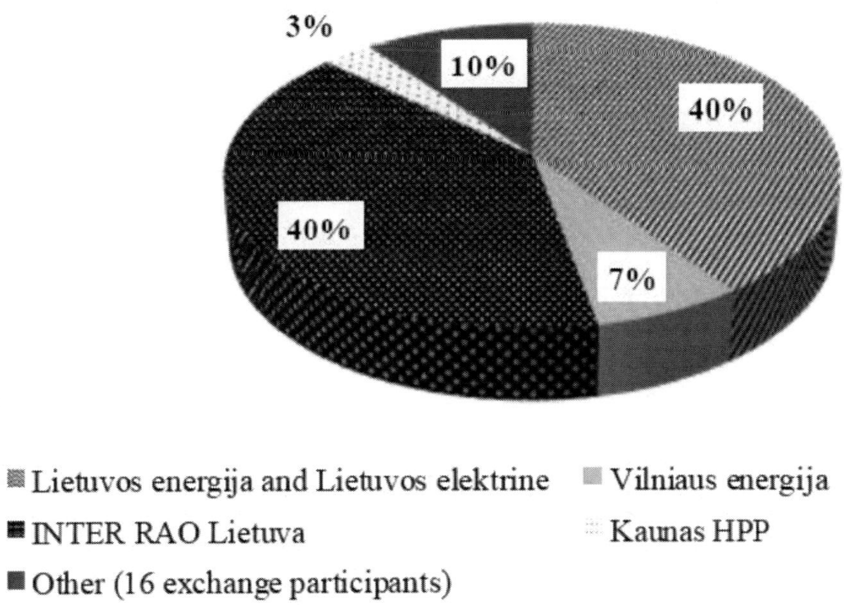

Source: author.

Figure 7. Structure of wholesale electric power market in 2010.

In 2010 and 2011 one player covering approximately half of electricity power market was INTER RAO Lietuva UAB in Power Exchange sales and buys.

With the increase of electric power market opening and elimination of public regulated prices, competition will increase among suppliers; however there will be no more alternatives due to the small Baltic regional market until the electric power trade will extend to the Nordic and the Western European electric power markets.

The electric power market model of NORD POOL SPOT was introduced in Lithuania since 18 June 2012. In this year 15 independent electric power supply licenses were issued. In the end of year 2012 there were 65 licensed suppliers in the market. The number of active suppliers has grown from 20 to 27 entities. In 2012 the market opening rate increased to 54% of total national energy consumption level, compared to 35% in 2010.

In 2011 Lithuanian electric power market electricity trade volume reached 8 TWh and was by 2% less than in 2010. In 2011 the average price on the BALTPOOL UAB electric power market was 45.24 EUR/MWh (3% lower than in 2010). The average electric power end price of independent suppliers increased by 1% and reached 4.9 ct/kWh in 2011.

Accoring to provisions of Electricity Trading Rules the retail electric market consists of the suppliers' trade in electric power with users carried out in line with the terms and procedure established in the Rules of Electricity Supply and Use, when electric power is sold to customers is an independent or public or electric power supplier. The retail electric power market concentration reduced in 2011-2012, however the company LESTO AB remained the main supplier in electric power market (Figure 8).

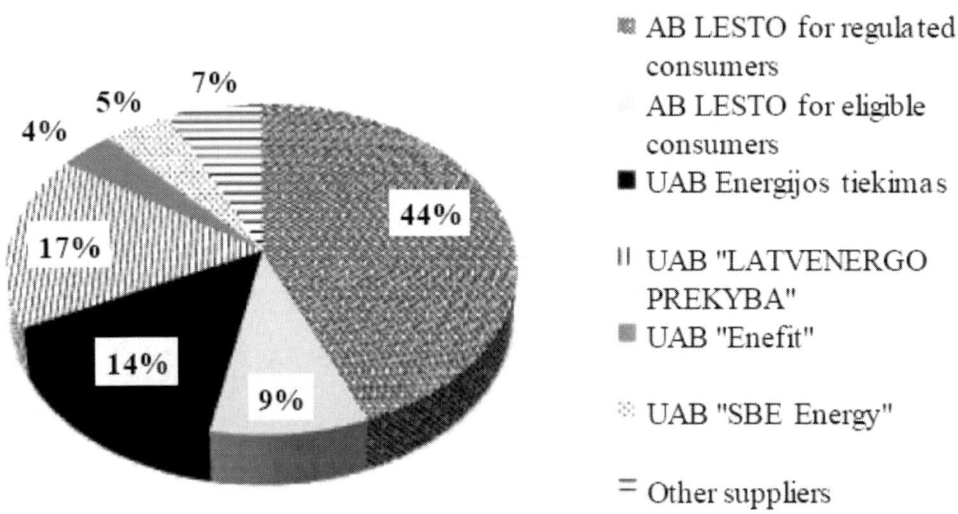

Source: author.

Figure 8. The structure of retail electric power market in 2011, %.

There were no big changes in electric power prices during investigated period. In 2010 the average electric power price sold to end users by independent suppliers was 4.38 ct/kWh, and in 2011 it grew by 12% and was 4.90 ct/kWh. In 2011 the actual buying price of the distribution grid operator (AB LESTO) applied to independent electric power users was 5.39

ct/kWh (In 2010 the price provided by Vakaru Skirstomieji Tinklai AB was 4.52 ct/kWh and by the one of Rytu Skirstomieji Tinklai AB - 4.52 ct/kWh).

Special Incentives

Special Lithuanian government incentives that affect the choice of generation:

- *Discount on the fee of connection of power plants to the* network. Generators whose power plants are using renewable energy sources for electric power generation are subject to a 40% discount for the connection to the network of operating energy plants.
- *Purchase obligation and transportation priority.* Pursuant to the Regulations holders of the electric power supply licence are obliged to purchase renewable electric power and sell it to their customers. The transmission network operator shall ensure transportation priority for the renewable electric power when the network throughput is limited.
- *Financial support for investments.* Financial support for investments is among the most important measures promoting the use of renewable energy sources (Lithuanian Environmental Investment Fund, EU Structural Funds).
- *Feed-in tariffs* are applied for wind power plants; biomass power plants, hydropower plants (only for hydro power plants of the capacity less than 10 MW). Electric power produced from wind, solar and biomass power plants with installed capacities not exceeding 30 kW is purchased at a fixed price (feed-in tariff), which is determined by the national regulatory authority (NCCPE). Feed-in tariffs are provided in Table 12.

Table 12. RES-E feed-in tariffs for 2012

Renewable energy technology	Support level (€/MWh)
Biomass	144,8
Biogas	185
PV (non-integrated into building)	417
PV (integrated into building)	521
Hydro	81
Wind	107,2

Source: author.

According to regulations the electric power produced from wind, solar and biomass power plants with installed capacities >30 kW is supported by feed-in tariffs and quotas that are established by auctions. The Govermnet approves quotas and geographical areas of auctions organised by the NCCPE. Auctions are open to all producers who have signed letters of intent and guarantee obligations. The winner of the auction is established based on the minimum feed-in tariff proposed by producer. The maximum amount of the feed-in tariff is determined by the NCCPE. The auctions are organised by the NCCPE. Also electric power from RES is exempt from excise tax.

Based on analysis of various studies and international market practice in Renewable Energy Sources (RES) sector the NCCPE established tariffs for electric power and biogas produced from RES, for 2012. The feed-in tariffs are differentiated by technologies and capacities. The amount of direct payments coming from the budget of the Public Service Obligations (hereinafter – PSO) to producers of electric power from RES for 2012 exceeds 33.3 million EUR and amounts to almost 16% of the total PSO budget. This amount does not include payments directly related to RES development in the electric power sector such as balancing costs of producers of electric power from RES, costs of connecting electric power producers from RES to the electric power networks, needs of making networks ready to connect producers from RES. These all are insignificant amounts and in future this component will definitely increase. It is forecasted that the amount of direct payments coming from the budget of PSO to electric power producers from RES will grow annually and in 2020 it will make 231.7 million EUR, in case of the forecasted annual growth of electric power exchange prices of 0.15 ct/kWh per year. The total market of electric power producers from RES will reach 0.51 billion EUR in 2020, excluding minor producers from RES with capacities < than 30 kW.

After the Law on Renewable Energy was passed in 2011 the NCCPE issued the related secondary legislation and approved new prices of buying electric power from RES. In 2011 the volume of electric power produced from RES was 0.7 TWh, amounting to 7.4% of the total national electric power consumption needs in Lithuania. The volume of electric power produced from RES in 2012 reached 0.82 TWh. In 2020 if objectives established in the Law on Renewable Energy will be reached and the incentivized volumes of installed capacities based on respective technologies, 4.4 TWh of supported electric power is likely to be produced from RES, excluding electric power produced by the smallest producers (up to 30 kW capacities). If the annual growth in electric power consumption will make 2%, in 2020 the total volume of supported electric power produced from RES will make 40% of the total electric power consumption in Lithuania.

In 2012 RES makes up ~14% of energy produced and approximately ~ 5% of electric power produced in Lithuania. The usage of RES in Lithuania is constantly growing. The biggest renewable potential in producing electric power in Lithuania is found in the field of wind energy. Up to 2004 in Lithuania the main kinds of renewable energy resources were wood and hydro power while the utilisation of other renewable energy resources was just at the beginning. In these latter years the electric power generation of wind energy and production of biofuel have been rapidly developing. The utilisation of biomass (wood, forest cutting residues, straw, energetic plants, etc.) as well as hydro power resources is being developed in Lithuania. There are constructed demonstrational geothermal and solar power plants, started the production of gas emitted from municipal waste dumps, expanded the amounts of biogas production (Table 13).

Lithuanian energy policy aims to ensure secure electric power supply at the lowest possible price for consumers and lowest possible impact on environment. State policy in electric power sector promotes use of renewable energy sources and construction of new nuclear power plant. The established mechanisms to support renewables had positive impact on investments in renewable based electric power generation. The favorable conditions were created by the Government of Republic of Lithuania to attract investments in construction of new NPP. Other factors which also have impact on choice of electric power generation technologies are related with public opinion. Up to now there was positive opinion regarding nuclear energy in Lithuania however after accident at Nuclear power plant in Fokusima has negative impact on public opinion regarding nuclear energy project in Lithuania however decision to buy new nuclear power plant in Lithuania is still being supported by the ruling Conservative party in Lithuania.

Table 13. Development of renewable capacities in Lithuania 2000-2010

	2000	2001	2002	2003	2004	2005	2006	2007	2008	2009	2010
Total solar capacity, kW	0.1	0.1	0.2	0.4	2	2.7	9	10	30	50	60
Total biogas el. capacity, MW	1.25	1.21	1.21	2.14	1.96	2.71	2.71	3.04	4.24	4.5	4.7
Total wind capacity, MW			0.16	0.16	0.85	1.1	48.1	52.3	54.4	62.8	92
Total small Hydro Power Plant (HPP) MW	13.1	13.4	16.5	18.3	19.6	23.5	24.4	24.7	25.0	26	27

Source: [182].

2.1.6. Electric Power Prices

From 01 January 2010 Regulated tariffs are removed for large consumers (consumption totaling 35% of Lithuanian demand). From 01 January 2015 Regulated supply tariffs for all consumers shall be abolished except the guaranteed tariffs for the groups designated by EU regulations (Table 14).

Table 14. Application of regulated tariffs

Starting from	Application of regulated tariffs
1st of January 2010	Regulated tariffs is going to be abolished for the consumption totaling 35% of Lithuanian demand (consumers with >400 kW capacity)
1st of January 2011	Regulated tariffs is going to be abolished for the consumption totaling 45% of Lithuanian demand (consumers with >100 kW capacity)
1st of January 2012	Regulated tariffs is going to be abolished for the consumption totaling 55% of Lithuanian demand (consumers with>30 kW capacity)
1st of January 2013	Only hausehold consumers shall fall under the regulated supply tariffs scheme
1st of January 2015	Regulated supply tariffs for all consumers shall be abolished except the guaranteed tariffs for the groups designated by EU regulations.

Source: author.

The development of electric power prices for households and industry is presented in Table 15. The electric power prices for final consumers were constantly growing in household's sector though in industry in 2005-2006 some tends of decease can be noticed.

Table 15. Electric power prices in Lithuania, €/kWh

Electric power prices for household							
2003	**2004**	**2005**	**2006**	**2007**	**2008**	**2009**	**2010**
	0,0535	0,0609	0,0609	0,0658	0,0729	0,0799	0,0955
Electric power prices for industry							
2003	**2004**	**2005**	**2006**	**2007**	**2008**	**2009**	**2010**
0,0550	0,0513	0,0498	0,0498	0,0548	0,0829	0,0924	0,0991

Source: [182].

Table 16. Electric power reform in Lithuania: summary

LITHUANIAN POWER MARKET	**Competition and consumer choice**								
	Degree of Competition				**Consumer Choices**				
	Generation		Retail		Small		Medium		Large
	Medium		Low		+		+		+
	Regulatory Frameworks								
	Independence of regulator	Monitoring & Compliance	Market Regulation	Network Regulation	Generation Tariff Regulation	T&D Tariff Regulation	End-user Tariff Regulation	Dispute Resolution	Licensing
	High	+	+	+	-	+	-	+	+
	Market Mechanisms								
	Power Exchange		Price-based Pool		Cost-based Pool			Contracts Auction	
	+								
	Capacity Payments								
	Pool Types				Capacity Payments				
					Price-based			Quantity-based	
	Net Pool							+	
	Transmission and Distribution Pricing								
	Regulator				Pricing				
					Transmission			Distribution	
	National Control Commission for Prices and Energy (NCCPE)				Price cap			Price cap	
	Instruments for Risk Hedging								
	Contracts for Differences		Bilateral Contract		Future Contract	Forward Contract		Options	
	-		+		-	-		-	

Notes: Large - large industry; Medium - commercial and small-scale industries; Small - households. High - more than 10 generators in a jurisdiction; Medium – less than 10 generators in a jurisdiction; Low – no competition.

High - the regulator is governed by statue and is overwhelmingly independent; Medium – the regulator is partially governed by statue and partially under government influence; Low – the regulator is largely under governmental control.

Quantity-based approach - the system operator estimates the need for capacity in the system. Price-based approach - generators receive directly payments for capacity.

Source: author.

In 2012, the adjustment of electric power prices was made for households predetermined by the following important circumstances: In 2012 the supported electric power as well as the electric power produced according to the quotas will amount to 3.23 TWh: the supported electric power produced from RES will exceed 0.8 TWh, the electric power produced in the combined heat and power plants - 0.9 TWh and 1.53 TWh - in Lithuanian Power Plant.

The supported electric power and electric power produced according to the quotas, which has to be obligatory purchased by the Public Supplier, covers the demand of the regulated customers, which for the year 2012 has been projected as 3.2 TWh. As the total demand of the regulated electric power customers is covered by the supported electric power, the imported electric power is not included into the electric power "pie" of this group of electric power customers. The supported electric power and the electric power produced according to the quotas are purchased at the uniform day and night prices during all week (this price significantly surpasses the prices set at the Power Exchange). The continuous balancing of the distribution service costs between the industrial and small customers has been further continued by reducing this unbalance up to 16% in 2012. The continuous balancing aims to reduce the barriers for access to the electric power market for alternative energy suppliers.

The electric power sector reform and its results in Lithuania are summarized in Table 16.

2.2. Natural Gas Sector

Lithuania in terms of the natural gas supply has to rely on two major wholesale suppliers, i.e., Lietuvos Dujos AB and Dujotekana UAB dominating in the natural gas supply market. Though the natural gas retail market is 100% open now in Lithuania because of the high concentration on the supply side, customers are not able to use the advantage of the open market. On the distribution side, about one third of the territory of Lithuania has not been gasified and this is main obstacle for further development of natural gas market in Lithuania.

2.2.1. Stages of Natural Gas Market Opening

Natural gas firstly reached Lithuanian consumers in 1961. In 1995 the state-owned enterprise Lietuvos Dujos was reorganised into the joint stock company (JSC) Lietuvos Dujos AB and has been running a natural gas business since then.

The company Lietuvos Dujos AB was privatised during two stages. The international energy companies have become its shareholders through a public call for tenders organized in 2002 and 2004. In 2002 a shareholding of 34% was acquired by the consortium Ruhrgas AG and E.ON Energie AG (Germany). In 2004 a shareholding of 34% was acquired by the natural gas supplier OAO Gazprom (Russia). Currently, OAO Gazprom has 37,1% of the shares of Lietuvos Dujos AB, E.ON Ruhrgas International GmbH has 38.9% of the shares of Lietuvos Dujos AB and the Ministry of Energy of the Republic of Lithuania - 17.7% and small shareholders - 6.3%.

In 2010 the Lithuanian government adopted a resolution approving the Law on Natural Gas concept establishing the provisions of the third legislative package on the energy market by opting to unbundle natural gas undertaking ownership. The provisions of ownership unbundling in natural gas sector were incorporated in the draft Law on Natural gas, which was approved in 2010. The draft Law on Natural gas was adopted by Lithuanian Seimas and entered into force from 1 August, 2011. The plan for unbundling the activities in natural gas sector was approved by the Lithuanian government on 28 October 2011. The plan foresees that the natural gas transmission and supply activities should be unbundled by 28 October 2014. Currently, the owner and the operator of the Lithuanian transmission network is company Lietuvos Dujos AB, a vertically integrated company engaged in the import, transmission, distribution and supply of natural gas in Lithuania.

According to Law on Natural Gas the Lithuanian government or its authorised institution can stipulate the necessary measures related to the transit of natural gas and its transportation through the Republic of Lithuania to ensure the safety and credibility of the natural gas sector of the Republic of Lithuania. In the case of a disruption of the gas supply, the amounts of natural gas transported by transit are proportionally limited to the amounts of natural gas limited to the country's users. According to this Law in the case of the termination of the natural gas supply, natural gas transportation by transit is cancelled immediately. Article 26 of the Law on Natural Gas sets requirements that the operator of the transmission system collect systemises and regularly provides information about the transit of natural gas in the territory of the Republic of Lithuania in accordance with the regulations established by the NCCPE. Article 40 of this law sets requirement that system operators provide the right to use the natural gas system according to the agreement with natural gas companies, users and persons transporting natural gas by transit.

Article 2 of the Law on Natural Gas regulates natural gas transit as transportation of gas through the territory of the Republic of Lithuania that is originated in the territory of a third state and intended for the territory of this and other third states. Article 18 of the Law on Natural Gas sets requirement that natural gas is transported by transit with the mutual agreement of the persons in the contracts and taking into account the capacity of the available transmission systems and the priority for meeting the demand of the country's system users.

Lithuanian Seimas has adopted the Law on Energy Resources Market in 2012, which establishes the legal framework for the creation of energy resources exchange. According to this Law the Energy Resources exchange is a centralised energy trade system, in which the trade of biofuels, petroleum product stocks, natural gas and instruments of auxiliary protection from energy price volatility shall be organised. The energy resources market started its limited operations in 2012, while achieving its full functionality on 1 January 2013. In March 2012, the natural gas exchange, operated by BALTPOOL UAB, was established in Lithuania in accordance with the provisions of the Law on Natural Gas, ensuring an alternative to bilateral gas purchase agreements.

Lithuanian Seimas adopted the Law on the Liquefied Natural Gas (LNG) Terminal in 2012. The Law ensures the required legal framework for the construction of the LNG terminal in Lithuania and establishes the financial and other conditions for the economically and technologically sound operation of the LNG infrastructure.

2.2.2. Market Structure and Ownership

The Lithuanian natural gas system is connected to the gas systems of Latvia, the Kaliningrad region of the Russian Federation and Belarus. All of the natural gas supplied to

Lithuania is sourced from the only company registered in Russia - OAO Gazprom. According to a long-term natural gas supply contract with Lietuvos Dujos AB, entered into force in 1999 and expired in 2015, natural gas is not only supplied to Lithuania but is also transited through Lithuania to the Kaliningrad region of the Russian Federation.

Lithuania has well-developed natural gas transmission and distribution network consisting of approximately 1,800 km of main natural gas pipelines and 8,000 km of distribution grids. Natural gas consumption in Lithuania in 2009 has decreased by 16% comparing with the consumption in year 2008 and amounted to 2.7 bcm from which 0.18 bcm being in the household sector. In 2010, natural gas consumption in Lithuania has increased by 14% and amounted to 3.1 bcm from which 0.2 bcm being consumed by the households.

According to the Law on Natural Gas, natural gas distribution, transmission, storage, liquefaction and supply are licensed activities. Licenses are issued and all licensed activities are being allocated under NCCPE control.

In 2010, Lithuania had one main natural gas transmission system operator (Lietuvos Dujos AB) and six distribution system operators. According to the Law on Natural Gas, natural gas transmission or distribution licenses are issued to undertakings that are in the defined territory and own natural gas transmission or distribution system installed under the requirements of the Law on Natural Gas, which must be connected to the operating transmission or distribution system.

The transit of natural gas to the Kaliningrad region is carried out according to the long-term agreement between the Russian company Gazprom and Lietuvos Dujos AB which was signed in 1999 and is valid until 1 January 2016. In 2010 transmission capacities for transit account 4.1 million m³/day. There have been 1387.2 million m³ of natural gas transported by transit to the Kaliningrad region of the Russian Federation. Compared to in 2009 transit of natural gas through the territory of Lithuania have increased by 15.9%.

Wholesale Natural Gas Market

The natural gas market's concentration is maximum in Lithuania because Lithuania is fully dependent on the sole natural gas supplier –Russian company Gazprom OAO, though natural gas is partly bought through LT Gas Stream AG. In Lithuania 13 natural gas companies were licensed as gas suppliers in 2013, but in real terms gas quotas were shared between Lietuvos Dujos AB and Dujotekana UAB. In 2010, the only company, Lietuvos Dujos AB, was licensed to be the transmission system operator in Lithuania.

The distribution market of natural gas is in the similar situation in Lithuania as company Lietuvos Dujos AB has 99% of the all distribution market share. Though there are five other companies entitled to engage in distribution activities, they provided distribution services only in individual regions with total distribution market share of 1%. At the same time in terms of distribution activities, approximately one third of the territory of Lithuania has not been gasified. To encourage competition and reduce the influence of dominating operators in natural gas market, a competition procedure has been prescribed by Law on Natural Gas therefore these unlicensed territories will be gasified through the development of an infrastructure.

There are two main suppliers in natural gas market, i.e., Lietuvos Dujos AB and Dujotekana UAB. These companies dominate the natural gas supply market and they have supplied 99% of the total natural gas sold to Lithuanian gas consumers. Haupas UAB has supplied gas to the Druskininkai region however this company has sold 1% of the total gas supplied to Lithuanian consumers.

In 2010 the natural gas market in Lithuania did not face any important changes — the same five companies were engaged in the import of natural gas, i.e., Lietuvos Dujos AB, Haupas UAB, Achema AB, Dujotekana UAB and Kaunas Thermal Power Plant UAB. Natural gas import volumes in 2010 have increased by 15% compared to year 2009 and amounted to 3,105.98 million m^3. Achema AB and Kaunas Thermal Power Plant UAB only use imported natural gas for their own use; the other three sell it to customers. Lietuvos Dujos AB experienced the highest increase of natural gas imports of 31.5% and covered about 50% of the natural gas market in Lithuania. All the natural gas distributed in Lithuania is purchased from Russia. More than 80% of all imported natural gas was purchased from Gazprom and the rest amount from Gas Stream AG LT. In Figure 9 the quantities of imported natural gas by the companies are presented in 2010.

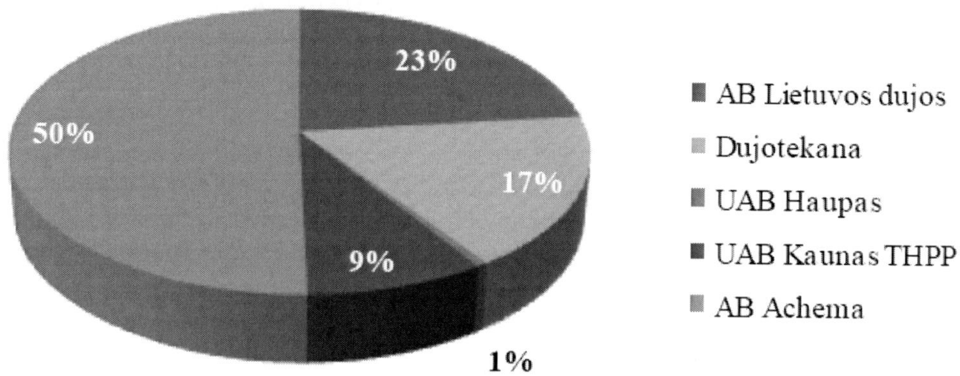

Source: author.

Figure 9. Natural gas import market in 2010, million m^3.

One can notice that Lithuanian natural gas wholesale market does not exist. In 2010, trade in natural gas between the natural gas companies amounted to just 0.3% of the total volume of imported natural gas. The main problem is that local natural gas companies buy and sell very small natural gas volumes to customers. Intergas UAB and Agrofirma Josvainiai AB purchased gas from Dujotekana UAB, Fortum Joniškio Energija UAB purchased natural gas from Lietuvos Dujos AB and Druskininku Dujos UAB purchased natural gas from Haupas UAB. Natural gas suppliers traded in natural gas only under long-term contracts in Lithuania. No other types of contracts have been established by natural gas supply undertakings. According to the Law on Natural Gas, the NCCPE has access to contracts concluded between natural gas undertakings and customers in Lithuania. There is requirement in the Law for natural gas undertakings to submit the main conditions of their natural gas purchase and sales contracts and other annual activity reports to the NCCPE for revision.

The only two natural gas supply companies, i.e., Lietuvos Dujos AB and Dujotekana UAB, supply gas to Lithuanian customers. Haupas UAB supplies natural gas only to the Druskininkai region, where the gas grid is not connected to the rest of the network. The annual natural gas consumption in Lithuania in 2010 totaled 28.74 TWh or 3.085 billion m^3. In 2010 the maximum daily consumption of natural gas in Lithuania reached 0.187 TWh. As it was mentioned before natural gas is not produced in Lithuania and the entire volume of natural gas is being imported from Russia. In 2010, imports of natural gas totaled to 41.86 TWh or 4,493 million m^3 and 12.92 TWh or 1,387 million m^3 was transmitted to the Kaliningrad region of Russia by transit through Lithuanian territory.

Retail Natural Gas Market

In Lithuania at the end of 2010 and beginning of 2011 there were 555 thousand of natural gas customers: 549 thousand households and almost 6 thousand industrial customers. The number of retail market participants did not change since 2010. There were seven natural gas suppliers in Lithuania the same as in the wholesale market. Two of them are dominant as in wholesale natural gas market, i.e., Lietuvos dujos AB (73.5%) and Dujotekana UAB (25.4%). All the other natural gas undertakings covered only 1.2% of the total natural gas sold to Lithuanian customers. The total volume of natural gas sold to Lithuanian customers in 2010 amounted to 19.6 TWh or 2 million m^3, and was by 27% bigger comparing with year 2009 level. Non-household customers consumed about 30% more natural gas in 2010 than in 2009. The closure of Ignalina NPP had a great impact on such a significant natural gas consumption increase as the Lithuanian Power Plant replaced Ignalina NPP and became the biggest electric power producer in the country. In 2010 Lithuanian households consumed 198 million m^3 of natural gas, which is about 10% more than in 2009. Due to a cold winter a peak in natural gas consumption occurred in the first quarter of 2010 and the natural gas consumption has increased by 41.5% compared the same quarter of year 2009. Lietuvos Dujos AB covers 99.9% of the total natural energy demand of Lithuanian households. In Figure 10 the structure of retail natural gas market in Lithuania is presented.

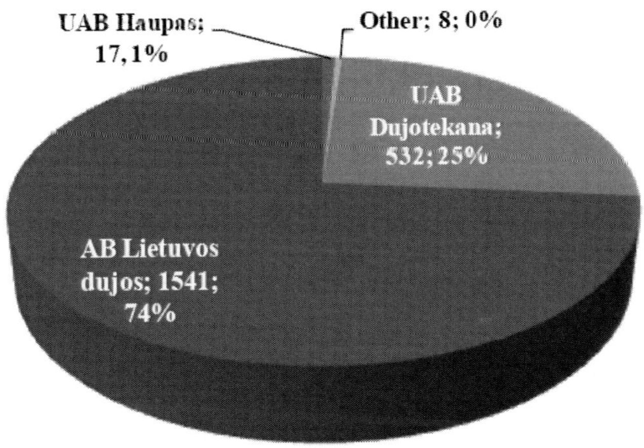

Source: author.

Figure 10. Retail natural gas market shares by natural gas undertakings in 2010, million m^3.

The largest natural gas company in Lithuania, i.e., Lietuvos Dujos AB, supplied 14.4 TWh or 1.6 billion m^3 in 2010 and 1.8 TWh or 197.8 million m^3 of this volume was sold to Lithuanian households and 12.6 TWh or 1348 million m^3 -to commercial consumers. At the same time Dujotekana UAB supplied about 5 TWh or 536 million m^3 of natural gas. All the natural gas was sold to just commercial consumers and 33 GWh or 3.6 million. m^3 from this volume was sold to other natural gas undertakings such as Agrofirma Josvainiai AB and Intergas UAB. Dujotekana UAB has just 15 consumers and the largest share of which are gas power plants.

Another natural gas company Druskininkų Dujos UAB purchased from Haupas UAB 2.4 GWh or 0.3 million m^3 of natural gas in the same year. It has supplied about 3000 households and 15 commercial consumers. In 2010 1.4 GWh or 147 million m^3 of natural gas was sold to households and about 1 GWh or 114 million m^3 to commercial customers.

Agrofirma Josvainiai AB purchased from Dujotekana UAB 25.3 GWh or 2.7 million m^3 of natural gas and supplied it to household and commercial customers. The Intergas UAB is engaged only in supply activities in Mažeikiai region and in 2010, the company sold 7.8 GWh or 836 million m^3 of natural gas to both household and commercial customers. Haupas UAB sold 156 GWh or about 17 million m^3 of natural gas. The company only supplied natural gas to two commercial customers. One of them was the gas supply company Druskininkų Dujos UAB. At the same time Fortum Heat Lietuva UAB purchased 47 GWh or about 5 million m^3 of natural gas from Lietuvos Dujos AB and has supplied it to household and commercial customers.

The Lithuanian natural gas system is interconnected with the natural gas systems of Latvia, Belarus and the Kaliningrad region of Russian Federation. Capacities located at the Lithuania–Belarus border ensure the full amount of capacities required by Lithuanian consumers for transit to the Kaliningrad region and to Latvia. From Russia natural gas is supplied to Lithuania through Belarus using the Minsk–Vilnius gas pipeline. The second interconnection with Belarus, i.e., Ivacevičiai–Vilnius, is currently not being used because of the unsatisfactory gas line status. In addition it has no gas metering station. In the north, the Lithuanian natural gas transmission system is connected to the Latvian natural gas system.

Currently, the Baltic States natural gas market does not exist because of the two reasons: the existence of isolated natural gas transportation system in Baltic States and the fact that all the countries are dependent on a single natural gas supplier from Russia, i.e., Gazprom. The diversification of the natural gas supply sources is one of the main requirements to ensure the proper functioning of the natural gas market in Lithuania. This purpose may be achieved by implementing strategically important infrastructure investment projects necessary in Lithuania: interconnecting the Lithuanian and Polish natural gas systems, using the Inčukalnis underground natural gas storage facility in Latvia and constructing a liquefied gas terminal in Lithuania. Diversification and liberalisation of the natural gas market would ensure natural gas supply security and reliability and make it possible for every natural gas user to freely choose a natural gas supplier and benefit from cheaper natural gas purchases. However, though Lithuania has opened its natural gas market, this has been just formality because of the existence of the only natural gas supplier – Russian Gazprom.

2.2.3. Natural Gas Demand

Natural gas has been used in Lithuania since 1961 when the gas pipeline from Dashava (Ukraine) reached Lithuania. After 35 years of service, this pipeline is worn out and is closed at the Belarussian border. Natural gas is imported to Lithuania by another pipeline from Belarus, which was commissioned in 1975. It connected the Lithuanian gas network to the "Northern Lights" pipeline transporting natural gas from Siberian gas fields. In the north of

Lithuania the natural gas network is connected to the natural gas system in Latvia. Natural gas pipelines connecting Lithuania and Latvia are closed at present. Lithuanian natural gas network is connected with the natural gas system of the Kaliningrad region in the west. Natural gas is also supplied to Lithuania from Minsk by a pipeline. Natural gas consumption is increasing since 2010 with the close of second unit at Ignalina NPP in 2009. Natural gas balance development in Lithuania is presented in Table 17.

The largest share of final natural gas consumption is in industry sector followed by households. Final natural gas consumption in 2011 has decreased in all sectors comparing with year 2010 (Table 17).

2.2.4. Regulatory Arrangements

Seimas of the Republic of Lithuania passed a new Law on Natural Gas on June 30, 2011 and it came into effect on August 1, 2011.

The Law on Natural Gas has been developed seeking to implement requirements of Directive 2009/73/EC of the European Parliament and the Council of 13 July 2009 concerning common rules for the internal market in natural gas and repealing Directive 2003/55/EC (OL 2009 L 211, p. 94) and Regulation (EU) No 994/2010 of the European Parliament and of the Council of 20 October 2010 concerning measures to safeguard security of gas supply and repealing Council Directive 2004/67/EC.

The Law on Natural Gas sets requirement for separation of the activity of natural gas transmission from the activities of natural gas extraction and natural gas supply by unbundling the ownership of the transmission system and TSO (transmission system operator) from the natural gas companies involved in the natural gas extraction and supply activities. Lithuanian Government based on the provisions of the Law on Natural Gas, approved the plan for implementing the unbundling of the activities of the natural gas companies, which do not comply with the provisions of the Law. In accordance with the mentioned plan, the natural gas undertakings, which do not comply with the requirements of the Law on Natural Gas, had to select the method of unbundling the natural gas transmission activity either by reorganizing control over the natural gas undertakings or by splitting the natural gas companies. According to the Law the NCCPE shall supervise the efficient unbundling of the relevant activities of natural gas undertakings by assuring independence of the transmission and distribution activities from the commercial interests.

In Lithuania there is only one natural gas company, which does not comply with the requirements of the Law on Natural Gas – Lietuvos Dujos AB. This company is involved in in natural gas transmission, distribution and supply activities. On May 31, 2012 the company submitted to the NCCPE the action plans for unbundling and reorganization, which had been approved on May 28, 2012. Pursuant to this Lietuvos Dujos AB have unbundled its natural gas activities in 2013 and unbundled natural gas activities and control in 2014.

The NCCPE by its Resolution as of June 15, 2012 resolved that Lietuvos Dujos AB has to unbundle the natural gas transmission and distribution activities in line with the methods and deadlines provided in the plans and has to submit the required documents by keeping to the deadlines indicated in the plans and notify the NCCPE about the cases of delays or failure to perform actions foreseen in the plans.

Table 17. Natural gas balance, million m^3

	2001	2002	2003	2004	2005	2006	2007	2008	2009	2010	2011
Imports	2681.6	2710.9	2944.3	2928.7	3116.2	3100.3	3719.6	3124.8	2736.8	3105.9	3407,4
Changes in stocks	1.7	2.1	-1.4	6.7	-20.0	-32.3	-104.5	120.1	-9.8	9,1	-8,9
Gross consumption	**2683.3**	**2713.0**	**2942.9**	**2935.4**	**3096.2**	**3068.0**	**3615.1**	**3244.9**	**2727.0**	**3115,0**	**3398,5**
Transformation	1382.4	1385.6	1577.8	1600.7	1689.9	1591.7	1494.3	1361.7	1349.9	1737,5	1433,4
Public TP plants	947.8	911.9	1081.4	1181.9	1270.1	1190.4	1090.0	1031.3	1026.5	1366,2	1111,3
Autoproducer TP plants	13.5	8.3	9.4	34.3	34.6	31.4	28.1	7.6	29.5	30,0	28,5
Public heat plants	407.9	438.9	452.7	346.7	340.8	340.1	355.9	299.6	263.3	314,3	268,5
Autoproducer heat plants	13.2	10.6	11.6	15.4	19.9	17.3	17.6	22.3	15.6	16,7	17,0
Geothermal plants	-	15.9	22.7	22.4	24.5	12.5	2.7	0.9	15.0	10,3	8,1
Used for transformation into methanol	10.9	13.5	15.2	17.5	16.1	11.7	0.8	9.0	3.1	-	-
Energy sector	4.0	4.0	3.9	3.8	3.9	3.0	2.9	2.9	2.1	1,9	6,0
Extraction of crude petroleum	0.1	0.1	0.1	0.1	0.1	0.1	0.1	0.1	0.1	0,1	0,1
Manufacture of refined petroleum products	0.8	0.9	0.9	0.8	0.8	0.2	0.1	0.0	0.1	0,1	0,1
Electric power, gas, steam and air conditioning supply	3.1	3.0	2.9	2.9	3.0	2.7	2.7	2.8	1.9	1,7	5,8
Non-energy use	761.7	755.7	766.5	675.8	725.2	747.2	1385.9	1172.1	721.2	666,1	1295,0
Distribution and transmission losses	30.9	19.0	29.8	26.4	12.6	2.0	0.9	-	0.1	0,1	0,1
Final consumption	**493.4**	**535.2**	**549.7**	**611.2**	**648.5**	**712.4**	**730.3**	**699.2**	**650.6**	**709,4**	**664,0**
Industry	263.1	292.4	298.1	324.7	347.0	371.9	352.9	338.2	314.7	343,4	330,1
Construction	8.3	10.9	12.2	14.7	15.3	18.3	19.5	20.2	12.7	15,0	13,7
Agriculture	34.9	34.9	32.9	38.5	35.6	47.2	49.4	42.7	33.8	39,1	38,0
Transport	10.1	11.2	9.6	9.6	19.3	32.6	34.2	30.0	30.3	30,7	25,7
Households	134.4	137.7	146.9	158.8	168.1	175.1	184.1	182.3	181.4	197,8	181,2
Commercial and public service	42.6	48.1	50.0	64.9	63.2	67.3	90.2	85.8	77.7	83,4	75,3

Source: [183, 184, 185, 186].

The new Law on Natural Gas does not provide for the regulation of the natural gas supply activities therefore since 1 August, 2011 the activity of natural gas supply has become unregulated in Lithuania. Natural gas supply has been functioning since that according to the principles of the competitive natural gas market. The price of natural gas supply can become regulated again if NCPPE during market research determines that due to the lack of efficient competition and natural gas operator is charging the prices that are too high or is using the price pressure thus causing damage to other natural gas market participants.

NCCPE has issued the natural gas market operator's license to BALTPOOL UAB on 23 November 2011. The primary function of the natural gas market operator BALTPOOL UAB is to organize trade in natural gas at the Natural Gas Exchange. When the Natural Gas Exchange becomes actually operating, all natural gas consumers, who have concluded yearly agreements with suppliers – natural gas importers (Lietuvos Dujos AB, Dujotekana UAB, Haupas UAB) and other economic operators of natural gas sector will be able to sell and purchase their yearly surplus or deficient quantities of natural gas at the Natural Gas Exchange, i.e., to balance their natural gas flows in Lithuania.

NCCPE has approved the Regulations of Trading at the Natural Gas Exchange in 2012, which had been developed by BALTPOOL UAB. This document prescribes the responsibilities and rights of the Exchange participants and of the natural market operator for trading in natural gas, procuring natural gas with the contract assignment rights, and establishes the procedure for settlement of payments for the transactions concluded at the Natural Gas Exchange.

To implement the requirements set forth in Regulation (EU) No 1227/2011of the European Parliament on wholesale energy market integrity and transparency and in performing its functions prescribed by the Law on Natural Gas the NCCPE approved the Rules for Supervising Trade in Natural Gas in 2012. These Rules aim to establish pre-conditions for efficient competition in the natural gas market, assuring transparency, reliability, settlement of payments among the participants of the Natural Gas Exchange. The Rules guarantee the equal treatment of market participants, transparency of information, avoiding distortion of natural gas prices and natural gas supply conditions. According to Rules the supervision of the natural gas market shall be ensured by NCCPE and the natural gas market operator. The natural gas market operator shall supervise natural gas trade at the Exchange, and the NCCPE – trade in natural gas based on bilateral selling-purchasing agreements.

Law on Energy Resources Market was passed in May 2012, which has established a legal framework for administration, regulation, supervision and control of the energy resources market. The Law regulates interaction of entities involved in centralized trading in biofuel and oil products stocks, trading in natural gas and in auxiliary instruments for hedging against fluctuation of energy prices. The Law on Energy Resources Market aims to provide the participants of the energy resources market with a possibility to compete in the energy resource market and to make use of the transparent, clearly regulated and non-discriminating centralized trade in energy resources.

These regulations opened the way for functioning of the natural gas market in Lithuania and established conditions for competition in the natural gas market; however the actual volumes of trading in natural gas at the Exchange are very limited. From the beginning of operation of the Natural Gas Exchange only one transaction was concluded.

The NCCPE supervises the natural gas market opening in the wholesale and in the retail markets. However in Lithuania the natural gas is being supplied from a single external source, therefore there is no real competition either in the wholesale or in the retail markets and there were no customers, who have changed their gas supplier since opening of natural gas market.

To assure that the natural gas market participants would have the reliable information, every quarter and after the end of the year the NCCPE uploads the market monitoring reports, on the NCCPE website. In these reports NCCPE summarizes the data about the import of natural gas, its consumption, transportation by the transmission and distribution gas pipelines, the respective market shares held by the natural gas market participants, the average prices of the imported natural gas and the investments made in the natural gas supply, transmission and distribution facilities.

After opening natural gas market, the participants of the natural gas import market were the same as in 2010, i.e., Lietuvos Dujos AB, Dujotekana UAB, Achema AB, Kaunas Combined Heat and Power Plant (Kaunas CHP), Haupas UAB. Natural gas was imported to Lithuania from the single external gas supplier – company Gazprom in Russia in accordance with the quotas set for each individual importer. Dujotekana UAB purchased imported natural gas not directly from the Russian company Gazprom, but through the intermediary – company LT Gas Stream.

2.2.5. Natural Gas Prices

In 2011 the average price of the imported natural gas not taking into account the price of Achema AB increased by 25.4% in average compared to 2010, i.e., from 249.65 thousand EUR up to 313.1 thousand EUR per 1000 m^3. The participants of the wholesale and the retail natural gas supply markets are Lietuvos Dujos AB, Dujotekana UAB and Haupas UAB. Lietuvos dujos AB and Dujotekana UAB supplied 99.2% of the total natural gas volumes sold to Lithuanian natural gas customers. At the same time company Haupas UAB supplied natural gas to Druskininkai region and sold 0.8% of the total natural gas volumes supplied to Lithuanian natural gas customers. Achema AB and Kaunas CHP have purchased natural gas for their own consumption and did not participate in the natural gas supply market.

In 2011, 3 407.46 million m^3 of natural gas were imported to Lithuania, i.e., by 9.7% more than in 2010. The import of natural gas to Lithuania has increased because of the natural gas volumes imported by Achema AB. In 2011 these volumes were by 81.3% higher comparing with year 2010. All other natural gas importing undertakings have decreased the import quantities. The total decrease of natural gas import, without taking into account the volumes imported by Achema AB, amounted to 11.7%. The sales to natural gas customers reached 1840 million m^3. The remaining volume of natural gas was consumed by the natural gas importing undertakings for their own demand. Only the volumes of natural gas, which from the importing company has been bought by other natural gas undertakings performing the natural gas transmission and distribution operations in the Lithuanian specific regions, can be categorized as belonging to the wholesale market. There was no natural gas trading transactions among the wholesale natural gas customers. 7.35 million m^3 of natural gas was sold in the wholesale market in 2011 or 0.4% of the total sold quantity of natural gas in Lithuania.

In 2011, like in previous years, 7 supply companies participated in the natural gas retail sales. In Lithuania the total number of natural gas customers reached 557 thousand in 2011. Among them 551 thousand were household customers and 6 thousand – commercial consumers. In Lithuania, in the retail natural gas market, 1 840.2 million m^3 of gas were sold in 2011, or by 12.2% less comparing with year 2010. In addition, in 2011 the income of the natural gas supply sector increased from 55 million EUR up to 603 million EUR or by 9.5%.

In the retail natural gas supply market, like in the wholesale market, there were the same two dominating natural gas suppliers in Lithuania. i.e., Lietuvos Dujos AB and Dujotekana UAB, which held 98.8% of the retail natural gas supply market. All the rest of natural gas supply undertakings shared among themselves 1.2% of the natural gas market. In the natural gas transmission market there is only one operating natural gas undertaking – Lietuvos Dujos AB. In 2011, 5 405 million m^3 of natural gas were transported via the natural gas transmission system in Lithuania. In 2011 the transported natural gas volumes increased by 21.3% in 2011 compared to 2010. 38% of the transported natural gas volume was the natural gas transmitted by transit. The natural gas transportation to the Lithuanian natural gas customers increased almost by 10% because of the bigger quantities transported by company Achema AB – from 3 069 million m^3 up to 3 361 million m^3 of gas. The natural gas transportation by transit increased in Lithuania by 47.3% in 2011 compared tom 2010. In 2011, the income for transportation earned from the Lithuanian natural gas customers reached about 40 million EUR or it was by 0.6% less than in 2010.

In the natural gas distribution activity 6 active natural gas market participants were operating. The biggest natural gas market share is held by Lietuvos Dujos AB – 97.6%. In 2011, 1 092 million m^3 of natural gas were distributed or by 9% less than in 2010. In terms of value, in 2011the income from distribution activity decreased by 11.0% or from 58 million EUR up to 52 million EUR.

In 2011, the investments in the infrastructure of the natural gas sector equaled to almost 19 million EUR. In the natural gas transmission activity – 9.6 million EUR, in the natural gas distribution activity – 9.4 million EUR and was by almost 46% less than in year 2010.

The main changes which can be noticed in monitoring the natural gas market in 2011, as compared to the data of 2010:

- the average natural gas import price assigned for production of energy increased by 25%;
- the volume of natural gas transported via the natural gas transmission network increased by 21% because of the bigger natural gas quantities purchased by Achema AB;
- the distributed natural gas volume decreased by 9%;
- the total natural gas volume imported to Lithuania increased by 9.7% because of the bigger natural gas volumes imported by Achema AB;
- in 2011 as in 2010, the wholesale natural gas market was insignificant and accounted for 0.4% of the total natural gas volume sold to natural gas customers;
- the quantity of the natural gas retail trade increased by 12%.

The natural gas market shares held by the natural gas undertakings operating in the natural gas market changed not significantly. In the natural gas supply market in 2011, like in

2010, Lietuvos Dujos AB and Dujotekana UAB remained the dominating natural gas undertakings.

Lithuania participates in the process of setting up uniform rules for natural gas tariffication at the EU level. Article 13 of Regulation (EC) No. 715/2009 of the European Parliament on conditions for access to the natural gas transmission networks and repealing Regulation (EC) No. 1775/2005 sets the main principles on natural gas tariffication, which are also applied in Lithuania. NCCPE participates in the process of developing framework guidelines, including a framework guideline on natural gas tariffs. In Table 18 the average natural gas transportation tariffs in Lithuania in 2011 are presented.

Table 18. Lietuvos Dujos AB average transportation tariffs for different consumer groups in 2011

Consumer group	Natural gas transportation price, EUR/MWh		
	Transmission	Distribution	Total
I4-1 (418,6 TJ)	1.55	3.86	5.41
D3 (83,7 GJ)	1.65	7.21	8.86
I1 (418,6 GJ)	1.55	7.21	8.76

Source: author.

The NCCPE prepares and approves the methodologies for setting the natural gas prices of the State-regulated activities, sets and approves the natural gas price ceilings of the regulated activities, approves the natural gas tariffs for Lithuanian household consumers.

Since 1 August 2011, when the new Law on Natural Gas came into force, the NCCPE has revised the Price Ceilings Calculation Methodology of the Natural Gas Transmission and Distribution Prices and introduced the principles of calculation of the reasonable return on investments made by the natural gas undertakings. The weighted average cost of capital (WACC) has been applied for the calculations of the return on investments, which is defined by applying the optimum structure of financing assuring the least costs of capital.

The NCCPE sets the natural gas transmission and distribution price ceilings for a five-year period, and once per year adjusts the price ceilings for five economic operators in the Lithuanian natural gas sector. The NCCPE inspects whether the specific prices of natural gas, which have been set by the natural gas undertakings, are not discriminating in respect to the individual consumer groups, and every six-month period approves the natural gas prices for household consumers. Every year NCCPE sets, adjusts or inspects about 100 prices applicable for economic operators or household customers in natural gas sector.

The end-user of natural gas prices and the natural gas transportation prices for customer groups in the period from 1 July, 2011 and from July 1, 2012 are presented in Table 19.

Lithuania is considering constructing a LNG import terminal in Klaipeda, which is expected to substantially strengthen Lithuania's energy security and diversify the gas supply. An Inter-institutional Working Group on the Construction of a LNG terminal in Lithuania was established in 2010. The group defined the most suitable location and technological solution for the LNG terminal in Lithuania. The site was selected in the southern part of Klaipeda Seaport for the offshore terminal with the possibility of storing LNG. The memorandum of understanding with the US Company Cheniere was signed in May 2011. Also a dialogue with major LNG suppliers has been already started.

Table 19. Natural gas price structure for consumers, EUR/MWh

	Price from 1st July 2011			Price from 1st July		
	D3	I1	I4-1	D3	I1	I4-1
Natural gas import	28.6	27.9	27.9	36.	35.72	35.72
Natural gas transmission	1.6	1.5	1.5	1.	1.55	1.55
Natural gas distribution	7.2	7.2	3.8	7.	7.19	3.85
Supply	1.0	0.3	0.3	1.	0.30	0.30
Equity	1.0	1.0	1.0	1.	1.06	1.06
Total:	**39.6**	**38.0**	**34.7**	**47.**	**45.81**	**42.47**
Taxes (VAT – 21%)	8.3	8.0	7.2	9.	9.62	8.92
Total:	**47.9**	**46.0**	**42.0**	**56.**	**55.43**	**51.39**

Source: author.

Klaipedos Nafta AB signed an agreement with the lead advisor for the preparation and implementation of the LNG terminal project in 2011. The international company FLUOR was selected. The agreement provides for the lead advisor to work together for four years in preparing the technical development plan for the project, assisting in the selection of technologies, performing actions in order to obtain obligatory permits, solving matters related to the safety of the project and on other issues associated with the technical implementation of the project. In addition the adviser shall perform works related to the economic part of the project. It will be responsible for the producing the business and financial models for the LNG terminal and developing a terminal's performance strategy. The adviser shall supervise the technical realisation of the project and participate during the entire execution period of the project, i.e., up to the year 2014. In July 2011, the government recognised LNG terminal as a project of state importance. In January 2012, the winner of the international tender for Klaipedos Nafta AB, 'Procurement of liquefied natural gas floating storage and regasification unit (FSRU)', was selected: an international Norwegian company, Hoegh LNG. In March 2012, Klaipedos Nafta AB entered into a lease agreement for a FSRU with Hoegh LNG. The lease of the vessel includes all the expenses for the FSRU operation, covering the maintenance, repairs and necessary materials for repairs, vessel crew and insurance. In 10 years of lease the Klaipedos Nafta AB will have the right to purchase the FSRU and operate it itself. In 10-year lease period, the FSRU should be able to operating LNG terminal for 30 more years. Hoegh LNG will, in addition to providing the FSRU, also provide the operation and maintenance, repairs and all necessary materials for the repairs, as well as a qualified vessel crew. This contract also includes training experts. The FSRU was ready to start operation before the end of 2014. Lithuanian Seimas adopted the Law on the Liquefied Natural Gas Terminal in 2012, which ensures the required legal framework for the construction of the LNG terminal in Lithuania and establishing the financial and organisational conditions for the technologically and economically sound operation of the LNG terminal and its infrastructure.

With the growing demand for the security of the natural gas supply, the construction of an underground natural gas storage facility has also become a priority project for Lithuania. Therefore Lithuanian government is carrying out preparatory works to implement it. In July 2010, a consortium of Lithuanian and international companies, MN, Odin and Acoustic Geofizikai Szolgalto Kft, began an evaluation of the feasibility of a potential site for the underground natural gas storage facility in Syderiai. The other preparatory works were completed by 2014. It is expected to have an underground storage facility in Syderiai with a minimum useful volume of 500 million m^3. It is expected that the underground storage facility will be constructed in Syderiai before the end of 2016.

Also the Lithuanian–Polish natural gas interconnection is one more priority project in order to diversify the natural gas supply in the Baltic Sea region. In line with the EU's Trans-European Energy Networks (TEN-E) Programme, almost EUR half million of support was received from EC in 2010 for the feasibility study concerning this project. The first phase of the feasibility study is foreseen for performing an economic analysis and the second phase will include the preparation of the feasibility study including three performance scenarios. A consortium of Gaz-System and Lietuvos Dujos companies in 2011 started to perform feasibility study of the Lithuanian– Polish natural gas interconnection project. It is expected that the Lithuanian–Polish natural gas interconnection will be built between 2018 and 2020. Among the priorities in the investment of EU funds in the EU financial framework for 2014–2020 it is foreseen that projects will be financed from EU funds. To increase the capacity of Lithuanian–Latvian natural gas interconnection, Lietuvos Dujos AB together with Latvia Gaze AS are implementing the project 'Improvement of Latvian– Lithuanian gas interconnection throughput capacity'. The companies received individually a decision by the European Commission (EC) in 2011 regarding the financial support allocation to the project. 50% of the project's value would be supported by EC. The project will be implemented during 2011–2013.

2.3. District Heat Sector

District Heat sector is one of the most important energy sectors of Lithuania. Its activities are closely related with other energy sectors, such as electric power supply, natural gas supply, oil, and renewable energy sources (RES). In Lithuania like in former soviet and socialist countries essential economic reforms took place in district heating (DH) sector. Former soviet and socialist countries had no experience in the conversion of DH as a public service to a financially viable business concern. The DH reforms in transition economies varies from the collapse of former large DH systems to effectively upgraded and efficient DH sectors in some countries. Lithuania together with the most former socialist states can be considered as country where state and municipal influence in the DH sector is quite high.

2.3.1. Restructuring of District Heat Sector

District heating (DH) sector reform in transition economies basically is related to changing from a "socially orientated" service to an "economically viable business." The process of restructuring the DH sector includes restructuring, ownership and organizational changes and also economic transformation supported by technical modernization. This should decrease the heat supply costs and ensure energy savings, as well as the environmental impact and increase the heat supply reliability and ensure high service quality to customer. Viability of the DH companies depends on heat price levels and heat sale, as well as heat supply costs.

Lithuanian DH sector passed abundant changes in course of the transfer from the Soviet methods of the activities to the market economy. In the transition period, a danger of liquidation of DH was obvious. The support of Scandinavian countries was very important for saving of DH sector in Lithuania since Restitution of Lithuanian Independence. At present, among the EI new Member States Lithuania is considered as an example of a well-managed DH sector capable to update it up to the level existing in countries of Western Europe. The heat transmission networks inherited from the Soviet Union contributed to preservation of Lithuanian DH sector, as well. The inherited heat transmission network enabled to extend and improve the DH sector after the Restitution of Independence, because of the existence of the initial investments in DH networks. At present in Lithuania, the total length of DH transmission networks of various diameters is about 2500 km. Otherwise as compared to natural gas or water supply pipes, in heat transmission systems double pipes are used for formation of closed circulation contour, because the cooled heat-carrying agent comes back to the boiler-house through the parallel return pipe. Therefore due to the former reason, the total length of DH pipes doubles and achieves up to 5000 km. Its weight is about 113 thousand tons.

Between the years 1991 and 2009, abundant works have been completed in all segments of Lithuanian DH sector. Automatic heat equipment of buildings maintains the required temperature in flats independently on the changes of the outdoor temperature that is particularly important during the spring and autumn. Because of the automatic heat equipment buildings are not overheated anymore in Lithuania. Earlier some Lithuanian DH consumers requested to disconnect them from the DH system, while at present, requests on connecting to DH system are provided. In course of liquidation of block substations and carrying out other modernization works, the heat losses in the heat-supply were considerably reduced (from 32% to 15%) in Lithuania. Though slowly but successfully Lithuanian DH is being transferred to using local fuel in heat production, increase capacities of cogeneration facilities and perform other modernization works. All these activities resulted in the reduced consumption of fossil fuel for heat production.

DH system was established in Lithuania in 1947, when supply of steam from Petrasiunai CHP to the Paper Factory was started. In 1948 the Petrasiunai CHP started supplying hot water for heating dwelling-houses. In the years 1949-1955, first DH systems appeared in the biggest Lithuanian cities: Vilnius, Klaipeda, Panevezys and Siauliai. Later, DH was rapidly developed in Lithuania and the today level was achieved by the year 1990.

The process of DH reforms in the new EU Member States was implemented in the last two decades and, consists of the following actions:

- Ownership of DH enterprises was moved from federal state control to local governments (cities, municipalities) and in some cases into private strategic investor hands.
- Separate institutions - Energy regulator (NCCPE) - have been established in most cases with the role of economic and legal regulation of the DH sector.

- The general energy policy issues and support schemes remain in the hands of government;
- Department responsible for the DH policy is set in the responsible ministry.
- All participants in the regulated DH sector have to ensure implementation of state policy in this sector.
- General support subsidies were removed from the DH sector and social support systems based on individual customer approach were introduced in most cases.
- General regulatory (tariff authority) principles were established: setting of heat prices and tariffs must ensure economic viability of DH operators and financing of long-term stability and modernization of DH sector. Pricing regime should give adequate incentives for DH undertakings to increase their efficiency.
- Municipalities (cities) can sell or lease DH undertakings to private business if it's feasible or necessary.

After reforming DH regulation and establishment of NCCPE the important results were achieved: implementation of technical-economic parameters of DH schemes were improved, the DH sector became economically viable, attractive for investments and now further successful modernization of the DH systems is taking place in Lithuania. Heat prices for final customers have increased significantly during period of reforms. NCCPE accepted all of the justified cost elements and in spite of these changes DH customers were usually not satisfied with these changes. Some customers tried to find alternative heating methods. Despite successful reforms some of the problems in DH remain in Lithuania. The most important problems define very high thermal energy consumption in residential and commercial buildings. The high heat demand cause of inefficient buildings resulted in relatively high energy bills to customers, especially compared to low household income in Lithuania. Most customers were not able to install individual heating systems that regulate heat demand. Therefore high heating bills do not match the low economic power of most Lithuanian heat customers. In addition, the renovation rate of older buildings that improves the insulation capacity of older buildings was quite slow in Lithuania and due to this reason energy demand has remained high in the country.

The main authorities regulating the energy sector in Lithuania are the Government, the Ministry of Energy, the Ministry of the Environment, the National Control Commission for Prices and Energy (NCCPE), the State Energy Inspection and the Council of the 60 Municipalities in Lithuania. The Ministry of Energy implements the State energy policy in the DH sector, drafts and approves legal acts regulating the DH sector. The Ministry of the Environment decide on issues relating to reduction of environmental impact, construction and fulfil functions, organise and carry out monitoring of environmental effects in increased pollution areas of the energy sector. The NCCPE approves methodologies and procedures for setting state regulated DH prices and must set heat prices if the municipality does not it, or sets incorrect prices; approve charges for connection of energy facilities; grant licenses for DH companies. The State Energy Inspectorate provides state control over energy facilities and establishes the technical reliability standards for equipment. The management of the DH sector at the municipal level is allocated to the individual Municipalities. Within their respective territory, municipalities organize the supply of DH to consumers including DH price setting, according to methodology adopted by NCCPE.

2.3.2. Structure and Ownership of District Heat Sector

A municipality, following the DH sector plan, organises the supply of DH to heat customerss according to their needs for heating and ventilating the premises and for hot water preparation. A heat supplier must hold a licence for the supply of heat in Lithuania. The procedure and rules for issuing licences are approved by the Lithuanian government. Licences for the DH supplier supplying at least 10 GWh/year, taking into account the recommendations of the municipalities, are issued. Their validity can be suspended and the licensed activities are controlled by the NCCPE. Licences for the DH supplier of less than 10 GWh/year are issued, suspended and cancelled and the licensed activities are controlled by the municipality. Licences for the activities involved in DH supply are granted for an unlimited amount of time for one person only in certain specified territories.

DH supply networks in Lithuania provide energy for heating and hot water preparation for almost 51% of all households and public sector buildings. DH supplies 20,100 buildings, in Lithuania out of which:

- 1,100 are business undertakings buildings;
- 3,100 public buildings.
- 2,600 are individual houses;
- 17,500 are apartment blocks.

Almost all of the small DH companies in Lithuania or about 300 of them belong to municipalities. In 2010 there were around 50 bigger DH supply undertakings supplying at least 10 GWh of DH per year and their activities were regulated by the NCCPE. The major part of DH undertakings or 33 were managed by municipalities. 17 DH undertakings were leased from municipalities by some private companies and others were independent heat producers. DH suppliers are regulated by the NCCPE and have served 638,000 customers, 96% of which are households.

The biggest DH supplier in Lithuania is Dalkia group of companies, which manages UAB Vilniaus energija and eight UAB Litesko branches: in Palanga, Telšiai, Vilkaviškis, Kelme, Marijampole, Biržai, Alytus and Druskininkai. In 2010 Dalkia group of companies have supplied 4% of all DH required by Lithuanian customers. During 2010 all the DH supply companies supplied 10,245 GWh of heat. 97% of the total DH supplied to the country's networks was supplied by NCCPE regulated companies.

There are about 2,500 kilometres of DH supply networks in Lithuania. The amount of DH supplied to the networks per year comprises 9,000–10,000 GWh, losses in the DH networks make around 1.5 TWh or 16% of DH supplied. The technical losses of heat transmission in modern and optimally sized pipelines and those having thermal insulation comprise around 10–12% of the DH volumes supplied to the DH network. The optimal level of heat losses has still not been reached in Lithuania and further improvement, renovation and modernization of DH supply system necessary. The experience of former social countries shows that when public DH suppliers are in difficult situations, and in desperate need for investment, experienced private partners with capital are very useful and desired. Private investors usually seek for higher profits; therefore the DH regulatory system must create conditions for private investors to earn money by increasing efficiency, reducing DH losses but not by abusing their monopolistic position in the market. Private undertakings should follow clear and detailed plans regarding investment, improvement of efficiency, upgrade of the main assets etc., which have to be fixed in appropriate agreements. When the economic situation in the DH sector has been stabilized in Lithuania and DH undertakings have good perspectives for profitable operations, private capital is often considered a disadvantage due to monopolistic market position. For example, in Lithuania new leasing agreements in the DH sector were discontinued in 2004 when the NCCPE assured the economic viability enterprises operating in this DH sector. There are examples, illustrating very low competence of the municipality in the privatization process in Lithuania. A poorly prepared tender, specification and contract can become a long-term disadvantage for the local community.

In some countries better results of modernizing and commercializing DH were achieved by leasing of DH undertakings to private business. In this case, the municipality remains involved through terms and conditions attached to the lease contract such as provisions based on: DH tariff calculation rules, investment requirements, service quality and reliability indicators, accounting provisions, reporting directions, oversight, timeframes, fees, and other issues.

Privatization in the DH sector could be controversial and frequently accompanied with disputes and conflicts, usually resulting from the improper preparation of the privatization process and a lack of experience in this field. The privatization processes takes different form depending on the limitations set by legislation and the authorities in charge of the privatization. According to Heat Law Lithuanian municipalities have to keep 100% ownership in DH transmission networks and no less than 30% in DH production facilities in order to secure the heat supply process.

In contrast, promotion of private capital participation in the DH production can form the basis for wholesale competition with the licensed DH undertaking. If the DH strategy is clear and appropriate, private investors are interested in the development of CHP plants, waste incinerators and other business related to DH schemes. Regulation and pricing systems should promote such competition in DH sector.

2.3.3. Regulatory Arrangements

The Heat Law in Lithuania was adopted and came into force in 2003. It splits responsibilities between NCCPE and municipalities. Licensing rules approved by the government describe all aspects of license conditions, termination etc. A licensee in the DH sector must fulfil the following requirements:

- ensure continuous supply of DH meeting consumers' demand. Must connect all new DH customers in the DH zone and connection cost is included in the general DH price;
- should have technical, economical and managerial potential to carry out duties related to licensed activity in DH sector;
- purchase of heat from independent producers if it reduces DH prices for final users;
- be ready to restore outages and to compensate losses to DH customers in case of DH supply disruption or failure in parameters;
- licensed activity in DH sector should be accounted separately and regularly reported;
- fulfil other economic and legal requirements of DH sector regulation.

As it was mentioned above the DH sector is managed by the Municipalities in Lithuania according to specific plans for the DH sector that are approved by municipal councils. The main task of the DH sector plans is to satisfy the DH customer at the lowest DH supply cost and within the allowable range for negative environmental impacts. The specific plans for the DH sector are reviewed by NCCPE at least every 5 years, depending on DH production and technology development, environmental impact and changes in other factors relevant to municipality spatial planning. DH supply in the concrete municipality is organized according to general planning documents or a specialized local DH plan. DH supply and competition zones are drawn in the territory of municipality and the only licensed company in the DH zone must connect all new DH customers. Connection to DH network cost is included in the general DH price or paid by special fee. DH customers in the competition zone could be connected and DH supplied on the basis of individual cost and prices.

There are different licensing approaches for DH around European countries. In Lithuania DH license for the companies who sell heat above 10 GWh/ year are issued by the NCCPE. The amounts below this level are done by the municipality. Licensed DH undertakings must ensure a reliable DH supply to the customers, to properly operate a DH network and to regulate the DH supply regime. Licensed DH undertakings in Lithuania have many other obligations and requirements, such as purchasing heat from independent heat producers (IHP), transparent accountancy and pricing systems, public openness etc. Disputes between DH companies and other parties are resolved by NCCPE and consumers safety authorities in a juridical process.

DH price regulation is based on cost-plus approach and benchmarking in Lithuania. DH undertakings are required to submit their cost estimates in accordance with regulatory guidelines set by NCCPE. The NCCPE benchmarks these costs, controlling for differences in company sizes (measured by output volumes). In Lithuania the price 'baseline' is typically agreed upon for duration of three to five years and is updated annually in order to reflect changes in inflation and quantities and monthly to reflect also changes in fuel prices. The price baseline is assessed primarily by reference to costs and volumes recorded over the previous three years, but may also take into account of planned investment and efficiency measures for the duration of the price control period. The NCCPE also regularly verifies that NH undertakings have sufficient financial resources to carry out their licensed activities. The Regulatory Asset Base (RAB) is based on depreciated historical costs and includes mandatory fuel stocks in Lithuania. The allowed return on equity includes a measure of country risk based on the spread between Vilibor and Euribor, but no specific measure of the business risk of DH sector. The allowed return has recently been reduced from 8% to 5% for DH undertakings in Lithuania.

2.3.4. Heat Demand

All DH companies supply around 8–9 TWh of heat to heat consumers per year in Lithuania. Around 40% of the total DH volumes are produced in CHPs. DH supply development during 1996-2010 in Lithuania is presented in Figure 11.

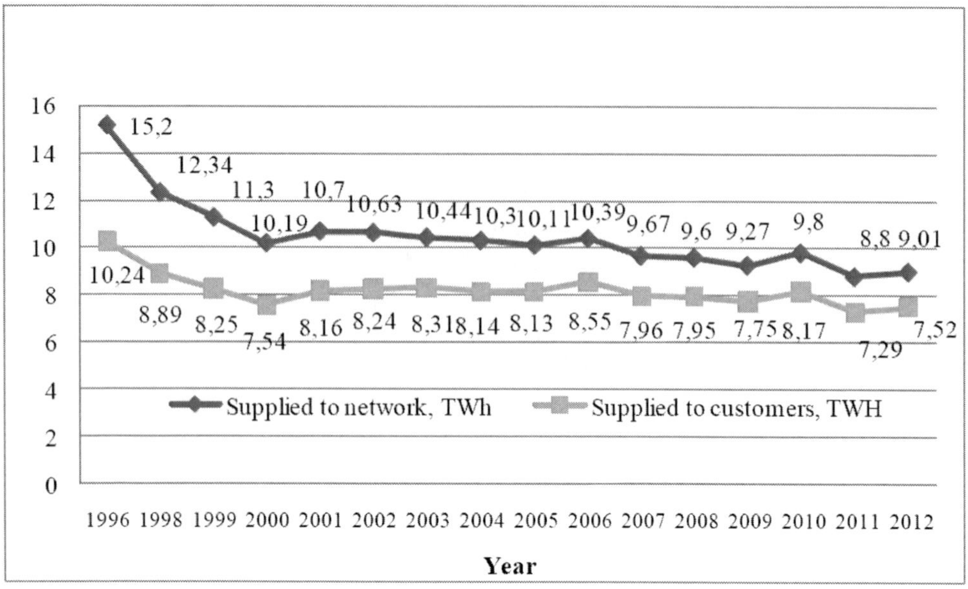

Source: author.

Figure 11. DH supply development in Lithuania during 1996–2012, TWh.

DH balance development in Lithuania during 2001-2011 periods is presented in Table 20.

Natural gas was the main fuel according to the balance of fuel for the Lithuanian DH supply during the period 1996–2010. Heavy Fuel Oil (HFO) consumption for heat production fell from 38% in 1996 to less than 5% in 2010 and is constantly falling. HFO usually remains a reserve fuel or is used for a short time during the coldest period only. It is related to its comparatively high price and strict environmental restrictions implemented by EU legislation.

DH production from biofuel has significantly increased since 2002 in Lithuania. It has been determined by the lower prices of the biofuel, favorable pricing, investment subsidies and the possibility of selling saved GHG pollution permits and other factors. An EU requirement concerning the limitations of burning high amounts of sulphur-containing fuels, in particular in the areas where natural gas networks are absent, has also contributed to increased heat production from biofuel in Lithuania.

2.3.5. District Heat Prices

In view of the sustained losses the costs of heat may be differentiated according to DH supply systems, customers groups, the place where the purchase–sale of DH took place, the ownership of the DH point, the supply–consumption limit, the scope of DH consumption, heating mediums and their quality, the reliability of the DH supply, the seasonal character, the periodicity of consumption and types of accounting. When differentiating the prices, cross-subsidisation between groups of customers is prohibited.

A supplier of DH who annually sells at least 10 GWh of heat shall, according to the methodologies of pricing and taking into account the notes of the municipal institution and the NCCPE, prepare and present to the NCCPE and the municipal institution a draft of the heat basic price.

Table 20. Heat balance, GWh

	2001	2002	2003	2004	2005	2006	2007	2008	2009	2010	2011
Total gross production	**13285.4**	**13976.7**	**14267.3**	**13764.7**	**13861.2**	**14521.7**	**13655.1**	**12863.3**	**13147.8**	**13557.3**	**12746,1**
Nuclear power plant	614.3	640.2	603.0	549.9	536.1	553.7	535.4	521.3	540.3	-	-
Thermal power (TP) plants	5357.0	5284.8	5689.8	6420.0	6428.8	6921.9	5624.6	5576.0	5731.2	6273.6	5453,8
Public TP plants	5200.4	5125.7	5529.9	6306.2	6336.7	6869.1	5583.0	5569.9	5684.0	6226.3	5445,8
Autoproducer TP plants	156.6	159.1	159.9	113.8	92.1	52.8	41.6	6.1	47.2	47.3	8,0
Heat plants	6053.2	5978.2	5683.1	4763.3	4718.5	4904.9	5009.4	4430.1	4214.4	4728.2	4360,5
Public heat plants	5748.3	5682.9	5351.4	4393.1	4302.7	4515.6	4612.1	4030.3	3896.7	4374.5	4036,6
Autoproducer heat plants	304.9	295.3	331.7	370.2	415.8	389.3	397.3	399.8	317.7	353.7	323,9
Geothermal plants	-	189.1	214.9	225.0	234.1	121.5	32.4	10.8	166.9	120.5	91,6
Other plants	1260.9	1884.4	2076.5	1806.5	1943.7	2019.7	2453.3	2324.9	2495.0	2435.0	2840,2
Gross consumption	**13285.4**	**13976.7**	**14267.3**	**13764.7**	**13861.2**	**14521.7**	**13655.1**	**12863.3**	**13147.8**	**13557.3**	**12746,1**
Used in other plants	145.3	470.5	521.7	498.6	532.0	540.1	719.5	733.8	859.3	770.3	794,6
Energy sector	695.5	692.1	624.5	624.9	729.9	1020.7	397.8	416.8	386.5	351.0	231,5
Extraction and agglomeration of peat	1.0	0.9	1.1	1.0	0.5	0.8	0.8	0.8	1.0	1.1	1,1
Manufacture of refined petroleum products	308.2	318.5	316.1	323.5	376.0	650.8	-	-	-	-	0,3
Electric power, gas, steam and air conditioning supply	386.0	372.7	307.3	300.4	353.4	369.1	397.0	416.0	385.5	350.2	230,1
Distribution and transmission losses	2550.2	2465.4	2394.3	2226.9	2071.4	1981.8	1837.5	1680.7	1606.2	1718.3	1612,6
Final consumption	**9894.7**	**10348.7**	**10726.8**	**10414.3**	**10527.9**	**10979.1**	**10700.3**	**10032.0**	**10295.8**	**10717.4**	**10107,4**
Industry	1659.4	1855.7	2095.3	1846.6	1983.0	2086.5	2277.1	1898.4	1914.8	2080.3	2381,3
Construction	27.7	25 6	26.4	24.5	22.7	24.9	32.7	32.2	23.4	22.0	19,1
Agriculture	125.9	108.6	111.5	118.0	120.2	110.6	104.9	115.0	106.1	93.7	75,5
Commercial and public services	2067.1	2034.6	2166.7	2205.3	2219.9	2376.4	2452.8	2080.8	2236.1	2388.0	1984,3
Households	6014.6	6324.2	6326.9	6219.9	6182.1	6380.7	5832.8	5905.6	6015.4	6133.4	5647,2

Source: author.

The municipal institution presents to the NCCPE documents for the harmonisation of the reference DH price. The NCCPE, having considered the information submitted by the municipality, sets the basic price of DH. The organisations protecting customer's rights are invited to participate in setting the basic price of DH. The DH suppliers managing the DH provision systems located in separate municipalities may propose to the NCCPE that it should set different basic prices of DH for these systems. The cost price structure of DH is as follows.

Variable costs make around 70%. They are comprised of costs for fuel, acquired heat, electric power and water technology, which change depending on the amount of heat that needs to be produced and supplied to the DH transmission networks. In 2010 such costs comprised 332 million EUR within the DH sector or 71% of all costs, while costs for fuel and acquired heat were around 324 million EUR in Lithuania.

Fuel component in the DH price comprises from 50% up to 70% of the total DH price, depending on the type of fuel burned (Figure 12).

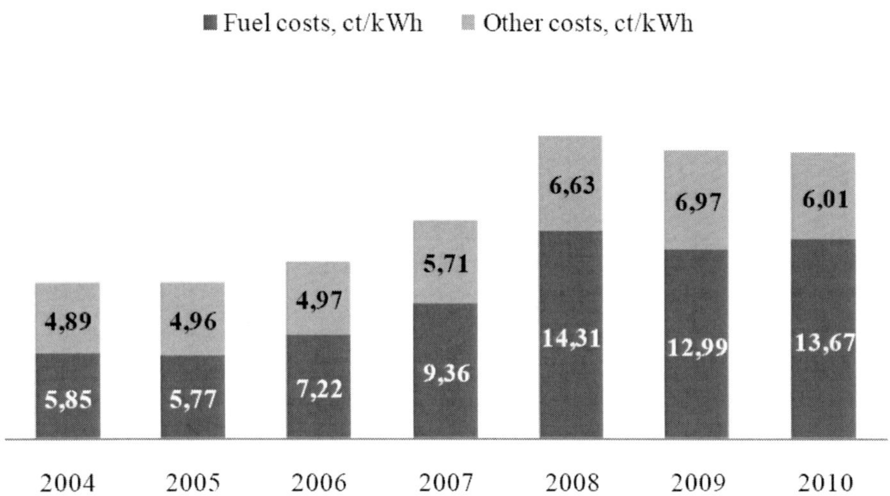

Source: author.

Figure 12. The development of ratio of fuel and other costs in the price of DH in Lithuania.

Fuel component for DH undertakings burning biofuel is lower than that that when producing heat using natural gas. DH undertakings that have a fuel structure comprised of more than 50% of biofuel usually can offer lower DH prices to the customers. However, by burning biofuel, the constant DH component is higher, since the operation of biofuel equipment is more expensive. Taking this into account, biofuel market prices are more stable and in the long run DH undertakings burning biofuel ensure lower DH prices for the customers.

As it was mentioned above natural gas is the main fuel for DH production in Lithuania. In 2010, natural gas comprised 74% of the heat production balance therefore the price of natural gas had a crucial influence upon the costs of the DH suppliers.

Technological losses in the DH supply, which comprised 15.7% in 2010, are also very important for the amount of variable costs of DH undertakings. Technical losses of heat transmission in modern and optimally sized pipeline and those having thermal insulation used in Western countries make about 10–12% of the DH amount supplied to the DH network. It is evident that the optimal level in Lithuania has not been reached yet, but DH undertakings further yearly decreasing losses and especially after increasingly accelerating investments in the transmission networks since 2004, heat losses has decreased by 4%.

Constant costs make around 25% of total DH supply costs. They include depreciation costs, work payments and social insurance fees, repair and other services, taxes, interests etc. The NCCPE controls these costs in particular and checks that unreasonable constant costs or excessive costs accumulating due to omission would not be included into the price of DH. Activity costs makes around 5%.

While calculating the price of DH supplied two main matters are taken into account: the amount of funds needed for the DH undertaking to increase the credibility of the DH supply or to renovate equipment by investments and necessary costs to produce and supply DH to the customer. By approving the price of DH the NCCPE establishes how much profit the DH undertaking can make therefore the profit rate is strictly regulated in Lithuanian DH sector.

When reorganising or privatising DH supply undertakings controlled by municipalities, it is necessary to ensure that the DH supply undertakings controlled by them should own DH transmission networks whereby at least 10 GWh of heat is sold annually and not less than 30% of the DH production capacity required for meeting customers' needs are owned in every DH network, including the necessary DH capacity reserve.

In Lithuania the basic long-term DH price are set by municipalities for a 3-5 years period. The NCCPE sets the DH price in case of incorrect setting and the DH price is adjusted every year with consideration given to fuel price, inflation, sold DH volume, other objective factors. The DH undertaking is allowed a maximum profit of 5% on the regulated asset value (using Weighted Average Costs of Capital or WACC). The DH price setting and control systems available in Lithuania and other countries are presented in Table 21.

Table 21. The DH price setting and control systems in selected countries and Lithuania

Heat price procedures	**Denmark** *DH market under regulation*	**Finland** *Free DH market*	**Poland** *DH market under regulation*	**Lithuania** *DH market under*
Methodology (determined by)	DERA	non applicable	ERO	NCCPE
Regulatory period (years)	not determined	non applicable	1-5	3-5
Minimal period of price adjustment	---	---	Annual	Monthly
Profit	0	not regulated	Reasonable	5% by WACC
Heat price setting	Company	Company	ERO above 5 *MW* Municipality below 5 *MW*	NCCPE
Control and final setting	DERA	Antimono poly agency	ERO	NCCPE
Supervision	DERA	Antimono poly agency	ERO	NCCPE and municipalities

Notes: DERA - Danish Energy Regulatory Agency. ERO - Energy Regulator Office. NCCPE – National Control Commission for Energy and Prices.

Source: author.

In all the modes of DH price regulation presented in Table 21 it would be useful to have the publication of data which demonstrates efficiency of different DH undertakings. This could create a viable benchmark and could form some pressure for other DH undertakings to increase their efficiency. Incentive instruments and figures could be derived from benchmarking analysis as well.

There are four groups of eligible households (defined by income categories) and the number of customers in each household is taken into account when applying subsidies for DH. The subsidy has an upper limit. In Lithuania social protection is implemented through compensations (e.g., compensation of DH expenditures exceeding 20% of the household's income). Support is allocated from the state budget and administrated by municipalities. Such schemes were not very well targeted and administration is very costly and the scheme was recently changed in Lithuanian in order to evaluate the householder's personal estate.

Table 22 that shows the customers DH prices in June 2010 for DH undertakings using biofuels for producing a considerable part of DH. In Table 23 DH prices are presented for DH undertakings using natural gas for DH production.

Table 22. DH prices of DH supply undertakings when biofuel predominates in DH production

No.	Heat supplier	Prices of DH since 1 June 2010 (US $ct/kWh), VAT included	The share of biofuel in fuel balance, %
1.	UAB "Ignalinos silumos tinklai"	**6.60**	**100.0**
2.	UAB "Moletu siluma“	**6.52**	**98.6**
3.	UAB "Sirvintu siluma"	**7.36[1]; 7.44[2]**	**98.0**
4.	UAB "Taurages silumos tinklai"	**6.68**	**87.0**
5.	UAB “Litesko” Branch “Kelmes siluma”	**8.05[1]; 8.38[2]**	**85.0**
6.	UAB "Raseiniu silumos tinklai"	**8.02[1]; 8.12[2]**	**84.0**
7.	UAB "Varenos siluma"	**7.30**	**80.5**
8.	UAB "Silales silumos tinklai"	**7.36[1]; 7.56[2]**	**80.6**
9.	UAB “Fortum Svencioniu energija”	**7.43[1]; 7.56[2]**	**77.8**
10.	UAB "Birstono siluma"	**7.87**	**76.8**
11.	UAB “Mazeikiu silumos tinklai”	**7.23**	**60.5**
12.	UAB "Silutes silumos tinklai"	**8.25**	**54.4**
13.	UAB "Utenos silumos tinklai"	**6.39[1]; 6.54[2]**	**43.8**

Source: author.

Explanations:

[1]- heat points owned by dwellers;

[2]- heat points owned by heat suppliers. US$=0.83 EUR

Table 23. DH prices for DH undertakings when natural gas predominates in DH production

No.	Heat supplier	Prices of heat since 1 June 2010 (US $ct/kWh), VAT included	The share of natural gas in the joint balance of fuel (%)
1.	UAB "Akmenes energija"	**9.96**	**99.9**
2.	AB "Jonavos silumos tinklai"	**9.22**	**99.5**
3.	UAB "Pakruojo siluma"	**10.62**	**97.2**
4.	UAB "Fortum Joniskio energija"	**10.28[1]; 10.69[2]**	**90.0**
5.	UAB "Anyksciu siluma"	**10.16[1]; 10.51[2]**	**82.5**
6.	UAB "Prienu energija"	**10.84**	**80.0**

Explanations:
[1]heat points owned by dwellers.
[2] heat points owned by heat suppliers. US$=0.83 EUR.
Source: author.

After generalization of the prices provided in the Tables above, it can be stated that when a major part of the balance of fuel is formed by natural gas, the consumer prices vary between 9.22 US $ct/kWh and 10.69 US $ct/kWh in Lithuania. When biofuel predominates in DH production, the customer prices vary between 6.39 and 8.38 $ct/kWh. The difference in DH prices is about 30%; therefore the benefit provided by biofuel to customers is obvious. In addition it should be noted that the price of natural gas in Lithuania is twice or more higher as compared to the price of biofuel. In Figure 13 the average DH price is presented for the selected European countries.

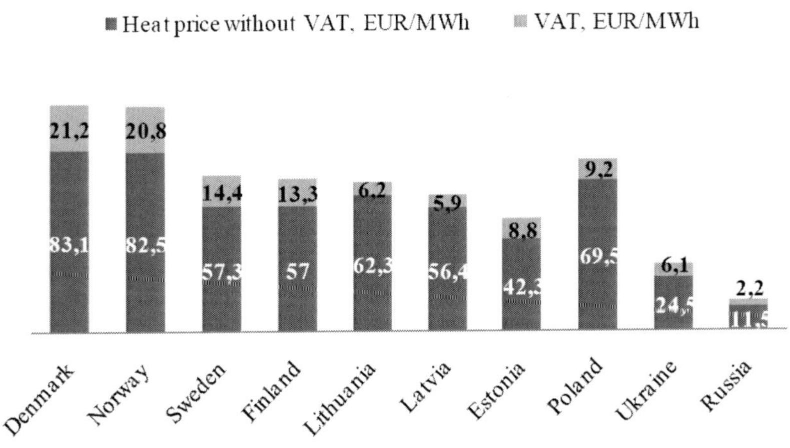

Source: author.

Figure 13. Average DH prices in the selected European countries.

As one can see from Figure 13 the lowest DH prices are in Russia, Ukraine and in Lithuania DH prices are the highest among Baltic States. Low DH prices are attractive for customers, it ensures social stability but the renovation rate of DH facilities is still rather slow in Lithuania. Having an uneconomic DH pricing regime restricts progress and can lead to the deterioration of existing infrastructure, as has happened in some transition economies.

Chapter 3

THE IMPACT OF ENERGY MARKET REFORMS ON ENERGY PRICES AND COMPETITIVENESS

> Apart from promoting the integration of EU energy markets, it is often said that the aim of liberalization is to create lower prices. In fact, the aim of liberalization is rather to create competitive, transparent and effective prices. It is therefore not the absolute price level that is important, but whether a price is "fair" and reflects real market conditions.
>
> (UNECE Committee on Sustainable Energy. Working Party on Gas. The impact of liberalization of natural gas market in UNECE region. Efficiency and security, 2012)

Regulatory reforms in the electric power sector have been observed in many parts of the world. In most countries, the industry had traditionally been characterized as a regulated monopoly, and reform has opened it to competition at the wholesale level as well as the retail level in electric power sector. The industry was also typically characterized as a vertically integrated structure, while reform has unbundled electric power generation and supply from transmission and distribution. The UK and Norway were among the first countries to introduce competition into the wholesale and retail electric power markets as well as unbundling services early in the 1990s. The UK also privatized the national electric power sector. Many countries have followed these regulatory reforms to achieve more efficiency in their electric power sectors. There is now a need for a detailed evaluation on the economic impact of the reforms, because such reforms appear to be costly and there seems to be a growing controversy as to their benefits. An increasing number of empirical studies have measured the impact of regulatory reforms in various ways. The following chapters present the review of energy market reforms and results of empirical studies dealing with the impact of electric power market liberalization on electric power prices.

3.1. ENERGY MARKET REFORMS

Experience from electric power sector liberalisation around the world has produced a measure of consensus over some generic measures for achieving a well-functioning market-oriented electric power industry. Liberalisation in energy sector generally requires implementation of one or more of the following inter-related steps: sector restructuring, introduction of competition in wholesale generation and retail supply, incentive regulation of transmission and distribution networks, establishing an independent regulator, and privatisation [187].

Under EU Electricity Market Directives, EU member countries were required to take at least a minimum set of steps by certain key dates toward the liberalisation of their national energy sector markets. Second, the EC has promoted efforts to improve the interfaces between national energy markets by improving cross-border trading rules, and to expand cross-border transmission links between countries. Trading rules are being developed with industry agreement and the EU has subsidised some cross-border transmission link upgrades like in the case of Ireland and Great Britain. The underlying aim of both of these policies was to extend the principles of the European Single Market to the energy market. The Directives were adopted to enable companies from across the EU to compete with national incumbents, while improved interconnection would reduce cross-border transport costs and increase competition.

The first and second EU Electricity Market Directives of 1996 and 2003 focused on unbundling the electric power industry and on a gradual opening of national electric power markets. The second EU directive further promotes competition by toughening regulation of access to electric power networks and requiring independent regulators. Regulation of cross-border trade aims to facilitate electric power market integration in EU. The second EU directive aims to achieve, by July 2007 at the latest: (I) unbundling of electric power transmission system operators (TSOs) and electric power distribution system operators (DSOs) from the rest of the electric power industry, (II) free entry to electric power generation, (III) monitoring of electric power supply competition, (IV) full electric power market opening, (V) promotion of renewable energy sources, (VI) strengthening the competition.

Table 24 outlines the measures for reforming a vertically integrated and publicly owned electric power sector into a competitive and privately owned electric power industry. In practice, the actual measures need to take into account both the specific characteristics of the national (or supra-national region) electric power industry and the general features of the liberalisation model.

Table 24. Main Steps in Electric Power Sector Reform

Restructuring	Vertical unbundling of electric power generation, transmission, distribution, and supply activities
	Horizontal splitting of electric power generation and supply
Competition and Markets	Wholesale market and retail competition Allowing new entry into generation and supply
Regulation	Establishing an independent regulator
	Provision of third-party network access in electric power sector
	Incentive regulation of electric power transmission and distribution networks
Ownership	Allowing new private actors to enter electric power market
	Privatising the existing publicly owned businesses

Source: author.

Liberalisation requires a suitable electric power market structure within which effective competition can be fostered. Usually, this involves restructuring the electric power sector by unbundling vertically integrated activities in electric power sector and reducing their horizontal concentration. The aim of vertical unbundling in energy sector is to separate potentially competitive electric power generation and supply from the natural monopoly activities of electric power transmission and distribution networks. The aim of horizontal separation is to create enough effective competition in electric power generation and retailing where economies of scale favour competition.

Many of the liberalisation initiatives in European energy sector and elsewhere began in the early 1990s in an atmosphere of reduced political concern over energy supply security. The ending of the cold war made imports of natural gas from Russia less risky in an environment where liberalisation favoured the building of new gas-fired power plants. An initial surplus of electric power generation capacity supported the reforms, as there was no pressing need to ensure guaranteed returns to support new investment in electric power sector.

The earliest introduction of market concepts and privatization to electric power systems took place in Chile in the late 1970s. Argentina built on top of the Chilean model and tried to privatize existing electric power generation assets which had fallen into disrepair under the government-owned monopoly, resulting in frequent service interruptions and to attract private investments needed for electric power sector rehabilitation and for system expansion. The World Bank was active in introducing a variety of hybrid markets in other Latin America countries, including Peru and Colombia, during the 1990s however with limited success.

Economic forces have been driving a dramatic restructuring of the electric power industry in recent years all over the world. Pioneers of the electric power system restructuring in different continents of the world embrace the idea of introducing competition in the wholesale supply and purchase of electric power combined with an open access regime for the use of electric power supply networks.

The diversity of the approaches can be seen in restructuring of electric power sector in Europe including the Nordic countries and Great Britain, North America, New Zealand and Australia. The creation of trading exchanges in electric power can offer the chance to build a truly open and competitive electric power market, guided by a global knowledge base of the successes and failures of other exchanges in other industries around the world. Electric power exchanges enable the development of the wholesale business. In addition to the trading of physical quantities, 'future' markets are created making extensive use of financial products.

Many energy exchanges offer multi-energy (i.e., electric power, gas, and oil) services, sometimes extending to other commodities as drivers as metal, pulp and paper. The number and nature of players will evolve as the electric power market continues to open and the liquidity of exchanges increases very often.

Competition in energy markets has driven the development of wholesale energy trading. There is an enormous variety in the speed and willingness of energy markets to deregulate, from across the world, country to country, and even from state to state. Many countries have already fully competitive and mature energy markets while other countries still do not plan to deregulate their natural gas and electric power sectors. In Table 25 some comparisons of liberalization of energy markets in EU and USA are presented.

Table 25. Comparison of energy sector liberalization models in EU and USA

	USA	EU
The year of liberalization start	Reform of electric power generation and transmission sectors started following order 888 in 1996. The other sectors were carried out separately by the state.	Electric power regulation reform of EU-wide started in 1996, according to provisions of EU Electricity directive. The enforcement time of regulatory reform was various depending on the country.
Main purpose of system reform	Correction of electric power price gap among the states.	Realization of single electric power market following EU economic integration
Framework of wholesale market	Regional Transmission Organizations (RTO) founded mandatory energy market within its area.	No regulation in all EU. But, most of countries have electric power exchange.
Unbundling of transmission sector	Functional and accounting unbundling were requested by 1996 order, however a wide area transmission organization RTO was proposed by 1999 order 2000. The Northeastern PJM Independent System Operator (ISO), Midwest ISO are approved as RTO.	Functional and accounting unbundling were obliged by 1996 EU directive. The legal and functional unbundling were obliged by 2003 EU directive.
Scope of retail liberalization	There is no unified movement at Federal level. Full electric power sector liberalization was carried out in the most states of the north-eastern area. The south-eastern area is not liberalized.	Full electric power sector liberalization is obliged to start by 2007. Especially, UK and Germany has already started full electric power sector liberalization.

Source: author.

The adoption of a electric power sector liberalization model affects electric power prices and electric power prices also affect the competitiveness of the country. In Figure 14 the several electric power sector liberalization stages are presented.

There are four main steps in the electric power sector liberalization model presented in Figure 14:

1) monopoly model - no competition in electric power sector;
2) single Buyer model. It means that mid- or long-term competitive bid is introduced to the electric power generation business and only unbundling between electric power generation and transmission is implemented;

3) wholesale market. It means that Power pool or bilateral contracts models are established and the wholesale market is liberalized;
4) retail market model means that the wholesale and retail electric power markets are liberalized.

The purpose of SB (Single Buyer) is to legally divide electric power generation, transmission and distribution, allowing fair, "equal" treatment for Independent Power Producers (IPP) and other power plants, thus promoting competition. The SB allows the reduction of the wholesale charge over several years in the beginning stages of development. Creation of the market for centralized transactions will serve as the foundation of subsequent electric power market developments. Once the SB stage has been passed, it will then become difficult for electric power producers to increase electric power prices unreasonably. This is achieved once the retail electric power market becomes liberalized, as the charge under the SB model becomes the base and centralization of transactions through the SB market system enable the reliable electric power price index in connection with electric power transactions to be established. On the other hand, Lovei [188] assumes the SB model is an artificial monopoly and cautions any country that selects this model. The SB model can be treated as electric power market transition measure toward the competitive electric power market.

There are several types of models in wholesale electric power market. In a power pool, all power generating undertakings offer price-quantity pairs for the electric power supply. This forms an aggregated electric power supply curve in the country. The offered electric power prices can be based on predetermined variable costs and such type of pools are called as Cost Based Pools (CBP). Also the electric power generators can be free to offer any electric power price they like and such types of electric power pools are referred to as Price Based Pools (PBP). On the energy demand side, the electric power market operator may forecast electric power demand and dispatch generating units against this. This is called a one-sided pool (OSP). In more sophisticated pools or two-sided pools (TSP), the electric power market operator may dispatch on the basis of a electric power demand curve created from price-quantity bids made by the electric power buyers on the electric power market, such as distribution undertakings and eligible customers. Bids are normally firm and they are matched in the electric power market clearing process and result in an obligation to take and deliver the matched electric power volumes and these electric power volumes will be financially settled [47].

A power pool can operate a day-ahead market (e.g., the former England & Wales Pool) or a close to real time market (e.g., five minutes-ahead). There can also be a combination of several electric power markets (day-ahead, intra-day and five minutes-ahead). There is a five-minutes-ahead electric power market. Other sessions can still be run on the basis of non-firm electric power offers and bids. Such sessions are used to create a forecast of the electric power market prices as an indication for the electric power market participants. Such electric power price seeking sessions are based on non-firm offers and bids and are important to allow for non-dispatched demand side response in case of high electric power market prices.

One of the main advantages of a pool model in electric power sector is that it allows for Locational Marginal Pricing (LMP). LMP is based on the marginal cost of supplying the next increment of electric power demand at a specific location in the electric power network accounting for both electric power generation and network characteristics.

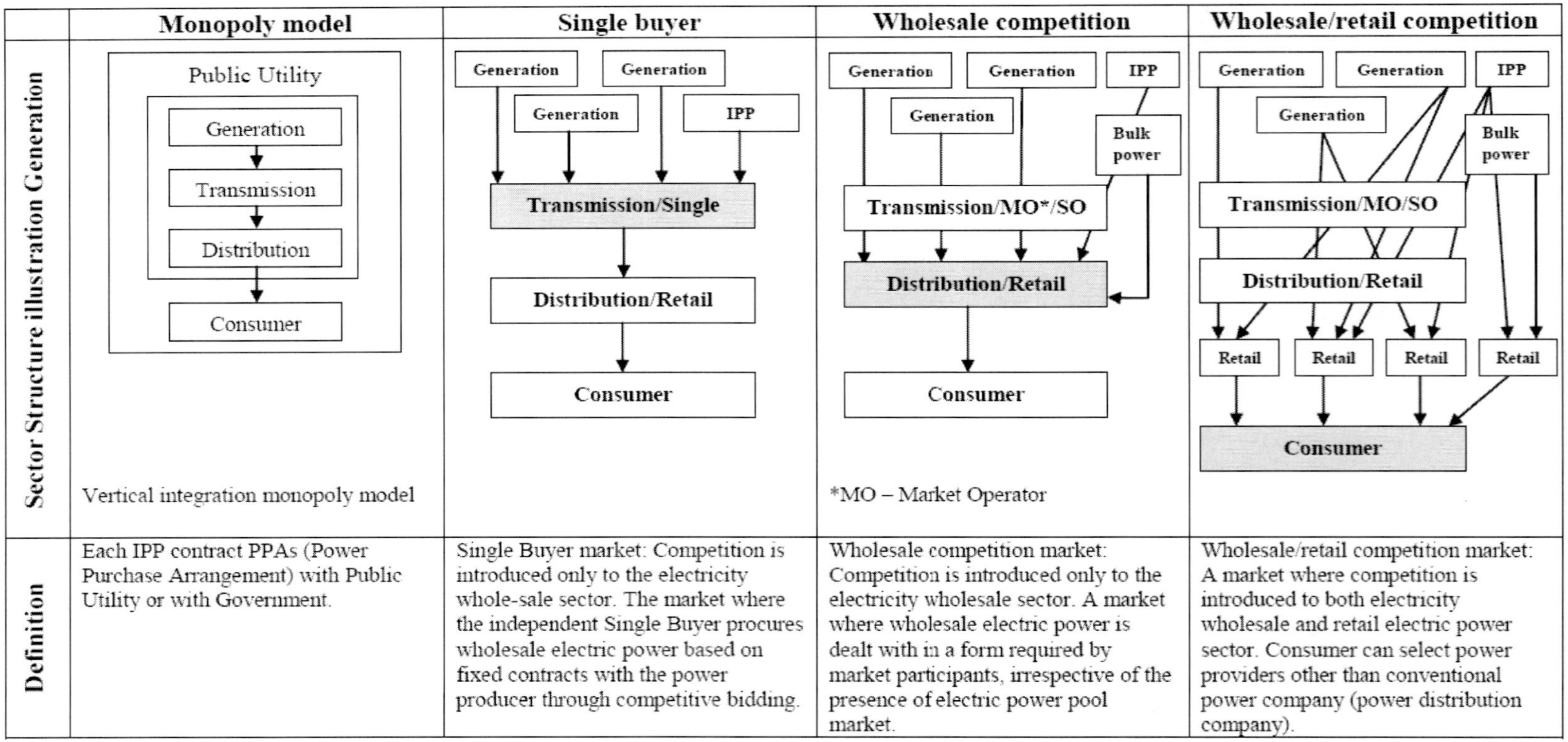

Source: author.

Figure 14. The stages of electric power sector liberalization.

The consequence is that instead of one uniform electric power price there is an electric power price per location, which can be at each node or on a wider zonal approach. In addition each market player pays for congestion caused. The congestion charge in a LMP-based electric power market is the difference between electric power prices at the generation and consumption zones. Electric power market participants can hedge against this congestion charge by entering into financial contracts. The objective of an optimization function is maximization of economic surplus subject to electric power generation and transmission capacity constraints. Detailed representation of a electric power network makes it possible to take losses, parallel flows, voltage stability and reliability criteria into consideration. As a result, first-order conditions associated with the maximization of economic benefits under constraints yield electric power prices, which represent the change in the total cost of meeting system energy requirements caused by a change in load or electric power generation at each zone.

A pool model with LMP defined for every zone is often considered as an ideal electric power market model as the nodal electric power prices perfectly reflect all costs of supplying electric; electric power at given nodes (zones) and, manage congestion at the same time. Nodal electric power prices send very clear signals to electric power market players regarding the location of a new electric power generating capacity or transmission lines. Zonal variant exist as well. The disadvantage is that a zonal approach averages the nodal prices within a zone, making the price signals less efficient.

In parallel to the pool, electric power market participants can enter into bilateral contracts. These contracts do not necessarily have to be financial bilateral contracts, but may also be bilateral contracts for physical electric power delivery. In this case, the electric power plants backing each contract are physically scheduled to supply the agreed electric power load and the electric power pool is responsible for the clearing of just “small” differences, due to differences in the amount of electric; electric power scheduled and the electric power observed in the real time operation. In this case only the differences are settled through the electric power pool, but the dispatch of plants is not affected by these physical bilateral electric power contracts. Pure financial bilateral contracts offer similar advantages, however they can offer maximum freedom to electric power market participants and due to this allow for physical bilateral contracts. These contracts allow electric power market participants the flexibility to secure electric power at prices independent of the electric power market.

The alternative to a electric power pool model is a market mechanism based on physical bilateral contracts. This model means that electric power sellers and buyers freely enter into bilateral contracts for electric power supply. Electric power sellers will normally be power generators and buyers will be distribution undertakings and eligible customers. However, power generators could also become a electric power buyer in the case they have a shortage of electric power generation. Likewise, customers can become electric power sellers. Brokers also can act as an intermediate between electric power buyers and sellers dealing in standard contracts. These types of transactions are referred to as Over the Counter (OTC). Usually, there will always be differences between the contracted volumes and the actual metered electric electric power volumes. Therefore the system operator will have to determine these imbalances and will have to settle them. In more advanced electric power markets, the system operator runs a electric power balancing market called regulating electric power market in order to establish a market based electric power price for the settlement of these imbalances.

In parallel to the bilateral contracts, a voluntary electric power exchange could be developed in the future on the initiative of the electric power market participants. An electric power exchange could offer day-ahead and intra-day electric power trade with the following benefits for the electric power market participants: anonymous treading; tool to optimize trading portfolio; more price transparency; no counter party risk.

However the electric power exchange will have no metered electric power generation or consumption and will therefore never have imbalances. This model with bilateral contracts and a voluntary electric power exchange has been implemented in several European countries, with exchanges in the Netherlands; France; the Scandinavian countries; Germany; Poland and Austria. One can even have several competing exchanges in one country, as was the case in Germany, England and Japan.

The two electric power market models (pools and bilateral contracts) are equivalent in a world without transaction costs. In a world with transaction costs however, the bilateral contracts model may result in a sub-optimal outcome, where electric power price and quantity that do not reflect real time electric power demand and supply. In a pool, electric power prices and quantities should reflect actual electric power demand and supply. Though electric power prices in a pool may be more volatile than in a contracts market, there are hedging instruments available. In terms of institutional capacity, a simple electric power contracts market is more straightforward and less expensive to set up than a electric power pool.

Both market models, pools and bilateral contracts, though so much different, can coexist. A electric power pool could have bilateral contracts alongside of it and in a bilateral contacts mechanism a voluntary electric power exchange could also be considered. Therefore to better illustrate the difference between both models one can draw a line between electric powers markets with central dispatch of electric power generating units and with self-dispatch. In general, central dispatch of all electric power generating units is related to mandatory pools. Self-dispatch means that electric power generators decide on the electric power dispatch of their own electric power generating units and this regime applies to bilateral contracts models.

In addition the central dispatch can offer important advantages as it allows for more integrated treatment of electric power generation units and transmission network. This in turn allows for the implementation of LMP and consequently a more efficient management of electric power transmission constraints. It also allows a better management of hydro electric power resources in hydroelectric power based countries.

The unbundled years and the introduction of foreign IPP with a competitive environment were selected as important preconditions for transition from the monopoly model to the SB model. The conditions for the transition to wholesale competition and retail/wholesale competition were set as the establishment of the Wholesale Market and the Retail Market, respectively. Many countries introduced retail competition gradually. However, it is important to distinguish the year when the liberalization law is enacted, not when it is fully realized.

Table 26 presents the main factors that influence the electric power prices in various electric power sector liberalization cases.

Table 26. The factors influencing electric power prices

Electric power price decrease	Electric power price increase
Free electric power market competition functions and competitive pressures become strong (new entries and productivity enhancement).	Associated with liberalization models. Exercise of market power entailed by the liberalization. High price with IPP. Profit guarantee to distribution companies Cost for rural electrification. Cost to promote to retail market. Introduction of cost reflective tariffs.
Rice of democratic movement. Price decreases through political pressure. Introduction of hydro power and coal thermal electric power generation. Decrease of capital costs. Decrease in price of fossil fuels. Price caps.	Not associated with liberalization models. Rise of price of fossil fuels.

Source: author.

The electric power price will decrease due to political pressure both in the industrial and residential prices and also by an effect of the electric power price decrease promoted by free market competition. Decreases in electric power prices are induced by electric power market competition. Increase in regulatory costs is associated with the unbundling, or the introduction of cost-reflective tariffs in each region, entailed by the liberalization of electric power sector. As the selected energy liberalization model develops, electric power prices are expected to decrease due to the development of liberalization and competition in developed countries. However, for some energy markets in developed countries with higher liberalization models, costs for the regulation are one of the factors responsible for raising the electric power price. In developing countries, there are also controversial questions that arise with liberalization. For example, to what extent should cost reflective tariffs for accelerating private investment be adopted? Electric power price increases are more likely to be associated with the restructuring of the electric power sector and the removal of subsidies. IPPs also often are conflicting with electric power liberalization due to structure of long-term contracts. As pointed out in Nagayama [189], the increase on electric power prices in Asian countries often resulted due to introduction of IPPs, since payments for IPPs are guaranteed for foreign investor under structure of long-term PPA (Power Purchasing Agreements) contracts.

Figure 15 summarizes the electric power sector structure and ownership in several world countries ranging from developed industrialized to developing economies.

One can notice that developing countries mainly apply Single Buyer model and public and private corporatization. The developed economics and EU member states apply retail competition and private ownership and private or public corporatization.

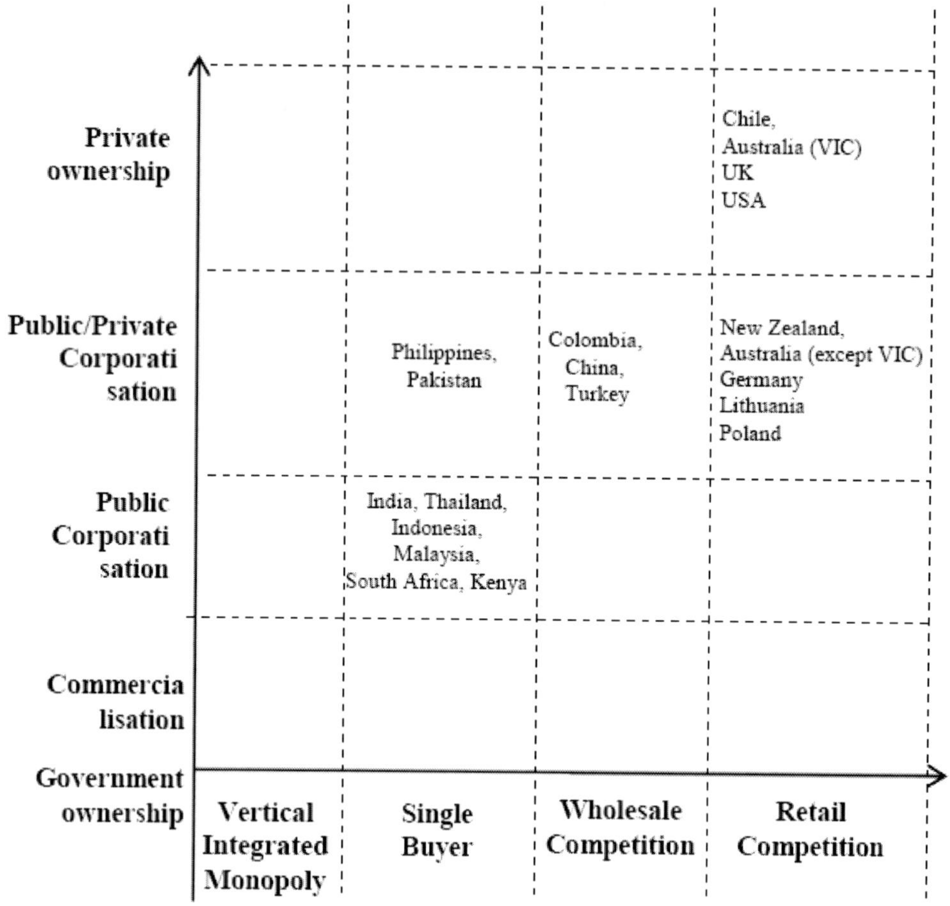

Source: Author.

Figure 15. Electric power sector structure and ownership in world countries.

The electric power prices have direct impact on economic growth, employment and competitiveness of the economy. The study conducted in US revealed the direct negative impact of electric power price increase on economic growth and employment [190]. The study finds an expected negative relationship between electric power prices and economic output. To summarize and illustrate results, several policy scenarios were conducted: based on either a 10% or 25% permanent increase in electric power prices. Because these policy scenarios look only at the electric power price shock and assume no changes in other factors such as technological innovations in electric power sector, these scenarios are simple simulations of future economic output under these assumptions rather than our forecast of expected future conditions. In terms of economic growth, the study [190] indicated that a 10% increase in electric power prices would decrease gross domestic product (GDP) growth from baseline value of 3% annual growth to 2.88% in the short run and 2.83% in the long run based on the U.S.-wide estimates. The drop in economic growth is more pronounced for estimates based on energy-reliant states. Turning to employment growth, a 10% increase in electric power prices decreases employment growth rate from the baseline value of 1% annual growth to 0.96% in the short run and 0.89% in the long run, based on U.S.-wide estimates. The resulting reduction in the long-run growth rate in employment growth is larger for estimates based on energy-reliant states and makes 0.84%. These policy scenarios provide valuable information on the possible effects of electric power price increases on competitiveness of the country. These scenarios illustrate that electric power price increases will have sizable negative effects on GDP and employment growth if the electric power price increases are not accompanied by other changes, such as technological advances, or other factors that might mitigate the consequences of electric power price increases.

However the study by Gil, de Souza [191] showed that, since the second half of the 1980s, energy prices have experienced very large changes, with arguably limited effects on global GDP developments. This argues that there are signs that the global economy is more resilient to commodity-price shocks than normally thought. This result finds support in both correlations and regression analysis, and had already been observed in several earlier works looking at the oil-price elasticities of GDP. This conclusion holds true for both developed and developing regions, and also broadly among different developing regions. The study found that the greater commodity efficiency since the 1970s, or more robust policy frameworks and responses, such as greater central bank independence and inflation-fighting capacities [192], floating exchange rates, or sovereign wealth funds and fiscal rules had significant impacts on such trends. In addition, a more geographically diversified and abundant set of sources for energy commodities, with the 'shale' oil and natural gas revolution, could be behind the changes in correlations. In addition, given the importance of developing economies for global growth, it should be pointed out that, while they are still converging to developed-country income levels, which implies that their growth process could become more commodity-intensive in some areas. They are also to experience this process with new technologies that are less commodity-intensive than those used by developed economies when they were at a similar level of development. Additionally, as development implies a convergence to an economic structure more concentrated on services and with less need of infrastructure investment, their sheer additional demand for commodities will abate. Therefore these factors combined may result in an even smaller sensitivity to energy commodity shocks.

The aim of electric power sector liberalization is improve economic efficiency and labour productivity; lower electric power prices; and provide better service to the customers and ensures security of electric power supply. The lower electric power prices and better service to customers including security of supply are the main drivers of competitiveness of the countries therefore it is important to assess the impact of electric power market opening on electric power price and other important issues relevant to the targets of electric power sector liberalization. In the next chapter the studies aiming at assessment of energy market liberalization impact on electric power prices and other drivers of competitiveness are outlined.

3.2. Review of Empirical Studies Dealing with Impact of Energy Market Deregulation on Electric Power Prices

There are a lot of studies conducted all over the world dealing with energy markets liberalization especially in electric power sector. One of the first studies aiming to develop models for assessing impact of regulatory regimes on electric power market environments and performances was conducted by Steiner [44]. He analyzed the effect of regulatory reforms on the retail price for large industrial customers as well as the ratio of industrial price to residential price, using panel data for 19 OECD countries for the period 1986– 1996. Steiner [44] found that regulatory reforms to introduce competition into the industry, including the creation of a wholesale spot market and the unbundling of electric power generation from transmission, generally induced a decline in the industrial price and an increase in the price differential between industrial customers and residential customers, indicating that industrial customers benefit more from the reform. These results support some policy recommendations currently made by the OECD [193]. For example, in its policy recommendation of structural separation in the network industries, OECD [193] judges that the results show signs of enhanced competition in the electric power supply industry from the unbundling of generation. Although the analysis was carefully conducted as a first step in assessing the impact of the reforms, it has several shortcomings and needs to be improved before reaching a consensus as to the policy recommendation.

The Steiner [44] applied regression analysis for assessing the linkages between electric power liberalization model and electric power prices for 19 countries. Steiner [44] used these indicators of competitiveness: industrial electric power prices, the ratio of industrial to residential prices, utilization rates and reserve margins. In his study the author concluded that the unbundling of generation and transmission, the expansion of third party access and introduction of electric power markets reduce industrial and-users prices. The Doove, Gabbitas, Nguyen-Hong, Owen [45] applied the extended Steiner model for 50 countries.

The Steiner model of the impact of liberalization on electric power prices:

$$p_e = \alpha + \beta R + \gamma NR + \varepsilon \quad (2)$$

Here: p_e – the industrial electric power prices, R – regulatory variables; NR- non-regulatory variables; α, β and γ are vectors of coefficients that were estimated and ε – is residual term.

The main regulatory variables according Steiner [44] are: unbundling of generation from transmission, Third party Access (TpA), Wholesale Pool, Ownership, Time to liberalization, Time to privatization. The main independent non-regulatory variables: hydropower share, nuclear share and GDP. The two share variables reflect differences in generating technologies across economies, which affect the marginal costs and hence the price of generating electric power. Finally the inclusion of GDP adjusts for differences in the size of economies and is also an overall measure of national income (Table 27).

Three of the six regulatory coefficients: for separating generation from transmission, allowing TpA to the transmission grid, allowing the wholesale electric power market are led to lower electric power prices. The coefficients on the three remaining variables – private ownership, time to liberalization and time to privatization – are less intuitive.

The regulatory variables in Steiner model focus on the key economic regulation needed to establish competitive generation sector- vertical unbundling of the generation system from the transmission system, whether third parties can access the transmission system, and whether a wholesale market exists. Dummy variables are used to indicate 3 key economic regulations needed to establish a competitive generation sector.

Table 27. The Steiner's model of assessing impact of electric power market liberalization on electric power prices

Variables	Measurements
Dependent variables	
Industrial electric power prices	Pre-tax industrial price (expressed in US$ PPP)
Independent regulatory variables	
Unbundling of generation from transmission	Dummy variable (1= accounting separation or separate companies; 0=otherwise)
Third-party access	Dummy variable (1= regulated or negotiated third-party access; 0=otherwise)
Wholesale pool	Dummy variable (1= presence of wholesale electric power markets; 0=otherwise)
Ownership	Discrete variable (4= private ownership; 3- mostly private ownership; 2= mixed; 1= mostly public; 0=public)
Time to liberalization	Negative of the number of years to privatisation (ranges from 11 to 0)
Time to privatization	Negative of the number of years to privatisation (ranges from 11 to 0)
Independent non-regulatory environmental variables	
Hydro share	Share of electric power generated from hydropower sources
Nuclear share	Share of electric power generated from nuclear sources
Gross domestic product	Gross domestic product (expressed in US$ PPP billion)

Source: author.

The unbundling of generation from transmission variable takes on a value 1 if separate companies are involved in the generation and transmission sectors, or if both sectors are managed by a single entity yet separate accounts are kept for each sector (accounting separation). Otherwise, it takes on a value of 0. The TPA variable takes on a value 1 if generators and eligible customers have a legal right to access the transmission grid on a certain pre-specified terms and conditions (regulated TPA) or can negotiate the terms and conditions under which grid access can occur directly with the operator of the transmission grid (negotiated TPA); otherwise it takes on a value of 0. The wholesale market variable takes on a value of 1 if generators can voluntarily sell or are obliged to sell their electric power into a wholesale electric power market, otherwise it takes on a value of 0.

Additionally to the above three regulatory variables needed to establish a competitive generation sector, Steiner included 3 market structure variables in the model: ownership variables takes on different discrete values ranging from 0 to 4, depending on the mix of public and private ownership. The time to liberalization and time to privatization variables measure the negative number of years to liberalization and privatization respectively. Indicators of the time remaining to liberalization and privatization are included as a proxy for the impact of expectations of liberalization and privatization on prices. These indicators are forward looking as they assess the effect of regulation on prices before liberalization or privatization. In Steiner model the time to liberalization is interpreted as being the time until the year in which key legislative changes are enacted, and time to privatization is deemed to be the time until the year in which the first sale of a public owned generators occurs.

The Steiner model also includes 3 non-regulatory variables – the share of electric power generated from hydro; the share of electric power generated from nuclear and the GDP. The two share variables reflect differences in generating technologies across economies which affect the marginal costs and hence the price of generating electric power. Finally, the inclusion of GDP adjusts for differences in the size of economies and is also an overall measure of national income.

The results of Steiner's model are summarized in Table 28.

Table 28. Effects of regulation on electric power prices: random effects model

Variable	Estimated coefficient	Z-statistic	Value under the benchmark regime
Constant	0.0667	7.104	0.0667
Regulatory and industry variables			
Unbundling of generation from transmission	-0.0011	-0.659	Separate
Private ownership	0.0029	2.7	
Third-party access	-0.0027	-1.357	Third party access
Wholesale pool	-0.0052	-2.306	Yes
Time to liberalization	0.0008	2.814	
Time to privatization	0.0006	1.51	
Non-regulatory environmental variables			
Hydro share	-0.0341	-3.252	
Nuclear share	0.0023	0.132	
Gross domestic product	0	1.011	

Source: author.

The Table 28 provides the impact of each economic regulation parameter on price. From these individual impacts it is possible to gauge the overall impact of economic regulation on price.

The indicators of regulation, industry structure, and performance were used to estimate equation (1) for the electric power supply industry. Initially, each equation was estimated using two regression models: a random effects specification and a fixed effects specification. In each of these specifications, the country-specific effect was assumed to occur in the constant term, so that slope coefficients are identical across countries. The random or fixed effects account for country-specific effects not otherwise included in the regressions. The random effects specification assumes that the relevant units (in this case countries) are drawn at random from a larger population, while the fixed effects specification is more appropriate if the focus is restricted to a specific set of units.

On the basis of Breusch-Pagan and Hausman tests, the random effects specification was chosen for the regressions in this analysis. Results for fixed effects estimation were not provided, though the signs, magnitude, and significance of coefficients were robust to the use of either specification [44]. The random effects specification makes sense in the context of this study if we consider that it consists of a sample of countries from a much larger population of OECD and non-OECD countries, so that country-specific constant terms are randomly distributed across cross-sectional units. Table 28 summarizes the estimated impact of regulation on industrial prices, industrial-residential price differentials, utilisation rates, and the gap between actual and optimal reserve margins, respectively.

The model was estimated separately for industrial prices and for the ratio of industrial to residential prices, changing the model specification to account for different expectations as to the effect of regulation and industry structure on the two price indicators. In the industry price regression, a number of control variables were included to account for cyclical economic variation and the impact of choice of generation technology. These controls were not included in the industrial-residential price differential regression, as the use of a price ratio should neutralise these effects, and the object of study is whether regulatory reform affects customer groups differentially. In both models, the explanatory variables are jointly significant in explaining the variation in prices, on the basis of the Chi-squared statistic, significant at the 0.01 level. Where they were included, the control variables had the correct sign but were generally insignificant. Only the share of hydro generation was significantly negative, a larger proportion of hydro-based generation results in lower industrial end-user prices, all else equal. This is consistent with expectations: the variable costs of hydropower are very low, except in drought years, so a large proportion of hydro generation should exert negative pressure on prices.

In the long run, liberalisation and privatisation may reduce electric power prices. Since there has been a gap between end-user power prices and the cost of power supply, this suggests potentially supra-competitive prices before deregulation and the possibility for downward movement of prices after. Unbundling of generation and transmission facilitates new entry into generation, so to the extent that entry intensifies competition, prices should decrease. Nevertheless, the estimated coefficient on unbundling of generation and transmission is statistically insignificant. While the negative sign of the estimated coefficient on the unbundling indicator was robust to different model specifications, its significance appeared to be affected by multi-collinearity with the other indicators of liberalization.

On the other hand, the positive and significant coefficient on ownership suggests that private ownership is not necessarily correlated with increased competition. This indicator reflects the influence of historic private ownership in addition to recent privatisation. The former could be correlated with higher prices due to a higher cost of capital, less tax advantages, and less access to low cost hydro resources. In fact, in many countries in the panel, private ownership coincides with a highly concentrated market (e.g., Belgium). Furthermore, privatisation of historically public generators may still result in high prices in the short run. Governments may actually increase electric power prices in order to sell assets and generate revenue. Furthermore, while governments may use privatisation as a platform for horizontal unbundling, if horizontal unbundling does not reach far enough, post-privatisation prices may remain high. For example, in the United Kingdom, the former state-owned utility, the Central Electricity Generating Board (CEGB), was broken up into only three competing generators (National Power, PowerGen, and British Energy). As a result, private companies with market power replaced a public company with market power, so prices did not respond immediately to privatisation. The model specification also permits assessment of the extent to which expanded legal rights to Third Party Access of networks and the establishment and operation of an electric power spot market are each effective in reducing prices. The estimated coefficient on these variables were negative, a expected.

However, the coefficient on TPA was not statistically significant. This may be because TPA will not make a difference in prices if legal TPA does not result in actual entry and if the incumbent retains practical control of the market. The coefficient on the spot market indicator was statistically significant. A real spot market should lower prices by inducing competition.

The Stneiner's study revealed that indicators of the time remaining to liberalisation and privatisation were included to proxy for the impact of expectations of liberalisation and privatisation on prices. Both coefficients were positive, and time to liberalisation was statistically significant. This suggests that as liberalisation and privatisation dates approach, power prices increase. In the case of privatisation, this is consistent with one potential policy goal underlying privatisation: to generate state revenue by selling assets, a goal that would be facilitated by higher power prices. Also, to the extent that time to liberalisation and time to privatisation are correlated, this may help to explain the counterintuitive sign on time to liberalisation. Alternatively, this empirical finding may result from a problem of reverse causality if high prices act as an incentive for liberalisation.

The regulation and industry structure indicators were used to explain the differential between industrial and residential power prices. To interpret the empirical results for this variable, it should be noticed that in all countries and time periods included in the sample industrial prices were lower than household prices (in US$ PPPs). Here, again, signs were largely consistent with expectations and statistically significant. The coefficient on private ownership was positive and significant. The coefficients on unbundling of generation and transmission, TPA, and the spot market were negative and significant, as expected.

The results underscore two important characteristics of reform in the power sector: first, the benefits of reform are disproportionately realised by industrial and residential customers. Second, power price discrimination can persist and even intensify under reform if market power is not reduced by structural measures such as horizontal unbundling in electric power sector. The fact that unbundling of power generation and transmission, TPA, and the existence of a spot power market all have a greater impact on industrial prices than on residential prices is consistent with expectations: industrial customers are larger than residential customers so they can benefit directly from TPA by arranging to have power wheeled by a generator, thereby avoiding other parts of the power supply chain. Additionally, commercial customers have the resources to participate in spot power markets. Furthermore, power prices to industrial customers should disproportionately reflect the effects of shifts in power generation regulation because for these customers, power generation makes up a larger proportion of end-user electric power prices. In contrast, small residential customers are less likely to be affected by these reforms because they continue to purchase power from local distribution undertakings so that they do not benefit directly from unbundling, expanded TPA, and spot power markets. There is evidence, therefore, that reforms may not have generally succeeded in eliminating market power in several cases.

This paper by Steiner [44] has provided a first attempt to assess, on the basis of international evidence, to what extent regulatory reform in the power industry can contribute to improved efficiency and welfare outcomes in the country. The comparative data on regulations presented in this paper showed that most countries have just begun to consider and to implement regulatory reform in the power sector. Furthermore, early efforts at liberalisation and or privatization in power sector, while creating legal access for competition in generation, are slow to meet with actual entry and competition in power generation. The most common pattern of liberalisation in power sector begins with attempts to introduce competition in power generation by unbundling power generation from transmission and expanding legal access to the transmission network. The most far-reaching power sector reforms also create spot power markets for trade in electric power and allow customer choice of power supplier. Preliminary exploration of the data using cluster analysis identified six groups of countries in 1996, with the United Kingdom as most liberal, followed by Finland, New Zealand, Norway, and Sweden. The least liberal group included Belgium, Canada, France, Greece, Ireland, Italy, Netherlands, Portugal, and Spain.

In summary, the primary empirical findings concerning the impact of regulatory reforms on efficiency and prices are as follows:

- The ratio of industrial to residential end-user power prices is reduced by the unbundling of power generation and transmission, expansion of Third Party Access (TPA), and introduction of power markets. The existence of these markets also tends to reduce the levels of industrial end-user power prices. However, a high degree of private ownership and imminence of both privatisation and liberalisation tend to increase industrial end-user power prices.
- Unbundling of power generation and transmission and private ownership each serve to improve the utilisation of capacity in power generation.
- Unbundling of power generation and transmission also brings reserve margins or the ability of capacity to handle peak load closer to their optimal level.

Taken together, these findings suggest that regulatory reforms in power sector involving vertical separation of the electric power industry, market price determination and privatisation impacted favourably on the efficiency. There are also signs that this power cost reduction translated into better opportunities for power price discrimination between different categories of customers and lower industrial end-user power prices. However, the effects of regulatory reform on power prices appear to depend crucially on the ability of regulatory policies to control market power after reforms have been implemented in electric power sector.

While the analysis conducted in Steiner's study serves as a first step in assessing the impact of regulation and industry structure on performance, much work remains to be done. The analysis could be enhanced by refining the regulatory indicators and finding a suitable proxy for assessment of quality of electric power supply and for market power. Additionally, the analysis could benefit from improved controls for the effect of regulation in the power transmission and distribution functions, particularly in the case of power prices are influenced by regulation outside of the electric power generation segment. A more complicated model that controls for the endogeneity of power generation technology choice across countries might also improve estimates by better controlling for factors that affect performance independently of regulation and power sector industrial structure. However, the most useful, would be to extend the analysis through time to include the many reforms which have just begun in East European countries.

Also, the Steiner model includes only a subset of economic regulations affecting the power generation sector, the impact measures calculated are unlikely to measure the full extent to which economic regulations impact industrial power prices. Dove at al. [45] conducted study to assess the impact of regulation on power prices by applying benchmark regulation. The appropriate benchmark against which the effect of regulatory regimes can be measured. This benchmark corresponds to the optimal level of regulation, namely socially least costly way of achieving the desired objectives. Dove at al [45] stressed that one practical option is to use the combination of regulation that minimize the power prices implied by the estimated equation. All regulatory regimes: separation of power generation from transmission, allowing TPA to the transmission grid and allowing for a wholesale power market are all found to lead to lower electric power prices. The other regimes: private ownership, time to liberalization, time to privatization is counterintuitive and Dove at al. [45] decided not to include them in the calculations of power price impacts.

Using the methodology described above power price impacts were estimated for industrial electric power sector for each of 50 countries during 1996. The power price impact of regulation in EU member states is presented in Table 29.

Table 29. Power price impact of regulation in power supply

Country	Power price impact, %
Austria	13.2
Belgium	15.4
Denmark	8.5
Finland	0.0
France	16.0
Germany	8.3
Greece	16.6
Ireland	13.9
Italy	17.1
Luxemburg	13.8
Netherlands	15.5
Portugal	17.9
Spain	9.5
Sweden	0.0
United Kingdom	0.0

Source: author.

The Table 29 indicates that as a result of regulatory regime implemented in power sector for example in Portugal, during 1990-1996 the power price was 17.9% higher than the power price in Sweden and United Kingdom.

Hattori and Tsutsui [194] applied the Steiner's model for the same 19 OECD countries and extended it through 1999. The study re-examined the impact of the regulatory reforms on power price in electric power supply industry and compares results with those found in an earlier study by Steiner [44]. The study provided results for both random and fixed effect estimation. They found significant positive impact on power prices in the presence of wholesale power market and that TPA has negative impact. In addition Hatori and Tsutsui proved that the private ownership coefficient is significantly negative for power prices. Some results obtained by Hatori and Tsutsui are contradictory to Steiner results. They also found that the extended retail access is likely to lower the industrial price and increase the power price differential between industrial customers and households.

The paper by Hattori and Tsutsui [194] reexamined the economic impact of the regulatory reforms in the power supply sector using panel data for OECD countries. The paper found that expanded retail access is likely to lower the industrial power price, and at the same time increase the power price differential between industrial power consumers and household customers, as expected. This result is largely due to the actual expansion of retail access after 1996—when we estimated the same model using data for the period to the end of 1996, the parameter estimate of the indicator of retail access was statistically insignificant.

Following Steiner, the regression equations were developed to analyze the impact of regulatory reform in the power sector on the level of the industrial power price and the ratio of the industrial power price to the residential power price. The two equations are estimated separately. Denoting the power price level or price ratio as *y*, the equation is written as follows:

$$y_{it} = a + X'b + Z'q + m_i + v_{it} \tag{3}$$

where *X'* is a set of regulatory reform indicators to reflect the degree of reform in various components of regulatory policy and Z' is a set of independent variables not directly related to regulatory reforms. Subscript *i* indicates the country and *t* indicates the time period; m_i accounts for an unobservable time-invariant country-specific effect, while v_{it} is the normal disturbance term.

It was assumed that the country-specific effect exists, and authors utilized some basic panel-data-estimation techniques, namely, a one-way fixed effect model and a one-way random effect model. The results indicated that the unbundling of generation and the introduction of a wholesale spot market did not necessarily lower the price, and may possibly have resulted in a higher price. The findings as to the unbundling and the spot market are not consistent with expectation and are different from those of Steiner. However, the results of Hattori and Tsutsui (2004) study are plausible in the light of the experiences in some countries. It is possible that the unbundling of generation from transmission increases transaction costs, which would be paid by final customers.

It has also been observed that power spot markets are vulnerable to the exercise of market power by electric power generators. In addition, these results indicated that there is a need for further analyses of the effect of reforms in the power supply industry. Hattori and Tsutsui [194] also indicated that it is too early to propose policy recommendation for countries considering such reform in the future. The power industry may yet be in a transitional state in which the policy makers are still working hard to "get it right". It may take much more time for the welfare enhancing effect of reforms to be realized. Estimation of the long-run effects of the reform on power prices will have to wait until a longer time series becomes available, although it should not be forgotten that power market participants will always respond very quickly to a changing regulation environment. The regulatory reform in the power supply sector is still an on-going process in many countries, and this underscores the importance of continuing efforts to analyze the net impact of the reform, as most of the reform policies are irreversible.

To determine if the difference between Steiner's results and Hattori and Tsutsui [194] study is caused by the different sample period, Hatori and Tsutsui [194] estimated the same model using the data for the period up to 1996. The parameter estimates for the regression equation (1) are shown in Table 30.

In Table 30 "The model 0" is the result from Steiner's study, in which few regulatory indicators are statistically significant. The existence of a wholesale power market statistically significantly lowers the industrial price. Unbundling and TPA have negative parameter estimates, but are not statistically significant. Time to liberalization and privatization are both positive, but the time to privatization is not statistically significant. As expected, the share of hydro generation has a statistically significantly negative coefficient. The share of nuclear generation and GDP are not statistically significant. In the next two columns (Models 1 and 2) of Table 30, the results obtained from other models that most closely replicate Steiner's model. These models are estimated using a data set extended to 1999. Model 1 is estimated as Model 3, is based on the random effect model, since the Hausman test statistics indicated that the random effect model is preferred. The unbundling of generation is statistically insignificant, as in Steiner's result. The retail access also is statistically insignificant, as was the TPA indicator in Steiner's study. On the other hand, the wholesale power market still takes a statistically significantly positive coefficient, and private ownership still takes a negative coefficient though it is insignificant. Based on this comparison, the effects of unbundling and retail access shown in Models 1 and 2 are at least partly due to the extension of our data set to 1999.

Comparing the results of Models 1 and 2 with those of Steiner's study, it is possible to observe several differences. First, the existence of a wholesale power market was statistically significantly negative in Steiner's study, but is significantly positive in 1 and 2 models. TPA in Steiner's model was statistically insignificantly negative, but our retail access parameter is statistically significantly negative in both Models 1 and 2. The share of private ownership was statistically significantly positive in Steiner's model, but is statistically significantly negative in our models. The share of hydro capacity is negative but not statistically significant. The share of nuclear capacity is not statistically significant, either. GDP is statistically significantly negative 1 and 2 models.

One of the potential problems with Steiner's model is that it includes both ''time to liberalization'' and ''time to privatization.'' These variables are highly correlated, and in fact, one of them (''time to privatization'') was statistically insignificant in his model as well as our Models 1–3. In Model 4 it was estimated the same model without ''time to privatization,'' and was found that the results (as shown under Model 4) are similar to those obtained in Model 2. The coefficient for ''time to liberalization'' appears to have changed from 0.001 to 0.002, but it actually changed from 0.00139 to 0.00169. Another potential problem is that the effect of ''time to liberalization'' may serve as the effect of a simple linear time trend, by which the effect of technological progress in the electric power supply industry throughout the world may be captured. To see if the effect of ''time to liberalization'' differs from the effect of the time trend, we replace the ''time to liberalization'' with the linear time trend and estimate the model again. Since the time trend is increasing over time while ''time to liberalization'' is defined to be decreasing over time, the estimate on the time trend takes the opposite sign but its magnitude (0.00180) is about the same as the estimate of the ''time to liberalization'' in Model 5 (0.00169). In addition the changing this variable does not very much affect the estimates of the other variables.

In more recent study by Nagayama [47] the effect of the selected liberalization models on electric power prices was investigated for 78 countries for period ranging from 1985 to 2003.

The ordered probit (random effect) model (Model 1) was developed to assess the impact of electric power prices on the selection of electric power sector liberalization models for each region. Denoting the liberalization model as γ^*_{it}, the following equation was developed:

$$\gamma^*_{it} = \alpha + \beta x_{it-2} + \epsilon_{it-2} \tag{4}$$

Here $y*_t$ is a latent variable which will not be observed as a continuous numerical data and the true measure of liberalization models adopted. B- is the vector of parameters to be estimated. X_{it} is the variable described above, y_i is an unobserved time-invariant country specific effect and e_{it-2} is an error term.

Y_{it}^* takes vales from minus infinity to plus infinity. To correspond Y_{it}^* to discrete selections, the Y_{it}^* was divided into 4 selections. The observed rating is determined by the cut-off point of the unknown threshold parameter μ_j $(j=1,2)$ which holds sequence restrictions. Categories 1, 2, and 3 are differentiated by μ_j.

$$Y_{it}^* = \begin{Bmatrix} 0(Y_{it}^* \leq 0) \\ 1(0 < Y_{it}^* \leq \mu_1) \\ 2(\mu_1 < Y_{it}^* \leq \mu_2) \\ 3(\mu_2 < Y_{it}^*) \end{Bmatrix} \quad (5)$$

Subscript i indicates the country and t indicates the time period. Independent variables are electric prices and GDP per capita with two years lag. The method of maximum likelihood is used to estimate the probit model. The likelihood is maximized by determining the joint distribution function of the explained variable. Since it is technically difficult to assume the fixed effect in the panel probit model, we take use of the random effects.

Endogeneity is not a significant issue in Model 1 as long as reform responds to price with the lagged term. In this paper, we took a two-year lag for all independent variables since there is thought to be some time lag for the selection of models. It is often the case that countries commence restructuring and raising prices well before reforms take effect, firstly, to act as a new energy policy and secondly, to attract foreign investors by signaling that secure returns can be obtained. Missing data are treated as missing values and are analyzed using unbalanced panel data. The first year of action was taken to shift from one model to another.

Estimation results of the ordered probit (random effect) model (Model 1) are presented in Table 31.

Table 31 demonstrates that, although there are some differences between the areas, the estimated results are generally in line with expectations. The higher the electric price, the stronger the impetus is to perform electric sector reforms. Electric power prices, for both industrial and residential prices, take a statistically significant positive value in Asian developing countries, the former Soviet Union and Eastern Europe. In developed countries and in Latin America, however, while the direction of the coefficients is as expected, statistically significant results are not evident.

In terms of the control variable for the industrial and residential prices, GDP per capita is statistically significant and positive, except for Latin America. Thus, a higher absolute level of GDP per capita is associated with liberalization models.

Table 30. Regression results for the analysis of the price level

Model	0	1	2	3	4	5
Sample period	1986–1996	1987–1999	1987–1999	1987–1996	1987–1999	1987–1999
Estimation	Random effect [44]	Fixed effect	Random effect	Random effect	Fixed effect	Fixed effect
Constant	0.067 (7.104)		0.077 (8.115)	0.078 (7.716)		
Unbundling	—0.001	0.004	0.003	—0.002	0.004	0.005
	(—0.659)	(1.940)	(1.509)	(—0.999)	(1.737)	(2.316)
Private ownership	0.003	—0.009	—0.007	—0.002	—0.009	—0.007
	(2.700)	(—6.583)	(—5.939)	(—1.118)	(—6.621)	(—5.544)
Retail access/TPA	—0.003	—0.005	—0.005	—0.002	—0.005	—0.004
	(—1.357)	(—3.251)	(—3.286)	(—1.031)	(—3.250)	(—2.339)
Wholesale market	—0.005	0.009	0.007	0.005	0.008	0.009
	(—2.306)	(3.188)	(2.619)	(1.643)	(3.063)	(3.483)
Time to liberalization	0.001	0.001	0.002	0.002	0.002	
	(2.814)	(3.773)	(5.233)	(4.871)	(9.145)	
Time to privatization	0.001	0.000	0.000	—0.001		
	(1.510)	(0.935)	(—0.120)	(—1.302)		
Share of hydro capacity/generation	—0.034	—0.027	—0.033	—0.029	—0.028	—0.031
	(—3.252)	(—0.484)	(—1.511)	(—1.276)	(—0.515)	(—0.572)
Share of nuclear capacity/generation	0.002	0.037	—0.004	—0.040	0.043	0.062
	(0.132)	(0.777)	(—0.122)	(—1.318)	(0.911)	(1.330)
GDP	0.000	—0.011	—0.006	—0.004	—0.010	—0.005
	(1.011)	(—4.217)	(—2.784)	(—1.468)	(—4.204)	(—2.184)
Time trend						—0.002 (—9.941)
Hausman test statistics	16.39		25.59	13.19	20.21[a]	13.48[a]
(P-value)			0.0024	0.1544	0.0096	0.0963

t-Values in parentheses..

Source: author.

Table 31. Estimation of results of the ordered probit (random effect) Model 1

Variables	Expected Sign	Total	Asian developing Countries	Latin America	Former Soviet Union and Eastern Europe	Developed Countries
Industrial prices						
(1) Electric power prices	+	0.00078228	0.00064687	0.3032956	0.00106781	0.00010113
		(11.625)	(3.864)	(0.884)	(11.103)	(0.614)
(2) GDP per Capita (%)	+	0.0000152445	0.00020521	0.0000050793	0.0000586226	0.0000181856
		(6.883)	(3.778)	(0.229)	(2.090)	(7.452)
μ (1)		0.63388377	1.40543487	0.81428672	0.65601919	0.19157673
		(17.083)	(11.097)	(11.788)	(8.148)	(6.034)
μ (2)		0.95781683	1.58793682	1.94249562	1.18255838	0.2455181
		(22.972)	(11.353)	(14.127)	(9.508)	(6.868)
Log likelihood		-1403.520	- 174.3765	-378.9503	-255.9733	-465.3292
Number of observations		1326	187	340	357	442
Residential prices						
(1) Electric power prices	+	0.00087861	0.00068838	0.00426032	0.00116709	– 0.0000432774
		(11.760)	(4.161)	(0.126)	(11.027)	(-0.2)
(2) GDP per Capita (%)	+	0.0000124402	0.00021224	0.0000135054	0.0000392415	0.0000174346
		(5.713)	(3.904)	(0.692)	(1.424)	(7.614)
μ (1)		0.63176010	1.40722826	0.80098849	0.67339108	0.19157673
		(19.079)	(11.096)	(11.815)	(8.273)	(6.034)
μ (2)		0.95413805	1.59004129	1.91573911	1.18620263	0.24551819
		(22.960)	(11.353)	(14.140)	(9.653)	(6.868)
Log likelihood		-1398.007	-175.4951	-378.5174	-248.0789	-459.0952
Number of observations		1326	187	340	357	442

Source: author.

The results Model 1 can be summarized as follows: the industrial/ residential prices of both Asian developing countries along with the former Soviet Union and Eastern Europe had an impact on the transition of the liberalization model (from monopoly model → SB model → Wholesale model → Wholesale/Retail competition model) as a result of the increase in the level of electric power prices, with statistically significant results as expected. Further, statistically significant positive results for the transition of liberalization models indured by high levels of GDP per capita in residential prices were observed in Asian developing countries, and in developed countries. Statistically significant results were not obtained for Latin American and developed countries. However, statistically significant results for industrial electric power prices obtained in all areas except for Latin American countries. This result may arise from heterogeneity in liberalization patterns in Latin America.

Nagayama [47] applied panel data from 78 countries, including developing nations. The effect of electric power prices on electric sector liberalization models and the effect of the selected liberalization models on electric power prices of each country for a period ranging from 1985 to 2003 was estimated. The endogeneity of electric power prices and power liberalization models has also been examined. The research findings suggested that higher electric power prices are one of the driving forces of adopting liberalization models. However, the development of liberalization models in the power sector does not necessarily reduce electric power prices. In fact, contrary to expectations prices had a tendency to rise. Therefore, when the selection of a liberalization model is discussed in developing or transition economies, careful consideration should be given to the types of reforms that would best suit the economic development or transition stage of each country.

It is necessary to take into account the fact that the change in prices, influenced by power sector reforms, has a dynamic impact on other factors as well. In developing and transition economies for example, the increase in electric power prices decreases electric power accessibility to the poor segments of the population. Alternatively in developed countries, the decrease in electric power prices mitigates the effort put forth toward saving energy. The decrease in electric power prices is clearly a negative factor for investors in terms of profit performance. This will almost certainly inhibit investment promotion in electric power fields. Dynamic aspects resulting from power sector reforms are also need to be investigated.

There is still much room for improvement within the models and data presented in the paper [47]. There is a need to further scrutinize the models against further data in the future. In addition in developed countries within the EU, the directives of the European Commission also had an impact on the adoption of the reforms, irrespective of prices. The policy which was intended to promote competition and efficiency ended up with compromising efforts to secure the additional power supply necessary for developing countries to achieve. It is necessary to understand that the number one root cause of the massive problems in a developing country's power sector is the high cost of electric power production which governments are unwilling to pass on to consumers for political reasons. Splitting public utilities into private companies in the name of power sector reform will not purely solve this problem. This problem can only be solved by pushing hard to implement low cost power generation projects. The results of study indicated that there is a need for continued analyses of the effect of reforms in the electric power supply industry. There is also an indication that it is too early to reach any concrete judgment for future policy recommendations based on the results of conducted study. An accurate calculation of the long-term effects of reforms on prices will require much additional study over longer periods of time. In many countries, regulatory reform in electric power supply is still an on-going process, a fact that also highlights the need for continued studies of electric power market reforms impact on electric power prices.

Zhang, Kirpatrick, Parker [195] measured the effect of such variables as the existence of an independent regulatory agency, a wholesale electric power pool market, private electric business, electric power generation per capita, installed capacity per capita, electric power generation per employee and residential/industrial electric power prices using data from 51 developing countries in the time frame ranging from 1985 to 2000. The study proved that neither privatization on it's own, nor regulation on its own leads to obvious gains in economic performance. This is because of the effect either of privatization or having an autonomous regulator is statistically insignificant. Zhang et al. [195], used real per-capita GDP, the urban population ratio, and the degree of economic freedom as well as three dummy variables relating to the competition and privatization used as the explaining variable. As pointed out in [195], privatization alone may not result in performance improvement. Competition and, in its absence, effective regulation may be required to capture any potential benefits privatization might bring.

In looking at the impact of unbundling on retail price, Bushnell, Mansur, Saraavia [158] found that had New England markets been forced to fully unbundle (as happened in California), retail prices in those areas would have been significantly higher due to production inefficiencies. Hogan and Meade [46] also found that generators tend to overstate their wholesale prices when there is unbundling, resulting in higher retail prices. On the other hand, Fiorio, et al. [196] examining the impact of energy market reform on household electric power prices in 15 EU countries over the period 1978 and 2005, found that less vertical integration is associated with lower prices. Joskow [197] used time series econometrics to find that competitive wholesale and retail markets reduced prices (relative to their absence) by 5-10% for residential customers and 5% for industrial customers.

International Energy Agency observed indications of cycles in liberalized electric power markets in some IEA member countries. Kadoya et al. [198] used a substantial excess of capacity as an indication for strong capacity boom and bust cycles. Arango and Larsen [6] showed in their study that deregulation and competition can lead to sustained cycles in electric power systems. They proved that deregulation and competition are actually the reasons for this long-term behavior. They proved that the introduction of deregulation in an electric power system leads to systematic fluctuations of over- and under-capacity. Such an occurrence of cycles is one of the major threats for electric power markets since it affects consumers and producers alike. The cycle hypothesis was formulated based on analogies with capital-intensive industries, behavioral simulation models, and experimental electric power markets. The support for this hypothesis was backed by examples of the English and Chilean markets, which comes from visual inspections of historical data, and autocorrelation analysis. Evidence from the Nordpool so far is not as clear as it is with the other two markets. Cyclical behavior in electric power markets has important implications for security of supply as well as for prices of electric power. For example, the consequences of wrong timing and insufficient generation capacity led to the well-known crisis in California [199]. Periods of low reserve margin may be triggered by external shocks, such as severe droughts in a hydro-based system, gas supply cuts, etc., but insufficient capacity at the time of the shock amplifies the security of supply problem (i.e., if the shocks hit when a country is at the bottom of the cycle). So far, there is no agreement on which market structure of an electric power system will lead to sufficient long-term investments. In deregulated electric power markets, investments are profit driven (at least for private firms), and in theory a well-functioning market should be resilient enough to guarantee sufficient generation capacity. The problem is that energy-only markets "rely on high prices during periods of capacity scarcity to remunerate peaking units" [200], in other words in many cases the cycles are necessary for the investors to recover their investment. On the other hand, regulators often look for a mechanism to prevent or cap the extreme prices. It is also widely accepted that many electric power markets have "market-failure", i.e., that they would not function properly, nor display the right signal for investments, and that regulators have an important function in correcting these market failures [201]. Moreover, the prevention of shortages of electric power creates the need for stabilizing policies, known as "keeping the lights on", which is the imperative of policy, market design, and regulation [200].

Though the long-term stability of electric power markets is a desired state, but it is a complicated topic [202]. In fact, the question about stabilizing policies is still open. There is no agreement as to whether there should be a coordination mechanism for investments or whether it should be left to the action of market forces [200, 203].

The study by Yarrow [204] provided that in terms of its implications for assessment of retail energy price deregulation in Victoria and elsewhere, the UK record since the lifting of price controls in 2000-2002 supports the view that effective competition provides strong protection for consumers generally, including domestic/residential consumers. Given the *ex ante* concerns about the likely efficacy of retail competition in protecting the interests of residential consumers – non -household markets have been open to competition for much longer – it is remarkable, only a few years after the ending of price controls, how generally accepted the notion of retail competition in energy has become. The last two years have seen very major swings in retail prices, similar to the swings in world oil prices, which would likely have given rise to some quite severe regulatory and political difficulties had public authorities been responsible for the supervision or determination of prices. Yet there has been no general call for a return to price control, and gas and electric power price movements have come to be accepted by the public in very much the same way that oil price movements are accepted. There is general recognition that, in competitive markets, prices go up and down, and that it is also recognised that, in the case of energy, there are powerful, global factors at work which are driving prices upwards. The complaints and concerns therefore tend not to be cast in terms of defensive requests for 'protection' against high prices, but rather in terms of a questioning as to whether markets are functioning reasonably effectively and hence whether or not the prices being charged do actually reflect underlying supply and demand conditions. And when problems are (rightly or wrongly) identified, there is an increasing tendency to see the appropriate policy response as falling within the domain of competition law, rather than as public price fixing [204]. Contrary to fears that household consumers would fare worse relative to no-household customers as a result of deregulation, the evidence suggested that, at least in the years immediately before and after deregulation, they fared better. As in the case of non-household customers, therefore, the evidence indicates that competitive, deregulated markets have served the interests of household consumers at least as well as, and most likely better than, regulatory supervision of prices. Although not directly comparable to the approaches to retail price regulation in Australia, the UK or the United States, the experience of retail market opening in Norway and Sweden, including in relation to the evolution of prices and price offerings, nevertheless provides some interesting information.

The Scandinavian developments have been low key and measured, but there have been relatively significant changes in market structures over a relatively short period of time, and some major price shocks have been absorbed without threat to the integrity of the overall market arrangements [204].

Over the last decades, important steps have been taken across Europe in order to liberalize the energy market at the national level of each member to make possible the birth of a common energy market at a European level, characterized by price alignment, market transparency, access of suppliers on every energy market in Europe, consumers' right to choose the best possible offer. Though the level of market liberalization reached by the members on their attempt to deregulate their national market is different from one country to another, the basic steps have been taken by most countries meaning that, in theory, each consumer can freely choose their supplier. In practice, this hardly applies, the markets are not that open and there are still several barriers that need to be overcome. The common energy market will not be achieved too soon. At the moment, prices are not sufficiently competitive, consumers have difficulties in adapting to the new situation and understanding their rights as they are used to the idea that decisions should be taken for them.

The energy market liberalization should bring benefits to both consumers and to the economic environment. But the liberalized markets cannot influence two important price components: the price of energy, often related to global/regional prices of fuels and the level of taxes and levies. This means that the price evolution cannot be determined. Competition and fair prices that reflect the real costs can only be achieved with a high level of commitment in this direction. Even when these conditions are satisfied, it takes a long time for markets to be fully implemented and developed so that consumers can benefit from competitive prices. The deregulation process in electric power markets is still in progress. The complexity of the analyzed sector combined with the resistance of the traditional market operators has made this process difficult. National interests represent another obstacle to liberalization. Although the first step in opening the market was successfully made by most European members, several measures still have to be taken so that consumers can enjoy the full benefits of a free market. Since empirical evidence suggest that, in general, deregulation has played a positive impact on efficiency and consumers welfare in other sectors – telecommunications, air transport – the same results are expected for the power sector.

The results of reviewed studies showed that the development of liberalization models in electric power sector does not necessarily reduce electric power prices and can cause economic cycles. In fact, contrary to expectation in some cases prices had tendency to rise. Therefore more attention has to be paid to selection of a liberalization model and careful considerations should be given to the types of reforms that would best suit to expected priority goals of EU energy policy. In addition it is necessary to mention that the aims of EU energy policy are conflicting as the decrease of electric power prices which is the main indicator of competitiveness mitigates the effort to go forward for energy savings, for investments in renewable energy and other new energy saving technologies. The decrease of environmental impact is related with the increase of electric power prices and consequently with decrease in competiveness. Therefore some trade of between EU energy policy goals is necessary when deciding on electric power market liberalization model. The multi-criteria assessment framework can help in ranking energy liberalization models.

Previous empirical studies on relationship between energy market reforms and energy prices provided that relationships between energy market liberalization and electric power prices are complicated and reciprocal. In addition the impact on other important issues such as energy supply security, sustainability needs more broad investigations.

3.3. Review of Empirical Studies Dealing with Impact of Natural Gas Market Deregulation on Natural Gas Prices

Natural gas is important for meeting the energy policy objectives of security, competitiveness and environmental sustainability. A liberalized market provides price signals that show its real value. Subsidies distort transparency and lead to unnecessary losses. Natural gas is not only the cleanest fossil fuel, but also the most flexible. Natural gas can provide the flexibility that wind and solar energy currently need as back up. Finally, biogas could partly replace fossil fuels. Natural gas is a bridge to a sustainable society and an integral part of a sustainable future.

Liberalization of gas markets is at various stages throughout the world countries. Most countries that have liberalized have done so formally but rarely claim to have reached a satisfactory end state. Liberalization takes time and continuous adjustment of means and goals. But customers, especially wholesale, benefit on prices where liberalization is most advanced. The downside is that natural gas prices tend to be more volatile and there are fewer possibilities for Governmental control. Liberalization leads to more integration and interconnection, as companies start doing business in neighbouring markets.

The main obstacle to gas market opening – long-term "take or pay" contracts-have been and continue to be the backbone of reliable gas supply. They will retain this important role for the next decade and probably longer. Nevertheless, liberalization in gas distribution has stimulated gas demand, expansion of local gas distribution infrastructure, and provision of more options for consumers. Finally, upstream market liberalization will grow in importance concerning the provision of the required quantities of gas supplies in an environment marked by increasing demand and increasing competition for natural gas between the regions. Liberalization has changed the legal and economic framework of the gas industry. In the EU, the gas sector has restructured from national monopolies to an EU oligopoly, and there is still no real competition. Huge investments are needed in networks (high pressure and low pressure) and gas storage capacities to address potential supply disruptions, which supports the case for an oligopoly organization. Conversely, growth in gas demand is expected to be driven by power generation in the future, and yet current pricing and market structures are not amenable to that outcome. The abundant availability of LNG quantities on the global gas market and the ongoing liberalization in Europe are mutually supporting developments.

Liberalization of natural gas markets was intended to introduce competitive forces and bring prices into line with costs. The expectation was that liberalization would lead to price reductions. However, according to the relevant Eurostat data on EU countries, prices increased significantly from 2000 to 2008. In particular, from 2004 to 2008 they increased by 50% on average and in the industry sector they increased by 60%. Liberalization led to concentration of the market into an oligopolistic structure dominated by a few major sellers. The persistence of oil-indexed contracts and the high degree of market concentration have prevented the expected price evolution from emerging.

The study of UNECE Working Party on Gas of Committee on Sustainable Energy [205] aimed to assesses whether liberalization has helped market participants improve their efficiency and grow market shares in order to determine, in their view, the real value of liberalization. Active participation of many experts from different counties confirmed the importance of liberalization for the international energy community [205]. The study revealed that in 2009, world prices for natural gas were roughly equivalent to their 2002 level. In the intervening period they varied by a factor of four were rising up to the start of the financial crisis. The price of coal has been more stable, but has known spikes of up to 300%. Oil prices rose up to four times their 2002 level and remain twice as high as they were in 2009. Other commodities, notably food products have seen similar substantial price changes. It is thought that the price rises were mainly caused by the economic growth in China, India and other developing countries, whereas the price decrease is attributed to a decrease in demand as a result of the financial crisis. Therefore in the period when market reforms in Europe took place, the main changes in prices reflected supply and demand fundamentals, making it difficult to filter out the effects of liberalization. Liberalization ensures that prices rapidly reflect the underlying costs of production, transport and storage, and enables investors and consumers to respond. In situations of supply surplus, liberalization leads to prices that reflect relatively low marginal costs of supply. In periods of tight supply the converse is true, where marginal costs include not just the commodity value but also the costs of investment [205].

The UNECE [205] study concluded that with the exception of North America, wholesale markets in the UNECE region remain dominated by incumbents. The lack of free firm transport capacity is often cited as one of the main reasons for the slow development of competition. As infrastructure projects have long lead times and incentives for companies to build new infrastructure are either unclear or unattractive, competition is increasing only slowly. Regulatory pressure on transport tariffs has obviously resulted in lower transport costs as part of the total bill, but care should be taken that this does not lead to a negative investment climate. The latter might prevent competition, thus leading to higher prices.

Even though the desired end state of liberalization has not been reached in many cases, the trend is towards more competition. Incumbents do try to enter new markets themselves, in most cases their neighbouring markets. They have a preference for large growing and changing markets. The best example is probably the United Kingdom, which is a large market, with a well-established demand and a near certainty that domestic production is less and less able to supply the market. Several neighbouring countries have built large pipelines to the United Kingdom and a number of large LNG receiving terminals are built as well. Large customers are often the first targets for new entrants who compete on price, as price can be the determining factor for choosing a supplier for large customers. Gas trading platforms (hubs) are developing everywhere and often show growing trends. Gas-on-gas competition leads to both up- and downward pressure on gas prices when compared to oil prices, but due to the depressed gas demand during most of 2009 the downward pressures have been the most obvious. As a result of the increasing importance of gas-on-gas competition and fast-changing market conditions, new contract types and pricing models keep appearing.

Regarding retail markets [205] study concluded that only a few retail markets are completely deregulated, most have some form of end user protection, either temporarily or continuous. Consumer protection can take the form of a maximum price or allowing consumers a choice between a regulated tariff and a free tariff or providing support for vulnerable customers. Competition is increasing in most European markets, although slowly, with the incumbent remaining dominant but losing share. As in the wholesale market, the most successful new entrants are incumbents from neighbouring markets. Some countries report large price differences in offers by suppliers to the benefit of the consumer who chooses the right supplier.

Nevertheless switching rates are seldom very high although they do vary from country to country. Consumers are not always well aware of the possibility to switch and of which benefits can be gained—which is a concern to policymakers. On the other hand, until recently, choosing a new energy supplier is low on the priority list of consumers, even if it can save substantial amounts of money. It is unknown how this attitude has changed as a consequence of the financial crisis.

There is a risk that suppliers anticipate this consumer behaviour in their price offers by giving more competitive offers to "active" customers. Since liberalization started, companies have successfully experimented with a range of new products in order to gain or maintain market share. Examples of this are the emergence of "green" energy, signing bonuses, energy-saving advice, and fixed and flexible tariffs.

The study by Department of Trade and Industry developed a model of the natural gas market for the EU in the year of 2005 and considered three scenarios in order to assess the impact of natural gas market liberalization on natural gas prices. The first scenario, which is called the 'constrained case', takes a pessimistic view of what competition in the gas market will be like by 2015. Although the second gas directive has been transposed into national law by all member states of the EU, there has been little real enthusiasm for competition and the European gas market continues to be characterized as a series of national markets. The second case, called the 'most competitive case, represents the most positive outcome from the point of view of competition in the gas market that can reasonably be expected over the next ten years. Long-term contracts continue to play an important part in the market but pricing terms move away from oil-price indexation to market-related pricing.

Liberalization within the EU itself is substantially complete but there remain problems beyond the EU's borders. Although some reform has been attempted in Russia, which in this outcome has signed the Energy Charter Treaty, Gazprom remains dominant over Russian production and effectively manages to exclude gas from the Caspian area from direct access to the European market. The third case, called the 'fully competitive case', represents the full natural gas market opening case.

After a series of events in the winter of 2005/06 (Hurricanes Rita and Katrina in the US, fire in rough storage in the United Kingdom, nuclear outages in Japan, shortages of hydropower in Spain and severe winter weather in Europe), the International Energy Agency concluded that the natural gas industry was globalizing, as price effects were passed on around the globe and demand for gas was soaring. A similar effect can be seen today as a global oversupply drives prices in the spot market down. Once again this influences the analysis of the effects of liberalization, as formerly separated markets started to interact with each other as liberalization kicked in. One could, of course, also argue that it was the liberalization in the first place which opened up markets for global competition and hence globalized the industry.

Using the Energy Markets' European Gas Model, the Department of Trade and Industry calculates in the year 2005 the spot price for each of 25 countries considered in the study to be the marginal cost of supply, including gas costs, transportation costs and storage costs. The marginal cost is calculated as the increase in total costs in the entire model that result from increasing the demand in a particular country in a particular quarter by a small increment (1 million cubic metres) while holding all other assumptions and constraints unchanged. The results are presented in Table 32. Considering the constrained case as the base case, it is possible to note by comparing the most competitive case with the base case that natural gas liberalization will led to a 59.6% reduction in spot price of natural gas in Turkey, 44% for Spain, 32% for Ireland, 45% for France etc.

Table 32. Natural gas prices by specific scenario (EUR/1000m^3)

Country	Constraint scenario or basic	Most competitive scenario	Fully competitive scenario
Austria	18.9	21.1	14.6
Belgium	31.0	19.5	15.3
Bulgaria	17.1	10.8	11.6
Croatia	19.9	12.3	16.3
Czech Republic	20.3	10.9	14.0
Denmark	17.7	13.8	13.8
Finland	11.6	88.2	9.1
France	37.4	20.6	16.1
Germany	22.8	14.6	14.2
Greece	18.6	11.9	12.9
Hungary	18.0	21.1	12.1
Ireland	36.6	24.6	18.2
Italy	19.7	10.0	14.1
Luxembourg	21.6	16.9	17.4
Netherlands	26.1	16.1	12.7
Poland	11.5	9.8	9.2
Portugal	12.7	20.5	17.6
Romania	16.5	20.0	11.2
Slovak Republic	15.8	8.6	11.7
Slovenia	20.5	13.2	16.2
Spain	30.6	13.6	15.0
Sweden	18.8	14.1	12.7
Switzerland	32.8	20.5	15.2
Turkey	34.9	14.1	11.2
UK	31.5	20.4	16.6

Source: author.

One can see from figures in Table 32 that the lowest natural gas prices are in fully competitive scenario for all countries. Most competitive scenario for some countries provides with higher natural gas prices comparing with constraint scenario.

3.4. Review of Empirical Studies Dealing with Impact of District Heat Market Deregulation on Heat Prices

Previous research has shown the effects of liberalization of electric power and natural gas markets, but very little regarding District heat markets.

Is DH a natural monopoly? Some would hold that the whole production system in the case of DH is to be considered a natural monopoly, while others would limit the monopoly to the distribution of the hot water [206]. A traditional definition of a natural monopoly is that it exists in an industry where a single firm can produce output to supply the market at a lower per unit cost than two or more firms could [207]. This is closely connected to the concept of *economies of scale.* In economic literature often cited examples of natural monopolies are gas companies, telephone companies and other so called *public utilities.* Public utilities include many different areas of business, e.g., telecommunications, different forms of energy systems, railroads, airlines, etc. They are characterised by having substantial *sunk costs* due to large infrastructures. The traditional (economist) way of understanding the nature of a public utility is that the operation can be divided into three different components: production, transmission and distribution (sales). For many public utilities the firms are vertically integrated and a recent issue has been the unbundling of these different components into competitive elements and "natural" monopolies.

Most commentators agree that the production state is "inherently competitive in most utilities." The opening of electric markets in Europe and elsewhere, illustrates a shift in common opinion about the nature of public utilities: "Where once regulated or government owned monopolies dominated because of the belief that most utilities were 'natural monopolies', there is now a growing consensus that competition can perform a broader and more effective role." Production and sales of electric power are nowadays considered suited for competition. The case of DH is not quite as clear-cut. Where electric power markets are national, sometimes cross-national (still with bottle-necks in the distribution systems) and consumers and suppliers can meet on functioning markets, e.g., NordPool, the DH markets are geographically much more limited.

In a multi product firm, economies of scope may also create a natural monopoly although there are no economies of scale with regards to the production of the goods separately. This last idea is of course very relevant when we are discussing DH in relation to e.g., the production of electric power and/or district cooling. Combined heat and power production (CHP) might more readily be considered a natural monopoly than simple DH, due to its larger complexity, although the electric power obviously can be produced and sold in competition with other firms.

The question of third party access (TPA) to the networks/grids has been central to the debate around the liberalization of the European electric power and gas markets due to the natural monopoly characteristics of these networks. The natural monopoly character of the grids prohibits the construction of parallel networks, and for this reason the possibility for new competitors to use the network of the incumbent monopolist is a necessary prerequisite for effective competition. Similar to natural gas, DH is an important network industry in a number of countries (e.g., Sweden, Finland, Denmark, Austria, Lithuania, etc.). In these countries DH represents an efficient technology for providing space heating and hot tap water [208]. Still, although the DH sector shares many of the above network characteristics, market opening and third party access in this industry has so far not been addressed to the same extent [209]. During recent years, though, appeals for the introduction of TPA in DH have become more frequent, not the least in Sweden. Since DH networks also offer the possibility of competition between natural gas and electric power in the market for space heating the economic efficiency of the DH sector is critical to a synergetic use of various energy carriers [210].

In 1996, when the Swedish electric power market was opened up for competition, the formerly regulated DH market was also deregulated in the sense that the firms (at the time typically owned by the respective municipalities) now could set their own prices, and free entry into the market was formally introduced [206]. This decision was motivated by a desire to secure efficient competition between electric power and DH in the space heating market segment. As a result of the deregulation some of the earlier municipality-owned companies were sold to private enterprises. The competitive situation in the Swedish DH market has since then been a highly debated topic, not the least considering the presence of large consumer price differences across different Swedish regions. The process industries in Sweden (e.g., steel works, pulp and paper mills, etc.), some generating considerable amounts of industrial waste heat, have been particularly strong promoters of the introduction of TPA [209].

In Sweden DH was an important energy source for the country's households, and several government investigations of how the competition in the DH market can improve have been conducted. The most recent one states that TPA would be technically feasible, but it would require substantial economic investments. It thus concluded that allowing TPA would increase the costs for the consumers, and only marginally increase the competitive situation. However, none of the suggestions brought up in these investigations tend to explicitly address the problem of monopoly prices in some networks. Although the new DH Act, introduced in 2008, offers a possibility for a weak form of negotiated TPA, a government commission was analysing the situation in 2010 and argue that one additional competitor of equivalent size can be enough to ensure a competitive situation in the market, and also that an opening of the network would increase the use of industrial waste heat and thus promote an overall efficient use of energy [209].

The possible impacts of a market opening of DH networks in Sweden, i.e., a situation in which production is subject to competition and non-discriminatory TPA to the network while the network itself is regulated was investigated in paper by Soderholm, Warell [209]. From a competition perspective, the separation of these two activities can be critical so as to avoid a situation where the DH company that owns the network keeps producer prices down in order to keep out potential competitors. In the new situation the price is divided into two parts: a regulated network price and a market price for the delivered heat. The central conclusion is that the net effect on consumer prices of the market opening is far from straightforward to assess, primarily since it is: (a) typically difficult to identify pricing strategies in a baseline scenario; and (b) the price impact of permitting new entrants is ambiguous since most networks are local (e.g., some networks may face no new suppliers).

One example of the difficulties in clarifying the consumer price impacts in the case of a market opening is when (in the baseline setting) a municipality-owned company operates the entire DH network in a mid-sized Swedish town and in doing this it applies a "fair rate-of-return" pricing policy [209]. When the market is opened up to competition, the price change following this will depend on the intensity of competition at the producer stage. The price will go down (ceteris paribus) only in the case where new suppliers connect to the network and compete with the existing suppliers. As was noted above, this may not occur in the smaller networks. If the company maintains its monopoly position (e.g., due to economies of scale) the impacts on the price can be moderate at least if the company continues to charge its customers on a cost-covering basis. However, an opening of the DH market through introducing TPA can also lead to a situation where the municipal owners choose to sell the DH activities to private investors (as they may not believe that it is part of their mandate to engage in competitive activities). With the deregulation of the Swedish electric power market in 1996, many municipality-owned electric utilities did exactly this, and if this occurs also in the DH sector prices are likely to increase unless the competition in the network becomes extensive. Thus, in some regions a cost-covering monopolist may simply be replaced by a profit-maximizing monopolist.

Another possible scenario is where the DH operations in a municipality are run by one private company that applies a monopoly pricing strategy. A separation of the production and network activities and the introduction of TPA, are here likely to increase the competition in the market. However, because of the presence of mainly local markets, a reasonable outcome is a situation of oligopoly competition (i.e., competition among two or few firms). Oligopoly implies, in principle, lower prices than a monopoly situation, but prices will also be more closely determined by how the competitive activities work in practice. A plausible outcome in the capital-intensive DH market is so-called Cournot competition in which each company's production level is the strategic choice variable. Such a situation leads to lower prices than in the monopoly case, but still prices that exceed marginal cost, and thus an output level which is lower than the economically efficient one.

The above illustrates that the effect on DH prices of introducing TPA is very much an open question, and will depend on the present pricing behaviour in each network as well as the dynamic competitive effects of opening up the producer market. Intense competition in Swedish DH is severely limited by the presence of many small, local networks. We should also remember that an economically efficient market is not necessarily a market where consumer prices are as low as possible; the key issue is that the prices are as close to the marginal cost of production as possible. The way in which this can be achieved in practice depends in turn on whether the production of heat is a natural monopoly or not.

The difficulties in attaining efficient competition are further complicated by the mere fact that a DH system constitutes an expensive physical infrastructure. One characteristic of the network is that it is far from clear whether one can arbitrarily provide TPA for any location and capacity. Some parts of a DH system, e.g., those remote from existing production, may have relatively small pipes and could only allow TPA given a significant modification of the system. This would imply an added cost for all users unless the third party pays, and could thus limit the possibility for TPA even if the cost of the heat is less than that of the existing producers.

Regulated TPA refers to the case of an unlimited access to DH networks. The network owner has an obligation to allow access to the network from the companies that so wish. The network access is *ex ante* regulated, which implies that the conditions for access are determined in advance. If these conditions are met by the third party company the network owner is obliged to provide access to the network [211]. This market form implies that the network fee is public and fixed for the companies that want to access the network to sell heat. In this scenario it becomes important to vertically separate the network and the production activities for a more efficient competition to occur. As such pricing behaviour would be similar to that in the Nordic electric power market; the customer pays a flat fee that represents the network cost, and a variable fee that represents the use of hot water. The variable component would differ depending on the production mix (low when a large proportion of waste heat and CHP is used and higher when the system needs to use reserve capacity such as oil-fired plants). Just as in electric power, it would be possible for consumers to choose fixed or variable price contracts.

In this scenario the possible benefits of TPA can be significant since this market form has the potentially greatest impact on the competition in the market. According to economic theory an unlimited access to the network will facilitate more efficient solutions, not the least since increased competition often creates new business opportunities and more efficient operators. In order for this to occur, however, the size of the market and the number of competing firms are important. As was indicated above, the introduction of regulated TPA may imply lower prices in some networks but also higher prices in networks formerly operated by municipality-owned companies.

The experience shows that the introduction of TPA in the Nordic electric power market has been overall successful [212]. However, the differences between the electric power and the DH markets are profound and it is unlikely that regulated TPA would have the same overall positive effects in the latter case. Technically the DH sector has a stronger resemblance to natural gas markets, and here the experiences of deregulation in Europe are less positive, despite the fact that there was a strong pressure from commercial operators to open up the market, and the relevant geographical market is significantly larger compared to DH. The presence of a few dominating companies in the respective national markets implies limited competition in the European natural gas market, and similar concerns could well apply to DH in the case of a market opening.

Therefore, the separation of production and distribution activities in DH makes it significantly more difficult to operate a cost-effective DH system. Similar system optimization effects are not as prevalent in the electric power sector. As has been noted above, the location and the size of the potential third party suppliers may have significant implications for the cost of network access (including any modifications of the system). These types of geographical differences make it hard to determine a uniform network fee that promotes an efficient market design throughout the country.

The main difference between regulated and negotiated TPA is that the latter implies that the network activity is regulated *ex post,* i.e., the conditions for access to and transmission in the network are negotiated between the network owner and the company requesting access. Compared to the case of regulated TPA this scenario is probably more suitable for the DH sector since it becomes possible to take into account any local conditions that exist for each network. The ability to address network-specific characteristics (e.g., networks with ample supply from industrial waste heat providers) is thus an advantage of this particular market design. In Sweden the respective networks tend to differ a lot in terms of both size and fuel supply mix, and over time the interests of the network owner and the producers may change thus inducing changes in the conditions for transmission. A negotiated TPA permits such changes in a way that an *ex ante* regulation does not [210]. With this form of TPA it is also easier to address any system optimization concerns that also tend to be specific to each network.

It should be noted that in practice a negotiated TPA means that the established company has a stronger position in the negotiations compared to a regulated TPA (unless a complete separation between production and network activities is introduced) [211]. Related to this is that the transaction costs, e.g., the costs of reaching an agreement, may be high, and it may typically be less costly for the incumbent producer to negotiate terms with the network owner than it is for any third party. Moreover, it may also become difficult and costly for a regulator to monitor and punish opportunistic behaviour.

The expected effects of this market design on competition between suppliers are overall similar to the case of regulated TPA, although the same increase in trade may not occur because of the above-mentioned transaction costs. Just as in the regulated TPA case it remains unclear whether the introduction of negotiated TPA would generate the desired competitive given the small market size of most Swedish networks. For this market form to be considered successful from a competitive perspective, it is necessary to vertically separate between the network and production activities, respectively. However, as has been stressed above, there is a risk that this will create inefficiencies in the operation of the entire DH system. There exists a stronger technical and economic interdependency between the different activities in the DH supply chain than is the case for other forms of energy distribution. Increased competition may thus be created at the expense of higher direct system costs, and the cost for network modifications in some parts of the system may even hamper competition in the first place.

In the Swedish debate it is typically argued that with the introduction of either regulated or negotiated TPA, the existing suppliers of industrial waste heat would be more active ‘players’ in the DH market and thus sell more heat to consumers. While several of the country’s industrial waste heat producers want to dispose its product, it is more doubtful how many of these who regard it worthwhile to engage in this type of direct business activities after having considered the additional costs that would be involved (e.g., for marketing and sales). For this reason many of these suppliers – with other core business activities – could well benefit from a market design more similar to the single-buyer concept. In both TPA cases the question about future investments in both production facilities and the network (new as well as reinvestments) is of great importance. In the case of investment in *new* production capacity, it is possible to foresee a situation with more private companies operating in the market and as a result the rate-of-return requirement on investments tends to increase. This implies in turn that it becomes more difficult to achieve profitability from new investments in relatively capital-intensive plants (including, for instance, waste-based CHP plants for base load purposes); instead, a more efficient and intense use of existing facilities may be given priority as will (if possible) incremental capacity additions in these plants. In the case of future investments in existing and new networks, it is important that a clear division of responsibilities is designed. Furthermore, the conditions under which such investments are made need to be clearly specified. In the case of investment in new networks there is a dilemma in the sense that in a TPA-setting many (new and existing) companies can benefit from the network investments of one single company, thus providing the latter with too few incentives to invest in the first place. For this reason Spanjer [213] proposes a solution for the European gas market where certain exemptions from the existing TPA rules are allowed during a certain time period, this in order for any private investor to be able to reap the benefits of its own investment. A similar type of exemption could be used also in the DH sector, notably as way of integrating currently separate networks and in this way expand the geographical scope of DH markets.

The single-buyer model is not very different from the above TPA models. It implies that all potential consumers in a network have the right to negotiate supply contracts with any eligible supplier [211]. However, only one company sells to consumers and this single-buyer is obliged to purchase the contracted volumes and sell to the consumer at a price that equals the negotiated price plus transport and system costs. In theory, this market form leads to an equally high degree of competition as in the cases of regulated and negotiated TPA. However, there are more similarities with negotiated TPA as transportation and system costs are negotiated separately for each DH network. What distinguishes this market form from negotiated TPA is that the new supplier does not sell to the final consumer. In other words, the single-buyer model is a form of TPA, which implies that there exists only a producer market but not a retail market [209].

The benefits of this market form are similar to those outlined in the case of negotiated TPA, not the least since it can take into account the local conditions of each network. This increases the likelihood of a cost-effective operation of the DH system. Moreover, a practical advantage in this context is that this market form does not imply that the potential supplier sells to consumers. The authors Soderholm, Warell [209] concluded that there are reasons to believe that many of the potential suppliers of heat (e.g., process industries supplying waste heat) do not necessarily have the intention to sell to the end consumer, because this would imply additional costs in the form of increased consumer contacts and any associated administrative obligations. The single-buyer model implies that an external part (not necessarily representing a heat producer) has the opportunity to sell heat to the consumers, and some of the financial burdens on the original suppliers are therefore lessened.

However, the company that acts as single-buyer has a strong incentive to exaggerate the system costs in order to cross-subsidize their own production and distribution activities, especially if vertical separation of grid operations from generation is not imposed. In order for a consumer to actually agree to a contract with an outside supplier the price offered must be significantly lower than the price the current DH company offers. This system provides, in other words, the existing DH company with a dominant market position, as this company has access to information about system costs that the third-party suppliers do not have. If the single-buyer company only owns the network part the problem of cross-subsidizing is avoided. It is thus unclear whether the desired impact on competition would be realized in a single-buyer model. The single-buyer approach to TPA implies thus a less open market compared to regulated and negotiated TPA, respectively, given that only one company sells to the consumers. This may not, again, be a major disadvantage in the Swedish DH market since it is likely that access to the DH network does not represent a core business for potential new suppliers of heat. It is therefore likely that the additional costs arising from the sale to consumers are gladly avoided. The single-buyer model can thus help increase the share of industrial waste heat in the DH network, because these potential suppliers face low marginal costs in supplying heat, which is a by-product of their main business.

In the case of DH an additional problem is that the system is typically optimized given the current conditions and production units, and an obligation to distribute and sell heat from a potential supplier may lead to increased total system costs for the network. A DH network is constructed and adapted to specific conditions and in many municipalities there exist also other production units that may be prioritized, such as waste incineration plants for base load.

Technically, a TPA model which does not address the DH system as a whole may increase total system costs. For this reason it is useful to also discuss a fourth possible future scenario for the Swedish DH market, namely a market design solution that is essentially based on an extended producer market [209].

The paper [209] proved that it is far from straightforward to introduce TPA in an unrestricted form in the DH market. The type of market design that was analysed in the paper is not equivalent to the earlier market forms, since it only involves a type of extended producer market. This scenario requires that the DH companies to some extent are vertically separated and that the heat is bought and sold between the production units and the network operators (but one company can still retain control over the entire DH system), similar to the situation in Finland. While this market design does not imply a major change from the present Swedish situation, it involves important new elements that are currently not required according to the country's DH Act. These include, apart from a vertical separation of network and production, increased transparency about the prices charged.

Given that transparency in information about prices and delivered transactions in all heating markets is introduced and the information is made public, the prices in the market should reach more economically efficient levels (compared to today's situation). It is important to note that the extended producer market presented here is not equivalent to a formal market place, like Nord Pool in the electric power case. Instead the extended producer market implies a greater transparency and information sharing regarding the network and production activities. In order to achieve this it is important that the DH companies keep separate accounts for these two activities. By creating a situation where new suppliers to the network have access to information about the transaction and system costs, the potential for a more competitive market situation is achieved. An enhanced regulatory control of DH pricing behaviour would further strengthen consumer confidence in the DH market.

The main benefit of the proposed market design is that a system optimization perspective can be maintained, while at the same time a more efficient pricing behaviour can be achieved. We have previously argued that there exist reasons to maintain a market solution where one company has the overall responsibility for the operation of the DH system in order to achieve lower total production costs. However, in order for this market form to ensure a competitive market structure it is important that the companies are open about their transactions and production costs, concerning both the network and production activities. If DH companies today charge prices that are in the vicinity of their marginal costs, this scenario ensures that this is made clear to both consumers and the competition authorities.

Some negative aspects of the proposed scenario, though, include the additional costs associated with the separation of production and network operations, and the requirement to report, for instance, transactions, investments, etc. For smaller DH companies this latter increase in the distribution of information can be seen as a burden and imply increased costs, especially in companies with few employees. An increased price transparency can also give rise to more opportunities for indirect (implicit) cartel behaviour, so called 'tacit collusion' [125]. The risk of such behaviour in DH should not be exaggerated, though, particularly since for many potential suppliers to the DH market (such as industrial waste heat suppliers) DH does not represent a core business activity.

The largest concern in introducing TPA in the DH markets according to [209] is that the various local networks differ regarding generation structure and local conditions. The municipality-owned firms often have other interests to consider, something which could distort competition in the market. It is therefore important to create an extended producer market so that any potential supplier and consumer of heat have the possibility to engage in trade in a non-discriminatory manner. For this to occur, a separation, at least with separate accounts, of the network and production activities is probably required, as well as transparency and information on prices and quantities of heat traded in producer market.

Icreased price transparency would provide just limited benefit and this is most evident at the national level. The Swedish DH sector consists of several local markets, many different types of production facilities (with varying costs), different age structures of the distribution networks, etc. What one hopes to achieve through enhanced transparency is some sort of 'benchmark' competition but given the above differences across the country's networks this may be difficult to pursue in practice. Still, in the separate local markets increased price transparency may play a more significant role in promoting, for instance, non-discriminatory access to the network [209].

An important conclusion from the paper [209] is that regulated TPA will have just a small positive effects on competition and it may have a significant impact on the possibility to run the integrated DH operations in a cost efficient way. This main conclusion is that most DH networks are local in scope. Even if the networks are opened up for competition, it is likely that one company would still be dominant in this limited local market. In adition, DH operations covering production and distribution are highly interdependent, this to a greater extent than, for instance, the corresponding operations in the electric power market. Therefore the changes in the organisation of the production mix may have a relatively large impact on system optimization throughout the DH network. A negotiated TPA and a single-buyer model will provide more efficient market designs, but also in these cases there would exist problems of achieving overall DH system optimization.

A possible development path that could support a system optimization perspective, while at the same time promoting more efficient pricing behaviour, is where the companies maintain separate accounts for their network and production activities, respectively. Furthermore, a type of producer market would be established in which the transactions of heat for DH networks and the corresponding prices are reported in a transparent manner. Given that transparency of prices and transactions in all DH markets is introduced, it is likely that a stronger pressure on prices will occur. This also creates an opportunity for potential new suppliers to sell hot water to the existing DH networks under reasonably competitive circumstances. An increased transparency of current pricing strategies and production costs will thus increase the probability that DH prices are set closer to the economically efficient levels.

Although the paper [209] has focused entirely on the prospects for a market opening and an introduction of non-discriminatory TPA to the network, policy makers also need to consider the option of an *ex ante* price regulation of heat. In the case where the entire DH system (production plus distribution) can be considered a natural monopoly, such a price regulation may be the only reasonable option available to protect consumers from being charged monopoly prices in DH systems not being operated under the fair rate-of-return principle. This view has been endorsed by the Swedish Competition Authority in 2009. Nevertheless, if there remains a strong political ambition to open up the DH market in a similar way as for electric power and natural gas markets, a reasonable suggestion is to introduce TPA (at least initially) only in the local markets that are most likely to realize the expected competitive effects. In Sweden this corresponds to the Stockholm area (with the possible integration with the Uppsala area). This district has the largest network and number of production units, and it has also witnessed the largest number of complaints concerning the DH prices facing consumers. By introducing TPA in this large-scale DH system lessons could be drawn regarding the possible effects of TPA in more small-scale DH systems. Due to the characteristics of DH systems (and the differences that exist across different municipalities and regions), it is likely that a negotiated TPA would be a more efficient alternative compared to regulated TPA. Overall, there are strong reasons to consider in detail the differences between the various DH networks; a uniform national TPA solution can easily lead to inefficiencies in many networks. Instead it might be useful to stipulate minimum conditions for access to the network (but where there exists a possibility for each region to go beyond these). Therefore while the paper [209] has mainly provided a conceptual discussion of the issue of introducing TPA in DH networks, future research ought to focus in more detail on the likely impact of opening up for competition in specific networks.

Many DH networks in Sweden are structured differently, and they thus face different conditions for competition. Some authors Grohnheit, Mortensen [210] concluded that in Sweden the effects on the national level of DH liberalization have been rather similar to those of the electric power market, with ownership changes, but also with concerns regarding pricing: mergers and acquisitions leading to ownership concentration—and the possibility of owning DH outside own municipality; International, and state, ownership in several systems—the "big three" in electric power becoming big in DH (E.ON, Fortum, and Vattenfall); around 40 percent of delivered heat from private or state-owned energy companies; price increases in several municipalities, especially in Fortum and Uppsala systems [214] complaints from customers regarding pricing policies and request for competition in DH systems [214]. No re-regulation, but modification of law in the form of demands for more transparency.

The DH market situation in Finland is more similar to the Swedish situation since there is no price regulation. Finland has, however, a relatively large producer market where almost one third of all heat in the DH networks is recorded. This market is characterized by transparency, and due to this it is argued that DH prices in Finland are kept at a relatively competitive level. The possible future TPA scenarios were also addressed the possible benefits and drawbacks of an extended producer market, similar to the Swedish one [209].

Chapter 4

THE MODEL FOR MULTI-CRITERIA ASSESSMENT OF IMPACT OF ENERGY MARKET LIBERALIZATION ON COMPETITIVENESS OF THE COUNTRY

Grid-based energy systems are problematic phenomena from a social science perspective not only because of their technological complexity but also due to the complexity of their social organization. They require cooperation among many actors who are interdependent upon one another in shaping and sustaining the systems.
Jane Summerton. DH comes to town: the social shaping of an energy system
Diss., Linköping University 1992.

4.1. ENERGY MARKET LIBERALIZATION AND ENERGY POLICY PRIORITIES

The first challenge facing Europe is the need to complete the internal gas and electric power markets. Many national energy markets are still beleaguered by protectionism and dominated by a few companies. These national reflexes are bad for consumers because they keep prices high and infrastructure uncompetitive. Opening up these markets will create fair competition between companies at European level and improve the security and competitiveness of the energy supply in Europe. Reliable energy supplies at reasonable prices for businesses and consumers and with the minimum environmental impact are crucial to the European economy. The European Union has therefore identified energy as one of its priorities. In the past, the electric power industry has been organized as vertically integrated monopolies that were sometimes also state owned. The growing ideological and political disaffection towards vertically integrated monopolies and the liberalization successes in other network industries have lead to liberalization initiatives world wide in the electric power industry. Vertically integrated utilities have been vertically separated or unbundled and barriers to entry in generation and supply are being removed to create competition, seen as a vehicle to increase the competitiveness of the electric power industry [215, 216]. The *first liberalisation directives* were adopted in 1996 (electric power) and 1998 (gas) and should be transposed into Member States' legal systems by 1998 (electric power) and 2000 (gas). The *second liberalisation directives* were adopted in 2003 and were to be transposed into national law by Member States by 2004, with some provisions entering into force only in 2007. The Third electricity directive adopted in 2009 confirms the trend initiated by the precedent 2003 Directive of setting general guidelines for the government of the sector and further strengthen consumer protection, innovation and makes an attempt to merge national systems into one European electricity markets. The 3 Directives discussed the following issues: market opening, third party access and the system operator. The Directive 96/92/EC introduced the concept of 'eligible consumers', being consumers who have the legal capacity to contract volumes of electric power from any supplier. The Directive aimed at a slow, gradual and partial opening of the Member States' electricity markets so that more and more generators and consumers have the opportunity to freely negotiate the purchase and sales of electric power. With the new Directive 2003/54/EC replacing the first Directive the process is dramatically accelerated and all non-households customers are eligible from 1 July 2004 and all consumers will be eligible from 1 July 2007. The suppliers and generators need to be assured they will have access to the grid to settle negotiated electrical energy transactions for delivering electric energy [217]. Directive 2003/54/EC therefore introduces one regime, being rTPA, and the requirement to appoint a regulator, who has to approve the tariffs, monitor congestion management and act as a dispute settlement authority [218, 219]. The second Directive 2003/54/EC can be characterized by shorter term deadlines and less freedom which should result in more convergence between Member States. The third energy liberalization package contains some commendable provisions on strengthening national regulators and on increased transparency in record keeping. However, its diluted unbundling ("unbundling" means that the same company cannot perform power generation – or supply – and transmission) provisions, in our opinion will not solve market concentration and vertical foreclosure. In addition, the package does little to enforce transparency in price formation or to break up regulated tariffs. With end-user tariffs set by regulators below market clearing price – because of protectionism and populist pressures – it is difficult to imagine how a super grid can be constructed, as economic agents have no incentive to really engage in a unified cross-border power market. Since the introduction of the first directive in 1998 opening EU energy markets to competition, the situation in energy sector has changed dramatically in member states.

The coherence among three pillars – competitiveness, security of supply and sustainability around which EU energy policy is built. Therefore it is important to assess the impact of energy market liberalization on the competiveness, security of supply and sustainability. Such type of assessment would allow to track the progress achieved in energy market liberalization in specific country and to assess the impact of this progress achieved on the main pillars of EU energy policy. Seeking to achieve this it is necessary to develop framework for the assessment of energy market liberalization on competitiveness, security of supply and sustainability, and to apply developed framework for assessment of impact of energy markets liberalization on progress in achieving EU energy policy goals in Lithuania. The assessment would allow to develope policy recommendations for Lithuania taking into account the main institutional and legal drivers of energy markets development and their positive impact on competitiveness of the country, security of supply and environmental sustainability.

4.2. Review of EU Energy Policy Priorities

The main EU energy policy documents are directives promoting energy efficiency and use of renewable energy sources, directives implementing greenhouse gas mitigation and atmospheric pollution reduction policies and other policy documents and strategies targeting energy sector.

The EU Green paper on European Strategy for Sustainable, Competitive and Secure Energy (SEC (2006) 317) sets the main priorities for EU energy strategy: competitiveness of the EU economy, security of supply and environmental protection. These objectives should help to address central policy concerns such as job creation, boosting overall productivity of the EU economy, protection of the environment and climate change [209].

The Commission's Green Paper on energy efficiency COM (2005) 265 stresses the importance of energy efficiency improvement for the controlling of demand growth and security of supply. According to estimates, the economic potential for improving energy efficiency in 2010 for all sectors combined is 20% of the total annual primary energy consumption of the current level. There are several directives aiming to implement Commissions Green Paper on energy efficiency: 2006/32/EC Directive on energy end-use efficiency and energy services, 2002/91/EC Directive on the energy performance of buildings and 2004/8/EC Directive on the promotion of cogeneration.

The 2006/32/EC Directive on energy end-use efficiency and energy services sets the targets for EU member states to reduce final energy consumption by 9% during the nine year period until 2015 and proposes set of measures to achieve these targets: voluntary agreements, white tradable certificates, energy service obligations, energy audits etc.

2002/91/EC Directive on the energy performance of buildings sets target to realize a savings potential of around 22% by 2010 for energy used in heating, air – conditioning, hot water and lighting. The main measures proposed for achieving this target are: improved standards, certification of buildings and information on energy consumption in buildings disclosure, subsidies form EU structural funds for energy efficiency improvements in public buildings, the incentive billing of residents of the buildings, soft loans for energy efficiency improvements in multi-flat buildings etc.

2003/30/EC Directive on the promotion of the use of biofuels or other renewable fuels in transport (*RF Directive*) sets that Member States must ensure by end of 2005 a 2% minimum proportion of biofuels of all gasoline and diesel fuels sold on their market. In longer term the target is to achieve a share of 5.75% of biofuels for transport in the total amount of fuels in Europe by 2010 and 20% by 2020. The main measures foreseen in directive include: excise, VAT, pollution and other tax exemptions for biofuels, financial (subsidies or soft loans) assistance for the processing industry and the establishment of a compulsory rate of biofuels for oil companies etc.

2004/8/EC Directive on the promotion of cogeneration based on a useful heat demand in the internal energy market aims to increase energy efficiency and improve security of supply by creating a framework for promotion and development of high efficiency cogeneration of heat and power based on useful heat demand and primary energy savings taking into account the specific national circumstances especially climate and economic conditions. The strategic goal of EU-15 is to double the share of electric power produced by combined heat and power pants (CHP) by 2010. The different mechanisms can be applied to support cogeneration at the national level, including investment aid, tax exemptions or reductions, green certificates and direct price support schemes, information disclosure etc.

White Paper for a Community Strategy and Action Plan on renewable energy sources COM (97) 599 final states that member states should formulate indicative targets contribute to the ambitious indicative target of doubling the overall share of renewables in the EU by 2010. It sets an indicative target of 12% for the contribution by renewables to the total primary energy consumption within EU by 2010 and contains a strategy and action plan to achieve this target. Pursuant to the White paper on Renewables the Directive 2001/77/EC on the promotion of electric power produced from renewable energy sources in the internal electric power market was passed in 2001. It adds the indicative target contribution of 22.1% by renewables-based electric power to total EU electric power consumption in year 2010. The main measures foreseen in directive: Feed-in prices for electric power produced from renewables, green tradable certificates, competitive bidding processes, voluntary agreements, generation disclosure rules, green electric power purchases, subsidies and soft loans for renewables projects etc.

The draft Directive promoting heating and cooling from renewable energy sources was put forward. The purpose of directive is to promote renewable heating & cooling. The EU target: 20% of heat and cold from renewables by 2020. National binding targets should be established by technology. National support mechanisms should be putted in place including green tradable certificates for heat produced from renewables, Feed-in prices for heat produced from renewables etc. Removal of administrative barriers, reliable statistics and monitoring of results are necessary.

In its Thematic Strategy on Air Pollution (COM (2005 446 final), the European Commission outlined the strategic approach towards cleaner air in Europe and established environmental interim targets for pollutants contributing to acidification, eutrophication and the formation of ground-level ozone in year 2020 compared to year 2000 levels. As one of the main policy instruments, the Thematic Strategy announced the revision of the Directive on National Emission Ceilings (2001/81/EC) with new emission ceilings that should lead to the achievement of the agreed interim objectives. In the meantime European Commission started the process to develop national ceilings for the emissions of the relevant air pollutants. The EU global goal in 2020 would make for SO2 - reduction by 87%, for NOx- reduction by 50%, for PM2.5 by 41%, for NH3 - by 25% and for VOC- by 46% compared to 2000. The main EU legislation for pollutants contributing to acidification, eutrophication and the formation of ground-level ozone relevant to energy production sector are Large Combustion plant (LCP) directive (2001/80/EC), Sulphur Content of Liquid Fuels Directive (1999/32/EC), and National emission ceilings directive (2001/81/EC), etc.

2001/81/EC Directive on national emission ceilings for certain atmospheric pollutants sets since 2010 the national emission ceilings for SO_2, NO_X, VOC and NH_3 which are very close to the limits of the same pollutants established by Gothenburg protocol to Long Range Transboundary Air Pollution Convention. This directive establishes national emission ceilings for EU member states for SO_2, NO_X, VOC and NH_3.

Directive 1999/32/EC relating to a reduction in the sulphur content of certain liquid fuels (Sulphur directive) is to ensure that as from 1 January 2004 the heavy fuel oil (HFO) used within territories of EU Member States do not exceed the sulphur content of 1,00% by mass. The requirement do not exceed the sulphur content of 1% shall not apply to HFO used in (large and small) combustion plants where the emissions of sulphur dioxide from the plant are less than or equal to 1700 mg/Nm^3 and for combustion in refineries, where the monthly average of emissions of SO_2 averaged over all plants in the refinery shall not exceed 1700 mg/Nm^3. According the requirements of EU Directive 88/609/EEC it is possible to burn HFO with a sulphur content exceeding 1% if it is co-combusted with either natural gas or with biomass. Thus, HFO - having a sulphur content of 2.2% - can be used by large combustion plants if it is co-combusted with at least 55% natural gas or 55% biomass (in terms of energy input). In this case, the concentration of SO_2 in the flue gas will be kept below 1700 mg/Nm^3.

In addition since 2008 the new norms for SO_2 emission will be established for large combustion plants based on Directive 2001/80/EC on the limitation of emissions of certain pollutants into the air from large combustion plans.

Besides that the implementation of all these directives and policy documents targeting specific but interrelated sustainable energy development targets described above and measures foreseen in these directives would interact with each other and this interaction is necessary to evaluate and address in setting harmonized reinforcing each other energy policies and achieving synergy effect implemented measures. Therefore before the implementation of policies and measures the evaluation of these policies impact on sustainable energy development targets needs to be addressed. The multi criteria decision aiding analysis would allow assessing impact of various energy technologies on sustainable energy development targets imposed by various EU policy documents.

On 10 January 2007 the Commission adopted an Energy and climate change package, calling on the Council and European Parliament to approve: an independent EU commitment to achieve a reduction of at least 20% in the emission of greenhouse gases by 2020 compared to 1990 levels and the objective of a 30% reduction by 2020, subject to the conclusion of a comprehensive international climate change agreement; a mandatory EU target of 20% renewable energy by 2020 including a 10% biofuels target. This strategy was endorsed both by the European Parliament and by EU leaders at the March 2007 in the European Council. The European Council invited the Commission to come forward with concrete proposals, including how efforts could be shared among Member States to achieve these targets. This package is the reply to that invitation. It comprises a set of key policy proposals that are closely interlinked. They include: (1) a proposal amending the EU Emissions Trading Directive (EU ETS); (2) a proposal relating to the sharing of efforts to meet the Community's independent greenhouse gas reduction commitment in sectors not covered by the EU emissions trading system (such as transport, buildings, services, smaller industrial installations, agriculture and waste); (3) a proposal for a Directive promoting renewable energy, to help achieve both of the above emissions targets. Other proposals that are also part of the package include a proposal for a legal framework on carbon capture and storage, a Communication on the demonstration of carbon capture and storage and new guidelines for environmental state aid.

The Commission's Green Paper on energy efficiency COM (2005) 265 stresses the importance of energy efficiency improvement for the controlling of demand growth and security of supply. According to estimates, the economic potential for improving energy efficiency in 2010 for all sectors combined is 20% of the total annual primary energy consumption of the current level. There are several directives aiming to implement Commissions Green Paper on energy efficiency: 2006/32/EC Directive on energy end-use efficiency and energy services, 2002/91/EC Directive on the energy performance of buildings and 2004/8/EC Directive on the promotion of cogeneration.

In 2008, the EU adopted the Strategic Energy Technology Plan (SET-Plan). This Plan is the energy technology policy of the European Union. Despite having been initially focused on power technologies, the European Commission has now received the mandate to investigate the role of technological innovation to achieve a more efficient energy intensive industry and with less CO2 emissions.

In 2011 EU has prepared the Roadmap and Energy Action Plan for moving to a competitive low-carbon economy in 2050. The European Commission is looking beyond these 2020 objectives and setting out a plan to meet the long-term target of reducing domestic emissions by 80 to 95% by mid-century. The plan indicates how the sectors responsible for Europe's emissions - power generation, industry, transport, buildings and construction, as well as agriculture - can make the transition to a low-carbon economy over the coming decades. The short-term priorities of Roadmap towards low carbon economy and Energy Roadmap 2050: energy efficiency, low carbon technologies. As future needs and supply are difficult to predict, the plan presents numerous scenarios examining the possible impacts, challenges and opportunities of modernising the energy system. They take into account potential changes in carbon prices, technology and networks. Scenarios were created by combining the four main decarbonisation options – energy efficiency, renewable energy, nuclear and carbon capture and storage.

The main findings suggest: decarbonisation is possible and could be less costly than current policies in the long-run; energy efficiency and renewables are critical, regardless of the energy mix chosen; investment to modernise infrastructure must start now to avoid more costly changes in the future and a common energy market is vital in keeping energy costs down and to ensure a secure supply – it should be completed by 2014. All the scenarios depend on every country taking action on climate change. And regardless of decarbonisation efforts, the EU's energy networks need investment to replace ageing infrastructure – some of which was built up to 40 years ago. With electric power prices set to rise until 2030, investment is needed now in "intelligent" electric power grids and improved technologies to produce, transmit and store energy more effectively. Together with a common energy market, these measures should ensure that prices fall in the long run. The costs will be outweighed by the high level of sustainable investment brought into the European economy, related jobs, and reduced dependency on imports.

EU energy security and solidarity action plan COM (2008) 781 final states that the EU produces 46% of its total energy consumption. 9% of the energy consumed within the EU comes from renewable sources. The EU intends to increase the share of these energy sources to 20% by 2020. To better promote these energies, the Commission will table a Communication on overcoming barriers to their use. The Commission is working with the European Investment Bank (EIB), the European Bank for Reconstruction and Development (EBRD) and other financial institutions to set up the EU Sustainable Energy Financing Initiative. Furthermore, the Commission intends to table new proposals:

- a Communication on Financing Low Carbon Technologies;
- a Communication on Refining Capacity and EU Oil Demand;
- a revised proposal for a Directive setting up a Community framework for nuclear safety.

In post-2020 period it is necessary to ensure that renewable energy is part of the European energy market, with limited but effective support where necessary and substantial trade. They must also ensure that Europe maintains its research and industrial leadership globally. Only in this way it is possible to continue to develop renewable energy resources in a cost effective, indeed, affordable manner and grasp the associated competitiveness, economic and job opportunities.

On 10 November 2010, the European Commission has adopted the Communication Energy 2020 - A strategy for competitive, sustainable and secure energy. The Communication defines the energy priorities for the next ten years and sets the actions to be taken in order to tackle the challenges of saving energy, achieving a market with competitive prizes and secure supplies, boosting technological leadership, and effectively negotiate with our international partners.

The new energy strategy focuses on five priorities:

1. achieving an energy-efficient Europe;
2. building a truly pan-European integrated energy market;
3. empowering consumers and achieving the highest level of safety and security;
4. extending Europe's leadership in energy technology and innovation;
5. strengthening the external dimension of the EU energy market.

On 8 March 2011, the EC adopted the Communication "Energy Efficiency Plan 2011" for saving more energy through concrete measures. The set of measures proposed aims at creating substantial benefits for households, businesses and public authorities: it should transform our daily lives and generate financial savings of up to €1000 per household every year. It should improve the EU's industrial competitiveness with a potential for the creation of up to 2 million jobs.

On 25 October 2012, the EU adopted the Directive 2012/27/EU on energy efficiency. This Directive establishes a common framework of measures for the promotion of energy efficiency within the Union in order to ensure the achievement of the Union's 2020 20% headline target on energy efficiency and to pave the way for further energy efficiency improvements beyond that date. It lays down rules designed to remove barriers in the energy market and overcome market failures that impede efficiency in the supply and use of energy, and provides for the establishment of indicative national energy efficiency targets for 2020.

The main priorities for EU energy strategy: competitiveness of the EU economy, environmental sustainability and security of energy supply. The main issues related with competiveness are energy prices, energy intensity of GDP, costs of energy imports etc. The main issues related with environmental sustainability are related with GHG emission reduction including measures to increase energy efficiency and enhanced use of renewables, reduction of emissions of classical pollutants such as SO2, NOx and particulates emissions. Security of energy supply is related with diversification of energy supply, energy import dependency, energy supply quality including outage rate, the structure of energy balance etc. Therefore seeking to assess the impact of electric power market liberalization of achievement of EU energy policy goals the integrated indicators approach can be developed allowing to integrate various indicators representing three pillars of EU energy policy.

Table 33 summarizes the priorities of EU energy policy and targeted indicators.

Table 33. Review of EU energy policy priorities

Indicators	Directive or policy document	Target	Date for achievement
Competitiveness			
Energy prices	EU Communication Energy 2020 - A strategy for competitive, sustainable and secure energy COM (2010) 639 final	Boosting the competitiveness of European industry by securing the availability of energy at affordable prices.	2020
Costs of energy imports	EU Communication Energy 2020 - A strategy for competitive, sustainable and secure energy COM (2010) 639 final	Reducing costs of energy imports	2020
End-use energy intensity of GDP	Directive 2006/32/EC on end-use efficiency and energy services	To reduce by 9% the current level (2006)	2016
Energy savings	Directive 2012/27/EU on energy efficiency.	To achieve energy savings of 20%	2020
Security of supply			
Energy independency	The EU Green paper on European Strategy for Sustainable, Competitive and Secure Energy	50%	2030
Environmental sustainability			
Energy saved in buildings	2002/91/EC Directive on the energy performance of buildings	22% of energy used in buildings	2010
Savings of primary energy supply	The Commission's new Green Paper on energy efficiency COM (2005) 265	20% from year 2005 level	2020
The share of CHP in electric power production	2004/8/EC Directive on the promotion of cogeneration national energy strategy	Double the current share	2010
The share of renewables in primary energy supply	The White Paper on renewable sources	12%	2010
The share of renewables in electric power generation	Directive 2001/77/EC on the promotion of electric power produced from renewable energy sources in the internal electric power market	22.1%	2010
The share of renewables in heat production	Proposal for Directive promoting the renewable heating and cooling	25%	2020
The share of renewables in fuel used in transport	2003/30/EC Directive on the promotion of the use of biofuels or other renewable fuels in transport	2% 5.75% 20%	2005 2010 2020
The share of renewables in final energy	EU energy and climate package: proposal for a Directive of EP and EC on the promotion of the use of energy from renewable sources {COM(2008) 30 final}	20%	2020

Indicators	Directive or policy document	Target	Date for achievement
Greenhouse gas emissions (CO_2 emissions from energy sector)	Kyoto protocol	Reduction by 8% of year 1990 level Reduction by 20% of year 1990 level	2008-2012 2020
SO2 emissions, NOx emissions, VOC emissions, NH3 emissions SO2 emissions, NOx emissions, VOC emissions, NH3 emissions	Gothenburg protocol NEC directive 2001/81EC	Reduction by 35%, 30%, 11%, 0% comparing to 1990 level, Reduction by 87%, by 50%, by 46%, by 41% compared to 2000 level	2010 2020

Source: author.

All these EU energy policy indicators can be connected to each other via the chain of mutual impacts seeking to develop comprehensive policy framework for monitoring implementation of EU directives and tracking various interacting policy measures targeting relevant indicators.

4.3. Framework for Assessing the Impact of Energy Liberalization on EU Energy Policy Priorities

Taking into account the priorities of EU energy policy the framework of indicators for assessing energy market liberalization impact on the three main pillars of EU energy policy needs to be developed. The success in achieving EU energy policy priorities can be treated as competitiveness of country in terms of energy sector.

There are several frameworks developed to assess the sustainability of energy systems or progress achieved towards implementing sustainable energy policy priorities. The World Economic Forum in collaboration with Accenture and a panel of experts have developed an Energy Architecture Performance Index (EAPI). The EAPI benchmarks and ranks 105 countries globally on how well their energy system delivers economic growth and development, environmental sustainability and energy security and access. In a changing global energy landscape, countries are seeking ways to manage the transition to new energy systems that better deliver on these core goals. The EAPI offers a tool for decision makers to monitor the performance of their energy system and a basis for assessing areas to improve.

The Global Energy Assessment (GEA) brings together over 300 international researchers to provide an independent, scientifically based, integrated and policy-relevant analysis of current and emerging energy issues and options. It has been peer-reviewed anonymously by an additional 200 international experts. The GEA assessed the major global challenges for sustainable development and their linkages to energy; the technologies and resources available for providing energy services; future energy systems that address the major challenges; and the policies and other measures that are needed to realize transformational change toward sustainable energy futures. The GEA goes beyond existing studies on energy issues by presenting a comprehensive and integrated analysis of energy challenges, opportunities and strategies, for developing, industrialized and emerging economies.

This first Global Tracking Report: Sustainable energy for all was compiled by experts from 15 organizations and led by the World Bank and the International Energy Agency, the report provides a comprehensive snapshot of the energy status of countries with respect to access, action on energy efficiency and renewable energy, as well as energy consumption. A major first step is the development of a Global Tracking Framework that establishes baseline energy data and provides regular bi-annual updates on trends in energy access, renewable energy and energy efficiency.

Sustainable Energy for all seeks to improve the lives of billions of people across the world and ensure a more sustainable future by working to achieve its three objectives: universal access to energy; greater energy efficiency; and increased use of renewables. Accountability and transparency are essential for tracking global progress towards the initiative's three objectives.

On the basis of global scenarios and multiple case studies the World Energy Outlook assesses how new development in foreign trade, energy markets and economic development might affect global energy and climate trends over the coming decades. It examines their impact on the critical challenges facing the energy system: to meet the world's ever-growing energy needs, led by rising incomes and populations in emerging economies; to provide energy access to the world's poorest; and to bring the world towards meeting its climate change objectives. It presents authoritative projections of energy trends through to 2035 and insights into what they mean for energy security, environmental sustainability and economic development. Oil, coal, natural gas, renewables and nuclear power are all covered, together with an update on climate change issues. Global energy demand, production, trade, investment and carbon dioxide emissions are broken down by region or country, by fuel and by sector.

All mentioned studies and frameworks aims at assessing sustainable energy development paths and sustainable energy policy performance. The studies present indicators and frameworks for the assessment of energy sector development trends. The Energy Architecture Performance Index developed by WEF was selected as the basis for the development of EU energy policy assessment tool which can be applied for assessing the energy markets liberalization impact on priorities of EU energy policy as the EAPI also measures an energy system's specific contribution to the three imperatives of the energy triangle: economic growth and development, environmental sustainability, and access and security of supply [220]. It comprises 16 indicators aggregated into three baskets relating to these three imperatives. The EAPI helps stakeholders as they look for performance areas to improve and balance the imperatives of the energy triangle over the long term. By measuring and reporting on a various set of indicators. Therefore the EAPI is a composite index that measures a global energy systems' performance across three imperatives: competitiveness, environmental sustainability, and energy access and security. The EAPI is split into three sub-indices. The score attained on each sub-index is averaged to generate an overall score. Within the aggregate score, each of the three baskets receives equal priority and weighting [220].

The Energy Architecture Performance Index (EAPI) uses a universal set of indicators to assess different countries' performances. Accepting the very different set of circumstances each country is in, all countries are heading for the same end goal of a high performing and balanced energy system across each aspect of the energy triangle, but each has a unique starting position on that journey. The EAPI measures an energy system's specific contribution to the three imperatives of the energy triangle: economic growth and competitiveness, environmental sustainability, and access and security of supply. It both scores and ranks the performance of a country's energy policy. The EAPI helps stakeholders as they look for performance areas to improve and balance the imperatives of the energy triangle over the long term.

Indicators were selected against the following criteria:

- Output data only: The measurement of output-oriented observational data (with a specific, definable relationship to the sub-index in question) or a best available proxy, rather than estimates.
- Reliability: The use of reliable source data from renowned institutions.
- Reusability: Data sourced from providers that the EAPI team can work with on an annual basis and that can therefore be updated with ease.

- Quality: The data selected represents the best measure available given constraints; with this in mind, the Expert Panel reviewed all potential datasets for quality and verifiability and those that did not meet these basic quality standards were discarded.
- Completeness: Data is of adequate global and temporal coverage; it has been consistently treated and checked for periodicity to ensure the EAPI's future sustainability.

The EAPI focuses on tracking specific and output oriented indicators to measure the energy system performance of a variety of countries. These include 16 indicators aggregated into three baskets relating to the three imperatives of the energy triangle economic growth and development, environmental sustainability, and access and security of supply to both score and rank the performance of each country's energy architecture. The EAPI is split into three sub-indices. The score attained on each sub-index is averaged to generate an overall score. The three sub-indices are:

1. Economic growth and development the extent to which energy architecture supports, rather than detracts from, economic growth and development.
2. Environmental sustainability the extent to which energy architecture has been constructed to minimize negative environmental externalities.
3. Energy access and security the extent to which energy architecture is at risk to an energy security impact, and whether adequate access to energy is provided to all parts of the population.

An index is a statistical measure of the changes across a portfolio of indicators reflective of an entity – in this case, energy systems. Indices serve the purpose of reducing complexity by tracking specific indicators representative of a whole system so that, ideally, a change in the index is reflective of a proportional change in the real world. In this context, the term indicator" provides empirical evidence that a certain desired outcome has been achieved or not, and that decision-makers within energy systems can use to assess progress towards their set objectives. The distinction here between "input" and "output" indicators is critical; the EAPI grades as "inputs" indicators that measure resources (human or financial) specifically deployed to a particular energy project or programme, whereas "output" indicators measure the quantity of energy-related goods or services produced and the efficiency of energy production.

The Table 34 below details each of the indicators selected, the weight attributed to it within its basket (or sub-index), what it measures and the energy system objective it contributes to, either positively or negatively.

Each indicator is equally weighted within the three baskets, with the exception of the economic growth and development basket. Here, indicators that correlated closely (due to their measuring similar, though not identical, aspects of energy architecture performance) had their weights "diluted" to prevent the double stacking of scores, for example a country receiving two high scores for subsidy/ high tax free pricing of both super gasoline and diesel. As such, the super gasoline and diesel indicators combine to form a mini-index within the economic growth and development basket, and this mini-index is allocated equal weighting with the other indicators. Where a country's scores across two similar indicators were likely to run orthogonal to one another (for instance across the fuel imports and exports as a share of

GDP indicators), the weights were again "diluted" so as to avoid a narrower statistical distribution of scores across the basket and to offset any double stacking of scores.

Table 34. Energy Architecture Performance Index (EAPI) framework

Energy system objective	**Measure (of)**	**Indicator Name**	**Indicator weight**
Economic growth and development	Efficiency	Energy intensity (GDP per unit of energy use (PPP US$ per kg of oil equivalent))	0.25
	Lack of distortion/ affordability	Degree of artificial distortion to gasoline pricing (index)	0.125
		Degree of artificial distortion to diesel pricing (index)	0.125
		Electric power prices for industry (US$ per kilowatt-hour)	0.25
	Supportive/ detracts from growth	Cost of energy imports (% GDP)	0.125
		Value of energy exports (% GDP)	0.125
Environmental sustainability	Share of low-carbon fuel sources in the energy mix	Alternative and nuclear energy (% of total energy use, incl. biomass)	0.2
	Emissions impact	Nitrous oxide emissions in energy sector (thousand metric tonnes of CO_2 equivalent)/total population	0.2
		CO_2 emissions from electric power and heat production, total/total population	0.2
		PM10, country level (micrograms per cubic metre)	0.2
Energy access and security	Level and quality of access	Average fuel economy for passenger cars (l/100 km)	0.2
		Electrification rate (% of population)	0.2
		Quality of electric power supply (1-7)	0.2
		Percentage of population using solid fuels for cooking (%)	0.2
	Self-sufficiency	Import dependence (energy imports, net % energy use)	0.2
	Diversity of supply	Diversity of total primary energy supply (Herfindahl index)	0.2

Source: [220].

Similarly, the fuel imports and exports as a share of GDP indicators are combined to form a mini-index within the economic growth and development basket, and this mini-index is allocated equal weighting with the other indicators.

Table 35 summarizes the indicators framework of EAPI index developed by WEF based on Table 34.

Table 35. Indicators framework of EAPI index

Economic growth and development basket					
Energy intensity (GDP per unit of energy use in PPP US $ per toe	Electric power prices for industry (US $ per kilowatt-hour)	Cost of energy imports (% GDP)	Value of energy exports (% GDP)	Diesel –level of price distortion through subsidy or tax (Index 0-1)	Super gasoline-level of price distortions through subsidy or tax (Index 0-1)
Environmental sustainability basket					
CO_2 emissions from electric power and heat, thou t/capita	Particulate emission country level, mcg/m3	NOx emissions from energy sector, thou t/capita	Alternative and nuclear energy share (% of total energy use)	Average fuel economy for passenger cars (1/100 km)	
Energy access and security basket					
Diversity of total primary energy supply (Herfindahl index)	Quality of electric power supply (survey score between 1-7)	Percentage of population using solid fuels for cooking (%)	Electrification rate (% of population)	Import dependence (energy imports, net % energy use)	

Source: [220].

Though EAPI index represents well the EU energy policy priorities: competitiveness, environmental sustainability and security of supply however some important indicators are missing in this framework therefore some modifications and simplifications were introduced seeking to develop index representing better EU energy policy priorities generalized in Table 33. Further based on the frameworks presented in Table 33 and Table 35 the index representing EU energy policy targets or EU Energy Policy Performance Index (EPPI) was developed (Table 36).

Table 36. Indicators for assessing progress achieved towards EU energy policy priorities

Competitiveness				
Energy intensity (GDP per unit of energy use in PPP US$ per toe	Electric power prices for industry (US $ per kilowatt-hour)	Electric power prices for households (US $ per kilowatt-hour	Cost of energy imports (% GDP)	Value of energy exports (% GDP)
Sustainability				
CO_2 emissions, thou t/capita	SO_2 emissions from energy sector, thou t /capita	NOx emissions from energy sector, thou t/capita	The share of renewables in electric power generation, %	The share of renewables in final energy consumption, %
Security of energy supply				
Diversity of total primary energy supply (Herfindahl index)	Quality of electric power supply (survey score between 1-7)	Percentage of population using solid fuels for cooking (%)	Electrification rate (% of population)	Import dependence (energy imports, net % energy use)

Source: author.

All selected indicators presented in Table 36 are useful for the assessing EU energy policy performance as they are related with three main pillars of EU energy policy and also represent the targeted indicators of EU energy policy presented in Table 33.

EU energy policy targets will be assessed by performing of comparative analysis of electric power market liberalization indicators and EU Energy Policy Performance Index (EPPI) developed in this chapter.

4.4. The Steps of Energy Market Liberalization and Indicators of Assessment

Many countries in the world have been restructuring their electric power markets to obtain a competitive market. One aim of this restructuring is to liberalise their electric power markets by opening the markets to the choice of both national and international customers and eventually to obtain a single market in a region or world-wide. Establishing a single electric power market, however, requires that all the countries that are members of the single market have their market liberalised to some extent so that competition is not distorted in the single market. The extent of liberalisation can be estimated by assessing the activities in the electric power market qualitatively. However, quantitative assessments, whenever possible, yield better results in comparing two or more articles. There have been attempts to measure the degree of electric power market liberalisation by using a range of electric power liberalisation indicators that represent the activities in electric power markets. Review of literature indicated that Oxford Economic Research Associates (OXERA) and Center for the Advancement of Energy Markets (CAEM) are the two institutions working on measuring the degree of electric power market liberalisation in the world. These two institutions employed the same technique and similar indicators in measuring the degree of electric power market liberalisation.

The liberalisation indicators used to asses electric power and gas market liberalisation is of both quantitative and qualitative nature. Quantitative indicators are used to represent objective and easily quantifiable data while qualitative indicators of liberalisation are used to summarise more subjective influences on liberalisation. For aggregating liberalisation indicators into higher levels, a score between zero and 10 and a weighting factor are assigned to each liberalisation indicator. Each indicator is weighed by multiplying its score by the decimal of its weighting factor and the resultant scores of indicators are summed up to obtained the score of the higher level indicator. Weighting and scoring process for each indicator is described in detail in this chapter.

As a general rule, the individual indicators in all market areas refer to two aspects linked to liberalisation and competition. Changes in market structures, from which conclusions about the success or failure of liberalisation can be drawn—an example of this group of indicators is given by the market concentration indicators: in countries where a monopolistic market structure prevailed before liberalisation, the number of independent generators or suppliers is expected to increase with successful liberalisation. Their number therefore provides an indicator of the successful development of competition. Another example is provided by price indicators: competition is expected to provide an incentive to lower prices, and the monitoring of price movements is therefore included in the indicators [221].

Framework market conditions enhancing the development of competition—an example of this second group of indicators is provided by the establishment of regulated third-party access (RTPA) regimes, or the introduction of standardised load profiling in the residential market, without which switching of small customers cannot be managed. Another example is the emergence of standardised wholesale markets, which can be the result of regulatory intervention, or be due to private market initiatives.

A special feature of the indicator framework developed is that, in each of the key market areas, certain indicators have the explicit objective of monitoring the integration of national markets into a single European market. Such indicators include the emergence of pan-European generators or suppliers operating in a number of national markets, the development of cross-border trade, or the importance of international participants in national wholesale markets.

The primary upstream and wholesale market indicators used to measure upstream and wholesale market competition can be grouped into four main areas [221]:

- compliance with the electricity directive on generation market openness (electric power only)—this measures the extent of implementation of the directive;
- market shares of the main generators/producers—this reflects the existing level of competition between upstream market participants;
- wholesale market existence and effectiveness—this identifies the impact of vertical links between producers and suppliers on upstream competition; and
- barriers to entry—this measures the likely barriers to future upstream competition.

For compliance with the electricity directive, a simple quantitative indicator is used to record whether the generation market has been opened to competition—countries score zero for non-compliance, 10 for compliance. Although it could be argued that a distinction should be drawn between tendering and authorisation, it is difficult to determine a priori which is more beneficial to competition. Moreover, the tendering procedure has only been adopted in a few (small) European countries.

In terms of measuring market shares, primary indicators for electric power focus on the share of the largest generator, and the three largest generators respectively, as proxies for overall market concentration. Although more comprehensive indicators of concentration, such as the Herfindahl Index, might be preferred, the choice of indicator was restricted by lack of available data. Market shares are based on output unless indicated otherwise. In order to quantify the different market shares, it is assumed that the largest firm in a liberalised market should have a share of 25% or less, and that a market share of 80% or more reflects a fundamental lack of competition. Therefore, liberalisation scores increase linearly between zero for an 80% market share and 10 for a 25% market share. For the market share of the three largest firms, scores range between zero for a 100% market share and 10 for a 50% share.

In gas markets, the market share of producers is an ambiguous concept. Given the specific geographic nature of gas production, indigenous gas production is very low in some countries. As a consequence, the measurement incorporates the number of producers actively trading in the country (accounted for within the wholesale market indicator and ease of access to the country's network), and the proportion of total expected demand that the largest producers have already contracted for within their portfolios—the revised concentration measure.

Weightings for aggregating the primary indicators into intermediate and high-level indicators are based on an assessment of the overall importance of the four main areas of analysis in driving liberalisation. The weightings attached to each of the indicators differ in gas and electric power—details are given in Table 37.

Table 37. Weightings of upstream and wholesale market indicators

Area	Electric power weighting (%)	Gas weighting (%)
Compliance with the directive	15	0
Market shares of the main generators/producers	30	30
Wholesale market existence and effectiveness	25	40
Barriers to entry	30	30

Source: author.

For electric power, most weight is placed on market shares of the main generators and potential barriers to entry by new generation. In contrast, the high-level gas indicator places more weight on the existence and effectiveness of a wholesale market. There is also no equivalent in gas to the need for compliance with the electricity directive on generation market opening. Table 38 summarises the primary upstream and wholesale market indicators, showing the weighting, scoring method, and comments. Indicators are broken down into quantitative and qualitative.

The primary indicators used to measure downstream market competition and customer impacts follow a similar analysis to that of upstream markets, again focusing on four area:

- compliance with the EC electricity and gas market directives on supply market opening—this measures the degree of implementation and speed of market opening;
- market shares of the main participants—this reflects the existing level of competition between downstream market participants;
- barriers to entry—this measures the likely barriers to future upstream competition; and switching/price impacts of liberalisation—this relates to the overall impact of liberalisation on consumers, and the opportunities for switching supplier.

Compared with the upstream analysis of market competition, the downstream indicators do not make explicit reference to the existence of a wholesale market. However, they include evidence of customer behaviour and impacts, which are absent from the upstream analysis.

Compliance with the energy directives is measured using two primary indicators. The first is a simple yes or no, where compliance with minimum market opening requirements scores ten and non-compliance scores zero. The second is a quantitative indicator of the extent of market opening, where 100% market opening scores ten and no market opening scores zero.

Table 38. Summary of upstream and wholesale market indicators

Primary indicator	Electric power weighting (%)	Gas weighting (%)	Data type	Scoring method	Comments
			Quantitative		
Compliance with the generation market directive?	15	0	yes/no	yes = 10; no = 0	Either authorisation or tendering.
Market share of largest upstream generator/producer	15	15	%	<25% = 10; >80% = 0; linear in between	Significant market power only emerges with a market share of 25% or more.
Market share of three largest generators/ producers	15	15	%	<50% = 10; 100% = 0; linear in between	Significant oligopoly power only emerges with a joint market share of 50% or more.
Existence of wholesale market?	15	20	yes/no	yes = 10; no = 0	Wholesale market preferred because it increases transparency and makes new entry easier.
			Qualitative		
New entry in generation/ production	20	20	high/ medium/ low	high = 10; medium = 5; low = 0	Takes account of change in ownership of existing plant by a new entrant. A high/medium score could be given if a new entrant succeeds in acquiring a (significant) stake in one of the large generators on the market.
Effectiveness of wholesale trading	10	20	high/ medium/ low	high = 10; medium = 5; low = 0	Includes variables such as volume traded, and number of participants. Allegations of gaming are taken into account.
Capacity constraints on the interconnectors	10	10	high/ medium/ low	high = 10; medium = 5; low = 0	Incorporates interconnector access if this facilitates competition.

Source: author.

Market shares of the main electric power and gas suppliers are measured in the same way as for upstream producers, with separate indicators for the market share of the largest supplier and three largest suppliers respectively.

As with upstream production, it is assumed that the largest firm in a liberalised market should have a share of 25% or less, and that a market share of 80% or more reflects a fundamental lack of competition. Therefore, liberalisation scores increase linearly between zero for an 80% market share and ten for a 25% market share. For the market share of the three largest firms, scores range between zero for a 100% market share and ten for a 50% share.

Barriers to entry are measured by two qualitative indicators, covering new entry to the supply market, and the potential for foreclosure through vertical integration. The assessment of new entry is scored as low, medium or high, and takes account of any available evidence on the number of new licences issued since the start of market opening. Ultimately, it should be possible to provide a quantitative indicator based on benchmarking market entry across the EU member states, but lack of data has led to the current compromise. The indicator of potential foreclosure is based on the theory that vertical integration can create barriers to entry for new suppliers owing to discriminatory or preferential practices. Ultimately, the indicator will have to be based on subjective judgement, but it should reflect the level of vertical integration between generation and supply, and an assessment of the market distortions created.

Finally, analysis of the switching and price implications of liberalisation is carried out using a range of primary indicators:

- the proportion of eligible industrial and domestic customers switching supplier since market liberalisation;
- the change in industrial and domestic consumer energy prices since market liberalisation;
- the rank in benchmarking of European prices;
- and tariff proliferation.

Most of these represent quantitative measures of market development. However, the degree of tariff proliferation is also measured, based on the number of tariff options and payment methods available, and growth of specialised tariffs in response to liberalisation (e.g., green tariffs).

Market Competition and Non-competitive Activities are called as high level indicators of electric power market in OXERA's terminology. These high level indicators are obtained by aggregating the primary indicators to intermediate level indicators first, and then by further aggregating these intermediate level indicators to high level indicators. High level indicators indicate the degree liberalisation in electric power market in terms of competitive and non-competitive activities.

Dividing the electric power market into two parts, indeed, matches with the objective of electric power market liberalisation, which is to separate the upstream (generation) and downstream (supply) markets and introduce competition into these markets while ensuring easy entries to noncompetitive areas through efficient regulation [221].

For (potentially) competitive areas of the supply chain, the areas identified were generation markets, wholesale markets, and customer supply the following three dimensions of indicators were developed [221]:

1. **Competition in energy generation indicators:**
   - ✓ market concentration;
   - ✓ generation market characteristics;
   - ✓ entry and decommissioning; and
   - ✓ pan-European integration, such as cross-border flows.
2. **Development of wholesale markets indicators:**
   - ✓ the emergence, growth and international character of standardized wholesale markets;
   - ✓ wholesale price movements;
   - ✓ the existence of balancing and penalty regimes.
3. **Competition in the supply of customers indicators:**

   Individual indicators in this market area refer to:
   - ✓ market opening and concentration;
   - ✓ entry conditions and the existence of customer load profiling;
   - ✓ internationalisation of supply markets;
   - ✓ customer switching and contract renegotiations; and
   - ✓ price and quality indicators.

The indicators measuring the impact of liberalisation in non-competitive, areas of the energy market also focus on three key areas, each encompassing a number of sub-groups summarising individual indicators. These areas refer to network activities, interconnection of national networks, and indicators of regulatory influence. Each set of indicators and their principal sub-groups are summarised below.

1. **Network activities**

   Individual indicators in this market area refer to:

   the degree of separation between network and other activities;
   the scope of monopoly rights;
   the type of access regimes and the publication of access tariffs;
   the cost of access; and
   the type of security-of-supply obligations (SSOs).
2. **Interconnection of national networks**

   Individual indicators in this market area refer to:

   technical openness (in terms of available interconnector capacity);
   foreign market participation (in terms of interconnector capacity accessible to non-incumbents);
   congestion management; and
   cross-border tariffication.
3. **Regulatory influence**

   Individual indicators in this market area refer to:

   the level of energy taxes;

the extent of public-service obligations (PSOs);
the scope of regulatory activities, and the division of power between different regulatory authorities.

The summary of indicators of electric power market liberalization is presented in Figure 16.

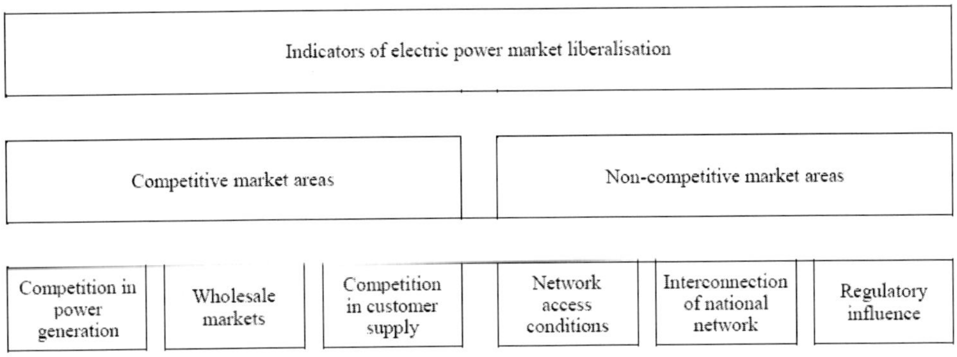

Figure 16. Summary of indicator framework.

Based on OXERA models [221] developed for measuring progress in energy market liberalization the following scoring system for energy market liberalization progress was developed (Table 39).

Table 39. Energy market liberalization indicators

MARKET LIBERALIZATION INDICATORS	SCORING METHOD IN OXERA
UPSTREAM (GENERATION) AND WHOLESALE MARKET	
Quantitative:	
Compliance with EU Directives	Yes=10; No=0
Market Share of largest upstream generator (%)	<25% = 10; >80%=0; linear in between
Market share of three largest generators (%)	<50% = 10; 100%=0; linear in between
Existence of wholesale market	Yes=10; No=0
Qualitative:	
New entry in generation	High = 10; medium = 5; low=0
DOWNSTREAM MARKET AND CUSTOMER IMPACT (RETAILING)	
Quantitative:	
Compliance with EU Directives	Yes=10; No=0
Degree of market opening (%)	100% = 10; 0%=0; linear in between

Table 39. (Continued)

MARKET LIBERALIZATION INDICATORS	SCORING METHOD IN OXERA
Market share of largest supplier (%)	< 25% = 10; >80%=0; linear in between
Market share of three largest suppliers (%)	< 50% = 10; 100%=0; linear in between
Industrial customers switching (%)	> 50% = 10; 0%=0; linear in between
Domestic customers switching (%)	> 25% = 10; 0%=0; linear in between
Change in industrial consumer prices (%)	> 20% reduction = 10; 0% reduction or increased; linear in between
Change in domestic consumer prices (%)	> 20% reduction = 10; 0% reduction or increased; linear in between
European rank in prices (average of domestic and industrial prices)	First tier = 10; second tier = 5; third tier = 0
Qualitative:	
New entry to the supply market	High = 10; medium = 5; low = 0

Source: author.

Aggregation to higher level is achieved by weighting the score of each primary indicator. This is done by multiplying the score of each indicator by its corresponding weighting factor and summing up the weighted scores of each indicator in that level to obtain a combined score for the level, which ranges between zero and 10. The equal scores were applied for all structural indices comprising the indicator. Further the electric power liberalization indicators will be assessed for EU member states.

4.5. Comparative Assessment of Electric Power Market Liberalization Impact on Success in Achieving EU Energy Policy Targets

The scores of electric power market liberalization for EU member states were developed based on simplified OXERA model presented in Table 39. The statistical data on energy provided by EUROSTAT was applied for the assessing electric power market liberalization indicators for year 2012. The scores of electric power market liberalization for EU member states and their ranking are provided in Table 40. In the same Table 40 the scores according three dimensions of EU EPPI for EU members states developed by applying EUROSTAT data were presented for year 2013.

As one can see from information provided in Table 40 the UK is ranked as the best performing country in terms of electric power market liberalization however the country is ranked as 6-th accordingly EU EPPI. The second mostly advanced country in terms of electric power market liberalization – Poland is ranked just as 19-th accordingly EU EPPI. The

Estonia which ranked as having the lowest electric power market liberalization indicator according EU EPPI is ranked as 17th [222].

Table 40. Ranking of EU member states based on electric power liberalization indicators and success in implementing EU energy policy targets based on EPPI

EU member states	Score of electric power market liberalization	Rank	Competitiveness	Sustainability	Security of energy supply	Overall score	Rank
Belgium	3.55	14	0.51	0.56	0.77	0.61	16
Denmark	5.24	10	0.64	0.56	0.82	0.67	4
Germany	5.88	7	0.6	0.58	0.79	0.66	9
Greece	1.73	20	0.63	0.48	0.7	0.60	18
Spain	4.83	11	0.71	0.55	0.75	0.67	5
France	3.18	17	0.58	0.76	0.8	0.70	2
Ireland	2.46	20	0.61	0.63	0.74	0.66	8
Italy	5.57	8	0.48	0.53	0.72	0.58	22
Netherlands	5.84	6	0.5	0.5	0.77	0.59	21
Austria	6.45	4	0.61	0.52	0.79	0.64	13
Portugal	2.55	19	0.64	0.56	0.75	0.65	12
Finland	6.5	3	0.58	0.47	0.81	0.6	20
Sweden	6.37	5	0.58	0.76	0.8	0.71	1
UK	7.69	1	0.59	0.63	0.78	0.67	6
Bulgaria	3.27	16	0.56	0.55	0.62	0.57	23
Czech Republic	4.46	12	0.5	0.4	0.78	0.56	24
Estonia	0.35	23	0.56	0.59	0.67	0.61	17
Hungary	5.46	9	0.53	0.67	0.76	0.65	10
Latvia	0.16	23	0.62	0.74	0.71	0.69	3
Lithuania	0.7	22	0.58	0.64	0.73	0.63	14
Poland	7.3	2	0.6	0.48	0.71	0.6	19
Romania	1.09	21	0.65	0.63	0.73	0.67	7
Slovak Republic	3.13	18	0.48	0.69	0.78	0.65	11
Slovenia	3.70	13	0.55	0.56	0.77	0.63	15

Source: [222].

In Figure 17 the relationship between EAIP and electric power market liberalization indicators is presented.

As one can see from Figure 17 the countries ranked with high energy market liberalization indicators not necessarily have been ranked with high scores according the EU EPPI Index providing for the evaluation of success of countries in implementing EU energy policy goals: competitiveness of the EU economy, environmental sustainability and security of energy supply. The low regression coefficient (R^2 = 0,0048) indicates that there is no statistically significant correlation between high level of electric power market liberalization and ability of country to comply with the main EU energy policy targets [222].

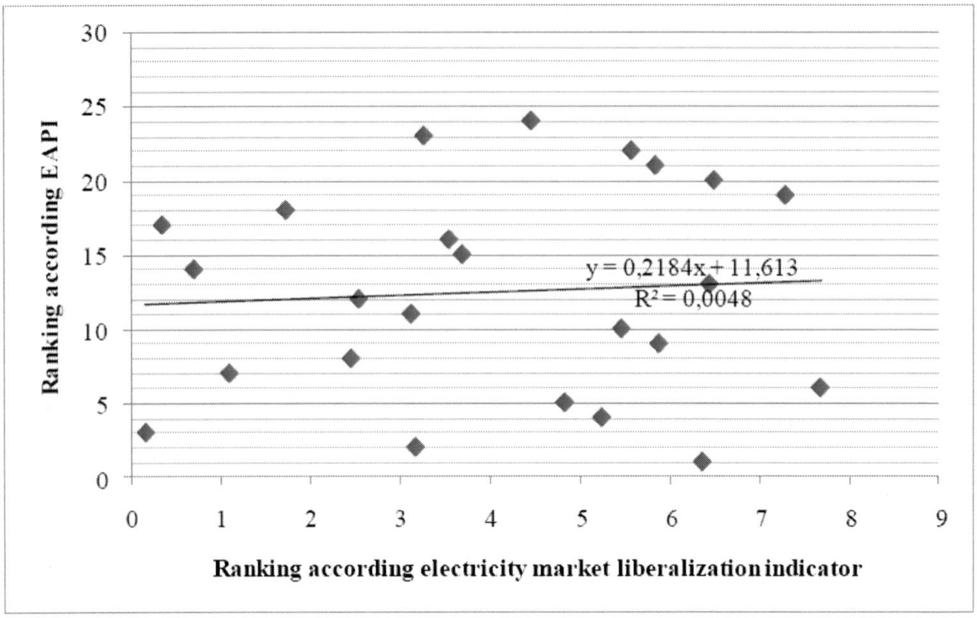

Source: [222].

Figure 17. The relationship between electric power market liberalization and success in achieving EU energy policy goals.

Therefore other important issues which are not addressed in electric power market liberalization index need to be addressed when assessing the impact of energy market liberalization on EU energy policy performance or the impact of specific indicators of energy market liberalization need to be investigated.

4.6. The Impact of Specific Energy Market Liberalization Indicators on Competitiveness

The Steiner regression analysis for assessing the impact of energy liberalization indicators on competitiveness expressed by EU EPPI can be assessed by applying EUROSTAT data. Steiner used as indicators of competitiveness: industrial electric power prices, the ratio of industrial to residential prices, utilization rates and reserve margins however we are more interesting in assessing overall energy market liberalization impact on EU energy policy performance including such important areas as security of supply, share of renewables, energy intensity etc.

The Steiner model of the impact of liberalization on EU EPPI

$$EPPI_e = \alpha + \beta R + \gamma NR + \varepsilon \quad (6)$$

Here: $EPPIp_e$ – EU EPPI, R – regulatory variables; NR- non-regulatory variables; α, β and γ are vectors of coefficients that were estimated and ε – is residual term.

The main regulatory variables were selected: unbundling of generation from transmission, Third party Access (TpA), Wholesale competition, Retail Competition, Ownership. The main independent non-regulatory variables: hydropower share, nuclear share and GDP. The two share variables reflect differences in generating technologies across economies, which affect the marginal costs and hence the price of generating electric power. Finally the inclusion of GDP adjusts for differences in the size of economies and is also an overall measure of national income. The modified Steiner model for assessing the impact of energy market liberalization on EU energy policy performance index is presented in Table 41 [222].

Table 41. The Steiner's model of assessing impact of electric power market liberalization on electric power prices

Variables	Measurements
Dependent variables	
EU EPPI	EU energy policy performance index
Independent regulatory variables	
Unbundling of generation from transmission R01	Dummy variable (1 = accounting separation or separate companies; 0=otherwise)
Third-party access R02	Dummy variable (1 = regulated or negotiated third-party access; 0 = otherwise)
Wholesale competition R03	Dummy variable (1 = presence of wholesale electric power markets; 0 = otherwise)
Retail competition R04	Dummy variable (1 = presence of retail electric power markets; 0 = otherwise)
Quality of regulation R05	Dummy variable (1= presence of high quality regulation; 0=otherwise)
Ownership R06 U1; U2; U3	Discrete variable (4 = private ownership; 3- mostly private ownership; 2 = mixed; 1 = mostly public; 0=public)
Independent non-regulatory environmental variables	
Hydro share N07	Share of electric power generated from hydropower sources
Nuclear share N08	Share of electric power generated from nuclear sources
Gross domestic product N09	Gross domestic product (expressed in US $ PPP billion)

Source: [222].

Regulation quality plays important role in ensuring that energy market liberalization would deliver EU energy policy priority goals. There are several important criteria which describe the quality of regulation: ensuring competition, efficiency and consumer protection.

In order to promote competition, a regulator must be able to assess how competitive a market is. It is necessary to watch three indicators to do this: barriers to entry; cross-subsidies between regulated and competitive activities; and collusion.

Barriers to Entry: Excluding economic barriers to entry (that is, the capital intensive nature of the industry, technical expertise, etc.), the ease with which producers and buyers can enter a market is a critical indicator of long-term competitiveness. It is necessary to strive in identifying and demoving barriers to entry. Although the regulator cannot assume responsibility for compelling new investment, he is responsible for ensuring it can occur.

Cross-subsidies: Revenues from regulated services must not cross-subsidize competitive or unregulated services. To eliminate this risk it is necessary to completely separate regulated and competitive activities by legislation. It is necessary continue to monitor compliance with the codes that define this separation, and to ensure new entrants of a level playing field.

Collusion: Credible monitoring of collusion - and real penalties for those who engage in it - must be both evident and effective. It is necessary to monitor participants, support the IMO in their market surveillance work and take action if needed. The fairness and transparency of prices is of paramount importance to the industry.

Faith in the integrity of the market is critical, not only for direct participants in the market but also for the governments that can overturn them. Regulators must therefore not only ensure that the competitive markets they oversee meet the three conditions above, but also prevent interference in the market when those conditions are met.

In measuring the effectiveness of regulator in promoting efficiency, there are four "vital signs" to monitor: investor confidence; asset management; price behavior and contract structures; and public confidence.

Investor Confidence: Investor confidence is reflected in the adequacy and pace of new investment, differences between rates of return demanded by investors at home and in other jurisdictions, and the creditworthiness of participating companies.

Asset Management: Asset management performance can be measured in terms of levels of reliability and security of supply, as well as the returns earned by owners on the services they provide under regulated rates.

A regulator must ensure that incentives are in place to drive innovation and efficiency, and that leaders in that race are rewarded sufficiently to encourage broader efforts. Defining performance benchmarks carefully is critically important. The regulator will work closely with the regulated companies to arrive at appropriate measures. Getting the measures and the framework right will be one direct contribution we can make to improve investor confidence.

Price Behavior and Contract Structures: In examining price behavior and contract structures, it is not the job of regulator to set market prices, but rather to ensure that the markets are sufficiently competitive that they do this well without outside assistance.

Public Confidence: While public confidence is difficult to measure directly it is essential – both in validating the integrity of the market, as well for maintaining stability and predictability.

The public confidence can be tracked by meeting with and listening to a wide range of stakeholders, assessing information collected from call centers, observing consumer behavior, following media reports on the industry, and closely monitoring political behavior on sector issues.

Consumer Protection can be ensured by controlling regulated prices, promoting industry health and policing interactions with customers.

Controlling Regulated Prices: Traditional regulation of distribution and transmission rates remains critical to maintaining consumer confidence. The task of regulator must surely be to find the appropriate balance between the objectives of maintaining the health of regulated entities while protecting consumers, thereby reducing uncertainty for both.

Promoting Industry Health: The consumers want assurances that power and gas will be available when needed, that price changes will be moderate and that market competition will be fair and managed in the public interest. It is the responsibility of regulator to create the policies and conditions needed to support the industry so that these objectives are achieved.

Policing Interactions with Consumers: With increased exposure to numerous energy retailers, consumers are facing a daunting array of complex products and sales approaches. It is now the added responsibility of regulator to define the terms of this trade and to monitor and, if necessary, discipline the participants who are not in compliance with the rules. To this end, the regulator license retailers and suppliers, have instituted Codes of Conduct that serve to protect consumers.

Regulation quality can be assessed by applying scores for criteria indicated above. Table 42 presents the scores for the assessing quality of regulation [222].

Table 42. Scores for assessing the quality of regulation

Indicators	**Scores**
Barriers to Entry	(1 = no barriers to entry; 0=otherwise)
Cross-subsidies	(1 = no cross subsidies; 0=otherwise)
Collusion	(1 = credible monitoring of collusion; 0 = otherwise)
Investor Confidence	(1 = high investor confidence; 0=otherwise)
Asset Management	(1 = no barriers to entry; 0=otherwise)
Price Behavior and Contract Structures	(1 = the regulator is able to ensure that the markets are sufficiently competitive; 0=otherwise)
Public Confidence	(1 = high public confidence; 0=otherwise)
Independent non-regulatory environmental variables	(1 = high independence; 0=otherwise)
Controlling Regulated Prices	(1 = efficient control of regulated prices; 0 = otherwise)
Promoting Industry Health	(1= regulator is able to create the policies and conditions needed to support the industry; 0 = otherwise)
Policing Interactions with Consumers	(1 = the regulator is able to discipline the participants who are not in compliance with the rules; 0 = otherwise)

Source: [222].

The 11 indicators of quality of regulation provide the scoring of countries in terms of quality of regulation. The scoring from 11 to 7 provides for high quality of regulation and scoring from 6 to 0 – for pour quality of regulation [223].

All six regulatory coefficients: for separating generation from transmission, allowing TpA to the transmission grid, allowing the wholesale and retail electric power market, the quality of regulator and privatization should lead to higher ranking of countries in terms of EU EPPI.

The regulatory variables in Steiner model focus on the key economic regulation needed to establish competitive generation sector- vertical unbundling of the generation system from the transmission system, whether third parties can access the transmission system, and whether a wholesale market exists. Dummy variables are used to indicate 4 key economic regulations needed to establish a competitive generation sector: Unbundling of generation from transmission (R01); Third-party access (R02); Wholesale competition (R03); Retail competition (R04). As quality of regulation has an important impact on effective functioning of electric power market the fifth independent regulatory indicator Quality of regulation (R05) also is included in Steiner model as dummy variable. The sixth independent regulatory variable Ownership (R06) is discrete variable. The prepared model as in the case of Steiner's also includes 3 non-regulatory variables – the share of electric power generated from hydro (NR07); the share of electric power generated from nuclear (NR08) and the GDP (NR09). The two share variables reflect differences in generating technologies across economies which affect the marginal costs and hence the price of generating electric power. Finally, the inclusion of GDP adjusts for differences in the size of economies and is also an overall measure of national income [223]. The model was tested for Lithuania for the period 1990-2012. Data for Lithuania provided in Table 43.

Table 43. Data for Steiner model (Lithuanian case)

t	Year	EPPI	R01	R02	R03	R04	R05	R06	NR07	NR08	NR09
1	1990	0.33	0	0	0	0	0	0	1.81	51.19	10395
2	1991	0.33	0	0	0	0	0	0	1.5	57.9	10287
3	1992	0.33	0	0	0	0	0	0	1.7	78.9	8562
4	1993	0.39	0	0	0	0	0	0	2,8	88	7424
5	1994	0.39	0	0	0	0	0	0	4.6	79	6958
6	1995	0.4	0	0	0	0	0	1	2.8	85.8	7904
7	1996	0.42	0	0	0	0	0	1	2	83.6	8429
8	1997	0.43	1	0	0	0	0	1	2	79	10128
9	1998	0.46	1	0	0	0	0	1	2.4	75.4	11254
10	1999	0.45	1	0	0	0	0	2	3.2	75.7	10971
11	2000	0.45	1	0	0	0	0	2	3	65	11500
12	2001	0.48	1	0	0	0	1	2	4.7	45.7	12219
13	2002	0.47	1	1	0	0	1	2	4.4	75.9	14251
14	2003	0.49	1	1	0	0	1	2	5	79.4	18704
15	2004	0.53	1	1	1	0	1	2	4.9	78.4	22654
16	2005	0.48	1	1	1	0	1	2	5.5	70	26094
17	2006	0.49	1	1	1	0	1	3	6.5	27.2	30250
18	2007	0.52	1	1	1	0	1	3	7.1	27	39329
19	2008	0.56	1	1	1	0	1	2	7.1	26	47486
20	2009	0.58	1	1	1	0	1	2	7.4	0	37067
21	2010	0.62	1	1	1	1	1	2	22.5	0	36568
22	2011	0.66	1	1	1	1	1	2	21.8	0	42861
23	2012	0.63	1	1	1	1	1	2	21.7	0	42234

Source: [223].

As one can see from information provided in Table 43 the impact of electric power market liberalization on EU EPPI index is assessed by several independent energy market liberalization variables. In our case these variables are mostly dummy variables. The linear regression model was applied. For the analysis of linear regression the discrete variable R06 (Ownership) was replaced by 4 fictitious dummy: U1, U2, U3, U4 (Table 44). The dummy variable U4 was not analysed as the private ownership value for Ownership indicator (R06 = 4) was not available for Lithuanian data (Table 43).

Table 44. The Fictitious variables for ordinal variables

Variable (U)	Private ownership	Mostly private ownership	Mixed ownership	Mostly public ownership	Public ownership
U1	0	1	0	0	0
U2	0	0	1	0	0
U3	0	0	0	1	0
U4	0	0	0	0	1

Source: [223].

The linear regression model according Steiner model was prepared based on Lithuanian data (Table 43):

$$EPPI=\alpha + \beta_1 R_{01} + \beta_2 R_{02} + \beta_3 R_{03} + \beta_4 R_{04} + \beta_5 R_{05} + \beta_{61} U_1 + \beta_{62} U_2 + \beta_{63} U_3 + \gamma_1 NR_{07} + \gamma_2 NR_{08} + \gamma_3 NR_{09} \quad (7)$$

Spearman's rank correlation coefficient allows us to identify whether two discrete variables relate in a monotonic function (i.e., that when one number increases, so does the other, or vice-versa). The close to 1 negative correlation; close to 0 - no linear correlation, close to 1 - positive correlation. If Spearman's rank correlation coefficient is lower than 0.1 – there is no correlation and if the value is in interval [0.1-0.4] – weak correlation, if the coefficient is in interval [0.4-0.6] – average correlation and if it is in interval [0.6-0.8] – strong correlation and very strong correlation exists when coefficient is higher than 0.8 [223].

The Spearman's rank correlation is provided in Table 45 and indicates the correlation between discrete variables however it does not provide for existence of causal relationships between variables [223].

As one can see from information provided in Table 45 there is strong correlation between variables N08 and N09 therefore because of multicollinearity just one of these variables needs to be included in linear regression (N09). One can notice that the closure of Ignalina NPP in 2008 has impact on reduction of GDP in Lithuania, i.e., reduction of the share of nuclear in electric power generation is directly related with GDP development trends in Lithuania [223].

As one can see from Table 45 there is strong correlation between variables R06 (ownership) and EPPI (Spearman's correlation coefficient =0.809). There is also strong correlation between all non regulatory variables (the share of hydro energy in electric power balance, the share of nuclear in electric power balance and GDP) and EPPI.

Table 45. Spearman's rank correlation between discrete variables of Steiner model

		EPPI	R06	NR07	NR08	NR09
	N	23	23	23	23	23
EPPI	Correlation Coefficient	1	0.808592	0.926679	-0.67238	0.913863
	Sig. (2-tailed)		3.03E-06	0.000001	0.00044	0.000001
R06	Correlation Coefficient	0.808592	1	0.770711	-0.54782	0.810758
	Sig. (2-tailed)	3.03E-06		1.68E-05	0.006809	2.71E-06
NR07	Correlation Coefficient	**0.926679**	0.770711	1	-0.65865	**0.841533**
	Sig. (2-tailed)	0.000001	1.68E-05		0.000632	0.000001
NR08	Correlation Coefficient	**-0.67238**	-0.54782	-0.65865	1	**-0.81794**
	Sig. (2-tailed)	0.00044	0.006809	0.000632	.	1.87E-06
NR09	Correlation Coefficient	**0.913863**	0.810758	0.841533	-0.81794	1
	Sig. (2-tailed)	0.000001	2.71E-06	0.000001	1.87E-06	

Source: [223].

Table 46. Unstandardized and standardized B coefficients for linear regression

Model		**Unstandardized Coefficients**		**Standardized Coefficients**		
		B	Std. Error	Beta	**t**	**Sig.**
6	(Constant)	0.295	0.013		23.253	0.000
	NR09	0.000	0.000	0.189	1.748	0.100
	U2	0.044	0.013	0.238	3.285	0.005
	U1	0.058	0.014	0.242	4.276	0.001
	NR07	0.019	0.005	1.315	3.877	0.001
	R04	0.209	0.075	0.770	2.801	0.013
	R01	0.035	0.015	0.178	2.410	0.028

Source: [223].

The standardized B coefficients for linear regression allow to define the independent variables having the highest impact on EPPI (Table 46).

The unstandardized coefficient of an independent variable (also called B or slope) measures the strength of its relationship with the dependent variable. It is interpreted as the size of the average difference in the dependent variable that corresponds with a one-unit difference in the independent variable. A coefficient of 0 means that the values of the dependent variable do not consistently differ as the values of the independent variable increase. In that case, we would conclude that there is linear relationship between the variables. The B column also shows the constant, a statistic indicating the intercept — the predicted value of the dependent variable when the independent variable has a value of 0. The intercept also has a significance level associated with it, but this statistic is usually ignored [223].

As linear regression analysis indicated that values of coefficients for other variables are not consistently differ as the values of the independent variable increase these variables are not included in Steiner model. The following model is obtained:

$$EPPI = 0{,}295+0{,}035R_{01} +0.209R_{04}+0{,}044U_1+0{,}019NR_{07}+1{,}6x10^{-6} NR_{09}. \quad (8)$$

As one can see from this linear regression (Table 46) the highest standardized B coefficient is obtained for variable NR_{07} (the share of hydro energy in electric power balance). As the share of hydro energy in electric power balance is also reflected in EPPI (as the share of renewables in electric power generation) therefore it is natural that this indicator has direct impact on development of EPPI therefore in the next stage just independent regulatory variables will be left in the Steiner model [223].

As one can see from Table 46 the independent regulatory variable R04 (Existence of retail market) has also strong impact on EPPI.

For assessment of dummy variables impact on EPPI the mean statistics analysis was applied (Table 47).

Table 47. The mean values of dummy variables

Dummy variables	Values	N	Mean	Std. Deviation	Std. Error Mean
R01	1	16	0.5188	0.07117	0.01779
	0	7	0.3700	0.03873	0.01464
R02	1	11	0.5482	0.06646	0.02004
	0	12	0.4050	0.05300	0.01530
R03	1	9	0.5633	0.06384	0.02128
	0	14	0.4157	0.05598	0.01496
R04	1	3	0.6367	0.02082	0.01202
	0	20	0.4490	0.07254	0.01622
R05	1	12	0.5425	0.06635	0.01915
	0	11	0.3982	0.04976	0.01500

Source: [223].

As one can see from information provided in Table 47 the dispersions of all variables are equal therefore the hypothesis about their equality is not being rejected [223].

In Table 48 the statistical significance analysis of mean differences by testing hypothesis about equalities of dispersions is being provided. First of all hypothesis about equality of mean differences is being tested. As obtained p values (the probability to make mistake by rejecting the null hypothesis) is lower than 0.005, therefore for each regulated variable mean differences are statistically significant.

In the last column of Table 48 the confidence intervals of the mean differences are presented, for example for variable R02 (Third party Access to the grid) the mean difference is (0.5482-0.4050) = 0.14318, therefore with probability of 95% we can say that mean difference for population is in interval [0.09128-0.19508] and is statistically significant [223].

Table 48. Levene's Test for Equality of Variances

	Levene's Test for Equality of Variances		t-test for Equality of Means						
	F	Sig.	t	df	P values Sig. (2-tailed)	Mean Difference	Std. Error Difference	95% Confidence Interval of the Difference	
								Lower	Upper
R01	2.770	0.111	5.160	21	0.000	0.14875	0.02883	0.08880	0.20870
R02	1.121	0.302	5.737	21	0.000	0.14318	0.02496	0.09128	0.19508
R03	0.245	0.625	5.846	21	0.000	0.14762	0.02525	0.09511	0.20013
R04	2.739	0.113	4.374	21	0.000	0.18767	0.04291	0.09844	0.27689
R05	1.784	0.196	5.856	21	0.000	0.14432	0.02464	0.09307	0.19557

Source: [223].

Therefore the analysis of mean difference presented in Tables 44-45 indicated that existence of all independent regulatory variables (R01, R02, R03, R04, R05) expressed as dummy variables has positive impact on increase of EPPI.

As the share of hydro energy in electric power balance is also reflected in EPPI (as the share of renewables in electric power generation, %) in the next stage just independent regulatory variables are left in the Steiner model. The standardized B coefficients for new linear regression are developed in Table 49. The linear regression can be applied for forecast of EPPI in the future. It presents the relationship between EPPI and independent regulatory variables [223].

Table 49. Unstandardized and standardized B coefficients for linear regression

	Unstandardized Coefficients		Standardized Coefficients		
	B	Std. Error	Beta	t	Sig.
(Constant)	0.398	0.018		22,370	0.000
R05	0.144	0.025	0.788	5,856	0.000
(Constant)	0.398	0.013		30,410	0.000
R05	0.113	0.020	0.616	5,786	0.000
R04	0.126	0.029	0,462	4,337	0.000
(Constant)	0.370	0.013		28,491	0.000
R05	0.064	0.021	0.347	3,081	0.000
R04	0.126	0.023	0.462	5,481	0.000
R01	0.078	0.022	0.390	3,599	0.002

Source: [223].

Therefore new linear regression has been developed:

$$EPPI = 0,370+0,078R_{01}+0,126R_{04}+0,064R_{05}. \quad (9)$$

As one can see from information provided in Table 49 the biggest impact on EPPI development has independent regulatory variable R04 (Existence of retail market). The other independent regulatory variables R01 (Unbundling of generation from transmission) and Quality of regulation (R05) have also significant impact on EPPI [223].

As values of other coefficients differ from 0 not statistically significant therefore these independent regulatory variable R02 (Third party access to the grid) and R03 (Existence of wholesale market) are not included in the Steiner regression.

The main conclusion based on analysis of electric power market development in Lithuania by applying Steiner model is the following: the biggest impact on competiveness of Lithuania measured by EPPI during the period of 23 years (1990 -2012) has the unbundling of generation from transmission (R01), introduction of retail market (R04) and quality of regulation (R05). The statistical analysis indicated that it is not possible to define that other regulatory variables such as wholesale market and third party access to the grid and privatisation have positive impact on growth of competitiveness of Lithuania. Therefore in the energy market opening in other sectors (natural gas and heat sector) the priorities should be allocated to unbundling of generation from transmission, introduction of retail market and quality of regulation [223].

The Steiner model developed for Lithuania should be further applied for all EU member states having the longer experience of electric power market opening. The results obtained for other EU member states and their comparative analysis would provide for more robust results in assessments of electric power market opening on competitiveness.

CONCLUSION

Conducted scientific literature research suggests that natural monopoly is excluded from other monopolies because of the fact that it can satisfy the whole market demand with lower average costs than the costs of two or more companies, had they had to supply the same amount of production. It has some specific characteristics: there is only one supplier of the good/service; goods or services are provided for a large number of customers; company's goods or services do not have close substitutes; high sunk costs; cost function subaditivity; decreasing average costs (economies of scale).

After assessing the indicators of natural monopolies it was determined that due to the importance of services provided by natural monopolies for economic subjects and due to monopolistic power, it is necessary to have regulations on natural monopolies and the following goals of natural monopoly regulation are distinguished:

1. Protection of consumer interest, pursuant to ensure quality consumption:
   a. Ensure the supply of natural monopolies' goods and services, by satisfying the interest of the whole society, legal economic subjects and individuals.
   b. Ensure proper quality of provided goods and services by natural monopolies.
   c. Ensure "reasonable" price for provided goods and services by natural monopolies.
2. Ensurance of companies' financial stability.
3. Facilitation of competition between producers, service providers and with some exceptions – between consumers.
4. Gathering and distribution of reliable information.

The range of analyzed natural monopolies sectors has changed. The technological progress has eliminated such sectors as telecommunications, cable TV and partly postal service from the range of natural monopolies. Most attention in the recent years is payed to the research which focuses on such natural monopolies as electric power supply, gas supply and heating. Water supply and sewage disposal is still treated as natural monopoly, but studies on these natural monopolies are more relevant for less developed countries.

Consumption of services provided by natural monopolies creates a closed circle. It becomes obvious when we analyze the increase in prices of these services. The services of natural monopolies are more or less necessary for all economic subjects: for households – final product consumption, for production and other business subjects, as intermediate consumption good. In a long run, the producers transfer higher costs to the final price of the product; consequently, the prices of goods and services increase. Thus, internal demand declines due to two reasons: increase of households' expenses for natural monopoly's services and increase in prices for goods and services.

Natural monopolies affect the growth of the economy by enhancing the productivity of production factors and also by providing goods and services that ensure country's economic activity. Natural monopolies assist in enhancing company's production volumes in two ways: the services of natural monopolies are intermediate production costs, goods or services of natural monopolies enhance the productivity of other production factors (labor and others).

Natural monopolies have both positive and negative impact to the economy of the state. As positive it is emphasized the existence of natural monopolies as such. It means that the state is endowed with the main infrastructure and its services for citizens and industry. The negative consequences of the natural monopoly cover topics, related to the price of services: dead-weight loss, lack of motivation to innovate and improve efficiency and distribution of social income.

The impact of natural monopolies on country's competitiveness is definitely significant and is included in many assessment models and factors of competitiveness assessment indices. It can be assessed by considering not only the price of its goods or services, but also by emphasizing the existence of its services, stability and other aspects.

In the past, the electric power industry has been organized as vertically integrated monopolies that were sometimes also state owned. The growing ideological and political disaffection towards vertically integrated monopolies and the liberalization successes in other network industries have led to liberalization initiatives worldwide in the electric power industry.

Vertically integrated utilities have been vertically separated or unbundled and barriers to entry in generation and supply are being removed to create competition, seen as a vehicle to increase the competitiveness of the electric power industry.

The *first liberalisation directives* were adopted in 1996 (electric power) and 1998 (gas) and were to be transposed into Member States' legal systems by 1998 (electric power) and 2000 (gas). The *second liberalisation directives* were adopted in 2003 and were to be transposed into national law by Member States by 2004, with some provisions entering into force only in 2007. The Third electric power directive adopted in 2009 confirms the trend initiated by the precedent 2003 Directive of setting general guidelines for the government of the sector and further strengthens consumer protection, innovation and makes an attempt to merge national systems into one European electric power markets.

The EU Third energy package requires: from 2011 at the latest the companies generating and supplying energy, will have to be unbundled from the companies owing or controlling the energy transportation system according unbundling model selected by particular MS; Full ownership unbundling; The independent system operator (ISO) model- vertically integrated companies may retain ownership of their network assets but the network is managed by ISO which is completely separate from vertically integrate company and performs all functions of SO; The independent transmission operator (ITO) model ;-compromise which preserves integrated supply and transmission companies but requires such companies to ensure that two activities: supply and transmission are operated independently.

Lithuania has liberalized electric power market and the spot-electric power market started operating on the 1 st of January 2010. There are about 30 participants in the spot-market. The market opening rate was 54% in 2011 of total national energy consumption level, compared to 35% in 2010. In 2011 Lithuanian power market trade volume amounted to 8 TWh, i.e., 2% less than in 2010. In 2011 the average price on the BALTPOOL UAB power market was 45.24 EUR/MWh (3% lower than in 2010).

30 June 2011 marked an important development in the natural gas sector, namely the Law on Amendments to the Law on Natural Gas and the Law on Implementation of the Law on Natural Gas passed by the Seimas of the Republic of Lithuania. Thus the unbundling of assets, which is the first and the main activity model of unbundling of the Gas Transmission System Operator's activities provided for in the EU III Energy Package will be implemented. On 31 May 2012 the only vertically integrated company submitted an unbundling plan and an activity restructuring plan to the NCCPE. The plans stipulate that no later than by 31 July 2013 the company must have its natural gas activities unbundled legally, functionally and organizationally, and no later than by 31 October 2014 it must have its activities and controls unbundled.

District heat sector is not liberalized in Lithuania however there are plans to stimulate competitive activities, wherever possible and regulate monopolistic behaviour seeking to solve fundamental problems in the DH sector of Lithuania. The restructuring of district heat sector is foreseen in 2014. The regulation and control in district heat sector will be implemented seeking to reduce district heat prices for households.

The results of reviewed studies dealing with the impacts of liberalization on competitiveness showed that the development of liberalization models in electric power sector does not necessarily reduce electric power prices and can cause economic cycles. In fact, contrary to expectation in some cases prices had tendency to rise. Therefore more attention has to be paid to selection of a liberalization model and careful considerations should be given to the types of reforms that would best suit to expected priority goals of EU energy policy. In addition it is necessary to mention that the aims of EU energy policy are conflicting as the decrease of electric power prices which is the main indicator of competitiveness mitigates the effort to go forward for energy savings, for investments in renewable energy and other new energy saving technologies. The decrease of environmental impact is related with the increase of electric power prices and consequently with decrease in competiveness. Therefore some trade of between EU energy policy goals is necessary when deciding on electric power market liberalization model. The multi-criteria assessment framework can help in ranking energy liberalization models.

Only a few retail natural gas markets are completely deregulated, most have some form of end user protection, either temporarily or continuous. Consumer protection can take the form of a maximum price or allow consumers a choice between a regulated tariff and a free tariff or providing support for vulnerable customers. Some countries report large price differences in offers by suppliers to the benefit of the consumer who chooses the right supplier. Nevertheless switching rates are seldom very high although they do vary from country to country. Consumers are not always well aware of the possibility to switch and of which benefits can be gained—which is a concern to policymakers. On the other hand, until recently, choosing a new energy supplier is low on the priority list of consumers, even if it can save substantial amounts of money.

Previous research has shown the effects of liberalization of electric power and natural gas markets, but very little regarding District heat (DH) markets. Nevertheless, if there remains a strong political ambition to open up the DH market in a similar way as for electric power and natural gas markets, a reasonable suggestion form Swedish experience is to introduce TPA (at least initially) only in the local markets that are most likely to realize the expected competitive effects.

An important conclusion from Swedish DH liberalization experience is that regulated TPA may have small positive effects on competition, and at the same time it may have a significant impact on the possibility to run the integrated DH operations in a cost effective manner. This conclusion stems from several different observations: the first is that most DH networks are local in scope. Even if the networks are opened up for competition, it is likely that one company would still be dominant in the local market. Moreover, DH operations (production and distribution) are highly interdependent, this to a greater extent than, for instance, the corresponding operations in the electric power market. This means that changes in the organisation of the production mix may have a relatively large impact on system optimization throughout the network. A negotiated TPA and a single-buyer model could likely provide more efficient market designs, but also in these cases there would exist problems in achieving overall system optimization.

Previous empirical studies on relationship between energy market reforms and energy prices provided that relationships between energy market liberalization and electric power prices are complicated and reciprocal. In addition the impact on other important issues such as energy supply security, sustainability needs more broad investigations.

WEF report on Energy Architecture Performance Index (EAPI) ranks energy systems of 105 countries from an economic, environmental and energy security perspective. Norway, Sweden and France top the ranking according to EAPI.

The scores of electric power market liberalization for EU member states were developed based on simplified OXERA model and using the statistical data on energy provided by EUROSTAT.

Analysis of electric power market liberalization impact on EU energy policy priorities indicated that countries ranked with high energy market liberalization indicator developed by OREXA not necessarily have been ranked with high scores according the EU Energy Policy Performance Index (EPPI) providing for the evaluation of success of countries in implementing EU energy policy goals: competitiveness of the EU economy, environmental sustainability and security of energy supply.

The Steiner's model was applied to assess the impact of specific regulatory and non-regulatory variables on EU Energy policy performance index in Lithuania to define the impact of specific regulatory variables impact on competitiveness.

The analysis electric power market development in Lithuania by applying Steiner model revealed that the biggest positive impact on competiveness of Lithuania measured by EPPI during the period of 23 years (1990 -2012) has the unbundling of generation from transmission, introduction of retail market and quality of regulation.

The statistical analysis also revealed that it is not possible to define that other regulatory variables such as wholesale market and third party access to the grid and privatisation have positive impact on growth of competitiveness of Lithuania. Therefore in the energy market opening in other sectors (natural gas and heat sector) the priorities should be allocated to unbundling of generation from transmission, introduction of retail market and quality of regulation.

REFERENCES

[1] Easterly, W., Rebelo, S. (1993). Marginal income tax rates and economic growth in developing countries. *European Economic Review*, Elsevier, vol. 37(2-3), 409-417. doi: 10.1016/0014-2921(93)90029-A.

[2] Canning, D., Fay, M. (1993). *The effect of transportation networks on economic growth*. Working Paper, New York: Columbia University.

[3] Canning, D., Pedroni, P. (1999). *Infrastructure and long-run economic growth*. CAER II Discussion Paper, no. 57, Harvard Institute for International Development, US.

[4] Ely, R.T. (1894). Natural monopolies and the workingman. *The North American Review*, 158 (448): 294-303. Retrieved from https://archive.org/details/jstor-25103294

[5] Ely, R. T. (1937). *Outlines of Economics*. New York, Maximilian.

[6] Farrer, T. H. (1902). *The state in its relation to trade*. London, Kessinger Publishing.

[7] Baumol, W., J. (1977). On the proper cost tests for natural monopoly in a multiproduct industry. *The American Economic Review*, 67 (5), 809-822. Retrieved from http://www.jstor.org/discover/10.2307/1828065?uid=3738480&uid=2134&uid=2&uid=70&uid=4&sid=21104345995847

[8] Schmalensee, R. (1979). *The control of natural monopolies*. Lexington Books.

[9] Sharkey, W. W. (1982). *The Theory of Natural Monopoly*. Cambridge, Cambridge University Press.

[10] Berg, S.V., Tschirhart, J. (1988). *Natural monopoly regulation. Principles and practice*. Cambridge university press. doi:10.1017/CBO9780511572067.

[11] Foster, C.D (1992). *Privatization, public ownership and the regulation of natural monopoly*. Oxford, Blackwell.

[12] Wilson, J., Capelik, V. (1997). Natural monopolies in Russia. *Russian and East European Finance and Trade*, vol. 33, no. 2, 7-17. Retrieved from http://www.jstor.org/stable/27749383

[13] Depoorter, B. (1999). *Regulation of natural monopoly*. Centre for Advanced Studies in Law and Economics, University of Ghent. Retrieved from http://encyclo.findlaw.com/5400book.pdf

[14] Joskow, P. L. (2005). *Regulation of Natural Monopolies*. Center for energy and environmental policy research, April. Retrieved from http://dspace.mit.edu/bitstream/handle/1721.1/45038/2005-008.pdf?sequence=1

[15] Joskow, P.L. (2007). Regulation of Natural Monopoly. *Handbook of Law and Economics*, vol. 2, p. 1227-1348.

[16] Robins, C. (2006). *Regulating utilities and promoting competition*. Edward Elgar Pub.

[17] Mosca, M. (2008). On the origins of the concept of natural monopoly: Economies of scale and competition. *The European Journal of the History of Economic Thought,* 15:2, 317-353. doi: 10.2139/ssrn.975461.

[18] Samuelson, P.A. (1948). *Economics*. New York, McGraw-Hill.

[19] Gary, H., Wolff, P.E., Palaniappan, M. (2004). Public or private water management? Cutting the Gordian Knot. *Journal of Water Resources Planning and Management*. doi: 10.1061/(ASCE)0733-9496(2004)130:1(1).

[20] Posner, R. A. (1999). *Natural monopoly and its regulation.* Cato institute.

[21] Posner, R.A. (1969). Natural monopoly and regulation. *Stanford Law Review* 21, 548-643.

[22] Panzar, J.C., Willig, R.D. (1977). Free entry and the sustainability of natural monopoly. *Bell Journal of Economics* 8 (Spring), 1-22. Retrieved from http://www.jstor.org /stable/3003484

[23] Joskow, P.L., Noll, R.G. (1981). *Regulation in theory and practice: an overview NBER chapters.* Studies in Public Regulation, 1-78.

[24] Kahn, A.E. (1988). *The economics of regulation: principles and istitutions.* New York, John Wiley.

[25] Aktan, C.C. (2004). *Privatization & the Turkish experience*. Ankara, Seckin Yayincilik, Saglik Sokak.

[26] Aktan, C.C. (2005). *Perspectives on economics, politics and ethics*. Ankara, Seckin Yayincilik, Saglik Sokak.

[27] Samuel, G. (2004). Some thoughts on economics and regulation. *Economic Papers,* vol.2, no.1, 13-21. doi: 10.1111/j.1759-3441.2004.tb00349.x

[28] Auriol, E., Picard, P., M. (2008). *Infrastructure and public utilities privatization in developing countries.* The World Bank Economic Review, vol 23, no.1, 77-100. doi: 10.1596/1813-9450-3950

[29] Auriol, E., Picard, P.M. (2005). *Government outsourcing: public contracting with natural monopoly.* Discussion Paper 5643, Centre for Economic Policy Research, London. doi: 10.1111/j.1468-0297.2009.02291.x

[30] Chang, H., Mashruwala, R. (2006). Was the bell system a natural monopoly? An application of data envelopment analysis. *Springer Science*, 251-263. doi: 10.1007/s10479-006-0033-8.

[31] Filho, C.S. (2011). *A legal theory of economic power. Implications for social and economic development*. Massachusetts, Edward Elgar Publishing, Inc.

[32] Mizutani, F. (2012). *Regulatory reform of public utilities. The Japanese Experience.* Chelrenham, Edward Elgar Publishing Limited.

[33] Demsetz, H. (1968). Why regulate utilities? *Journal of law and economics,* no.11, 55-65. Retrieved from http://www.sfu.ca/~wainwrig/Econ400/documents/demsetz68-JLE-utilities.pdf.

[34] Comanor, W. S., Mitchell, B. M. (1970). *The economic consequences of the proposed FCC regulations on the CATV Industry*. Attachment A to National Cable Television Association.

[35] Jankauskas, V. (1997). *Ekonominis komunalinių įmonių reguliavimas.* Kaunas, Lietuvos energetikos institutas.

[36] Jankauskas, V. (2000). Infrastruktūros šakų pertvarka, konkurencijos įgyvendinimas. *Ekonomika,* 114-127. Retrieved from http://etalpykla.lituanistikadb.lt/fedora/get/LT-LDB-0001:J.04~2000~1367181137536/DS.002.0.01.ARTIC.

[37] Simanavičienė, Ž. (2002). *Valstybinis verslo reguliavimas.* Kaunas, Technologija.

[38] Moreau, F. (2004). The role of state in evolutionary economics. *Cambridge Journal of Economics,* 28, 847-874.

[39] Menezes, M., F. (2009). Consistent regulation of infrastructure businesses: some economic issues. *Economic papers*, vol. 28, no.1. March, 2-10. doi: 10.1111/j.1759-3441.2009.00002.x.

[40] Vickers, J., Yarrow, G. (1988). *Privatization: an economic analysis.* Cambridge, MA, USA: MIT Press.

[41] Bishop, M., Kay, J., Mayer, C. (1994). *Privatization and economic performance.* Oxford, Oxford University Press.

[42] Cho, D.S. (1994). The nine factor model, reprinted in Cho, D.S, Moon, C.H. (2005). From Adam Smith to Michael Porter. Evolution of Competitiveness Theory. *Asia-Pacific Business Series*, vol.2, 135-160.

[43] Rugman, A.M., D'Cruz, J. (1993). The "Double Diamond" model of international competitiveness: the canadian experience. *Management International Review*, 1993, vol. 33, 17-39. Retrieved from http://www.jstor.org/stable/40228188.

[44] Steiner, F. (2000). *Regulation, industry structure and performance in the electricity supply industry.* OECD Economics Department Working Papers no. 238. doi: 10.2139/ssrn.223648.

[45] Doove, S., Gabbitas, O., Nguyen-Hong, D., & Owen, J. (2001). Price effects of regulation: Telecommunications, air passenger transport and electricity supply. doi: 10.2139/ssrn.287800.

[46] Hogan S., Meade R. (2007). *Vertical integration and market power in electricity markets.* ISCR Working Paper, 1 May, Wellington, ISCR. Retrieved from https://editorialexpress.com/cgi-[1]bin/conference/download.cgi?db_name=NZAE2007&paper_id=89.

[47] Nagayama H. (2009). Electric power sector reform liberalization models and electric power prices in developing countries. An empyrical analysis using international panel data. *Energy Economics* 3, 463-472. doi: 10.1016/j.eneco.2008.12.004.

[48] Cournot, A.A. (1960). Recherches sur le principes mathematiques de la theorie des richesses. Translation: N.T. Bacon (Trans.) (1960). *Researches into the Mathematical Principles of the Theory of Wealth.* New York, Kelley.

[49] Mill, J.S. (1849). *The principles of political economy: with some of their applications to social philosophy.* London, JohnW. Parker.

[50] Walras, L. (1936). L'etat et le chemin de fer. Reprinted: (1936). *Etudes d'economie politique appliquee*. Paris: R. Pichon et. R. Durand-Auzias, 193-236.

[51] Edgeworth, R.Y. (1897). The pure theory of taxation. *The Economic Journal*, 7 (25), 46-70. Retrieved from http://www.jstor.org/discover/10.2307/2957242?uid=3738480&uid=2134&uid=2&uid=70&uid=4&sid=21104351861007.

[52] Smith, A. (1776). *An inquiry into the nature and causes of the wealth of nations.* London, W. Strahan & T. Candell.

[53] Malthus, T.R. (1969). *An inquiry into the nature and progress of rent, and the principles by which it is regulated.* New York: Greenwood Press.

[54] Bastiat, F. (1864). Harmonies economiques. *In oeuvres completes*, vol. VI, 5th ed. Paris: Guillaumin.

[55] Waterson, M. (1988). *Regulation of the firm and natural monopoly*. Oxford: Basil Blackwell. doi: 10.1002/mde.4090130113.

[56] Lowry, E.D. (1973). Justifications for regulation: The case for natural monopoly. *Public Utilities Fortnightly*, 92, (8 November), 17-23.

[57] Kahn, A.E. (2002). The regulatory tar baby: the precarious balance between regulation and deregulation, 1970-2000 and Henceforward. *Journal of Regulatory Economics*, vol 21, 35-56. doi: 10.1023/A:1013674607038.

[58] Jamison, M.,A. (1997). *A further look at proper cost rests for natural monopoly*. Public Utility Research Center, University of Florida. Retrieved from http://warrington.ufl.edu/centers/purc/purcdocs/PAPERS/9703_Jamison_A_Furthur_Look.pdf.

[59] Evans, D.S., Heckman, J.J. (1984). A test for subadditivity of the cost function with an application to the Bell System. *American Economic Review*, September, *74*(4), 615-623.

[60] Evans, D.S., Heckman, J.J. (1986). Erratum: a test for subadditivity of the cost function with an application to the Bell System. *American Economic Review*, September, *76*(4), 865-858.

[61] Shin, R.T., Ying, J.S. (1992). Unnatural monopolies in local telephone. *RAND Journal of Economics*, Summer 1992, *23*(2), 171-183. doi: 10.2307/2555982.

[62] Armstrong, T.O., Leppel, K. (1994). Are regulated and potentially unregulated combination gas and electric utilities natural monopolies? *Journal of Economics and Business*, August, *46*(3), 195-206. doi: 10.1016/0148-6195(94)90012-4.

[63] Tschirhart, J. (1995). Monopsony power and the existence of natural monopoly in energy utilities. *Resource and Energy Economics*, December, *17*(4), 327-340. doi: 10.1016/0928-7655(95)00008-9.

[64] Newbery, D. M. (1996). *Privatization, restructuring and regulation of network utilities*. Paper presented for The Walras-Pareto Lectures, University of Cambridge, June 17.

[65] De Viti de Marco, A. (1890). L'industria dei telfoni e l'esercizio di Stato. *Giornale degli econoimsti*, September, 279-306. Retrieved from http://www.jstor.org/discover/10.2307/23217809?uid=3738480&uid=2134&uid=2&uid=70&uid=4&sid=21104351861007.

[66] Marshall, A. (1890). *Principles of economics*. London. Macmillian.

[67] Kahn, A. E. (1970). *The Economics of Regulation*. Vol. 1 – Economic Principles. New York, John Wiley.

[68] Kahn, A. E. (1971). *The economics of regulation*. Vol. 2 – Institutional Issues. New York, John Wiley.

[69] Baumol, W. J., Panzar, J. C., Willing, R. D. (1982). *Contestable markets and the theory of industry structure*. New York, Harcourt Brace Jovanovich.

[70] Laffont, J.J., Tirole, J. (1993). *A theory of incentives in procurement and regulation*. Cambridge, MSA, MIT Press.

[71] Laffont, J. J., Tirole, J. (2000). *Competition in telecommunications*. Cambridge, MSA, MIT Press.

[72] Armstrong, M., Cowan. S., Vickers.J. (1994). *Regulatory reform: economic analysis and British experience.* Cambridge, The MIT Press. doi: 10.1016/S0167-6245(97)00022-X.

[73] Baumol, W., J., Bailey, E., E., Wilig, R.,D. (1977). Weak invisible hand theorems on the sustainability of multiproduct natural monopoly. *The American Economic Review*, 67 (3), 350-365. Retrieved from http://www.jstor.org/discover/10.2307/1831405?uid=3738480&uid=2134&uid=2&uid=70&uid=4&sid=21104345995847.

[74] Becker, G.S. (1997, October 6). There's nothing natural about "natural" monopolies. *Business Week, (Industrial/technology edition),* 3547, pp. 26.

[75] Dupuit, J. (1852). Peage. *In Dictionnaire de l'economie politique*, vol. 2, 339-344.

[76] Dupuit, J. (1852). Voies de communication. *In Dictionnaire de l'economie politique,* vol.2, 846-854.

[77] Berg S.,V., Tschirhart J. (1995). A market test for natural monopoly in local exchange. *Journal of Regulatory Economics,* 8,103-124. doi: 10.1007/BF01072585.

[78] Train, E. K. (1991). *Optimal regulation.* Cambridge, The MIT Press.

[79] Chadwick, E. (1859). Results of different principles of legislation and administration in Europe; of competition for the field, as compared with competition within the field, of service. *Journal of the Statistical Society of London*, 22(3), 381-420. doi: 10.2307/2338385.

[80] Ely, R.T. (1886). Social Studies. *Harper's New Monthly Magazine*, 73, (436)-571-8.

[81] Ely, R.T. (1889). The telegraph monopoly. *The North American Review*, 149 (392), 44-53. Retrieved from http://www.jstor.org/stable/25101819.

[82] Hadley, A.T. (1886). Private monopolies and public rights. *The Quarterly Journal of Economics*, 1(1),28-44. Retrieved from http://www.jstor.org/stable/1883107.

[83] Adams, H. C. (1954). *Relation of the state to industrial action and Economics and jurisprudence: two essays.* Columbia University Press. Retrieved from Retrieved from http://www.jstor.org/stable/2560515.

[84] Agrell, P. J., & Bogetoft, P. (2004). Nve network cost efficiency model. Report, *Norwegian Energy Directorate NVE*, SUMICSID AB. Retrieved from http://www.sumicsid.se/web-files/docs/projects/SUMICSID_Report_Efficiency_Model_2005.pdf

[85] Friedman, M. (1962). *Capitalism and Freedom.* University of Chicago press, Business and Economics.

[86] Uekusa, M. (1991). *Economis of Public Regulation (Koteki Kisei no Keizaigaku).* Tokyo, Japan: Chikuma Shobo (in Japanese).

[87] Uekusa, M. (2000). *Economic of Public Regulation (Koteki Kisei no Keizaigaku).* Tokyo, Japan: NTT Shuppan (in Japanese).

[88] Konig, A., Taylor, A. (2003). *Impact of the general agreement on trade in services on developing countries*, Water 21, February 03.

[89] Noll, R. (1989). Economic perspectives on the politics of regulation, in R. Schmalensee and R. Willig, *Handbook of Industrial Organization*, vol. II, 1254-82; Amsterdam, North-Holland.

[90] Berg, S. (2000). Developments in best practice regulation: principles, processes, and performance. *Electricity Journal*, July: 11-18. doi:10.1016/S1040-6190(00)00120-2.

[91] Kerf, M., David Gray, R., Taylor, R. (1998). *Concessions for infrastructure: a guide to their design and award.* World Bank Technical Papers. doi: 10.1596/0-8213-4165-0.

[92] Joskow P. (2006). Introduction of to electricity sector liberalization: lessons learned from cross countries studies, in Sioshansi, F. P. and W. Pfaffenberger (Eds.), *Electricity Market Reform: An International Perspective*. Oxford, Elsevier.

[93] Bergara, M., Henisz, W.J., Spiller, P.T. (1998). Political institutions and electric utility investment. *California Management Review,* 40 (2). doi: 10.1225/CMR100.

[94] Posner, R.A.(1971). Taxation by regulation. *The Bell Journal of Economics and Management*, vol. 2, no.1, 22-50. Retrieved from http://www.jstor.org/stable/3003161.

[95] Fama, E.F. (1980). Agency problems and the theory of the firm. *The Journal of Political Economy*, vol. 88, no. 2, 288-307. Retrieved from http://business.illinois.edu/josephm/BA549_Fall%202010/Session%205/Fama%20(1980).pdf.

[96] Stigler, G. (1971). The theory of economic regulation. *Bell Journal of Economics and Management Science*, 2 (1), 3-21. Retrieved from http://www.jstor.org/stable/3003160.

[97] Menard, C.J.D., Ghertman, M. (2009). *Regulation, deregulation, reregulation*. E. Elgar Pub.

[98] Kornai, J. (1980). *Economics of Shortage*. Amsterdam: North-Holland. Elsevier Science Ltd.

[99] Dewatripont, M., Maskin, E. (1995). Credit and efficiency in centralized and decentralized economies. *Review of Economic Studies,* 62(4), 514-55. doi: 10.2307/2298076.

[100] Maskin, E. (1999). Nash equilibrium and welfare optimality. *Review of Economic Studies*, 66, 23–38. doi: 10.1111/1467-937X.00076.

[101] Kagami, M. Tsuji, M. (2000). *Privatization, deregulation and economic efficiency: a comparative analysis of Asia, Europe and the Americas*. Northampton, MA. USA, Edward Elgar.

[102] Kornai, J. Weibull, J.W. (1983). Paternalism, buyers' and sellers' market. *Mathematical Social Sciences* 6, 153-169. doi: DOI 10.1016/0165-4896(83)90003-3.

[103] Shleifer, A., Wishny, R.W. (1997). A survey of corporate governance. *The Journal of Finance*, vol. 52 no.2, 737-783. doi: 10.1111/j.1540-6261.1997.tb04820.x.

[104] Shapiro, C., Willig, R.D. (1990) Economic rationales for the scope of privatization. In E.N. Suleiman and J. Waterbury (Eds.), *The Political Economy of Private Sector Reform and Privatization*. Boulder, CO: Westview Press.

[105] Megginson, W. L., Netter, J.M. (2001). From state to market: a survey of empirical studies on privatization. *Journal of Economic Literature* XXXIX, 321–389. doi: 10.2139/ssrn.262311

[106] OECD (1992). *Regulatory Reform, Privatisation and Competition Policy*. Paris, OECD.

[107] Williamson, B., & Mumssen, Y. (2000). *Economic regulation of network industries* (No. 00/05). New Zealand Treasury.

[108] Pajarskas, Š. (1991). *Kontraktinė kainodara ir valstybinis reguliavimas*. Vilnius, Baltikon.

[109] Mueller, Charles E. (1996). *Antitrust overview.* Antitrust Law and Economics Review. Retrieved from http://www.faqs.org/abstracts/publication/antitrust-law-and-economics-review-1996/

[110] Leibenstein, F. (1966). Allocative efficiency vs. X-efficiency. *The American Economic Review*, vol. 56, no. 3, 392-415. Retrieved from http://www.jstor.org/stable/1823775.

[111] Zupan, M., A. (1990). On cream skimming, coase and the sustainability of natural monopolies. *Applied Economics*, 22(4) 487-492. doi: 10.1080/00036849000000006.

[112] Parker, D. (2002). Economic regulation: a review of issues. *Annals of Public and cooperative economics 73,* 4, 493-519. doi: 10.1111/1467-8292.00202.

[113] Winston, C. (1993). Economic deregulation: days of reckoning for microeconomists. *Journal of Economic Literature.* vol. 31 no.3, 1263-1289. Retrieved from http://www.jstor.org/stable/2728241.

[114] Winston, C., Peltzman, S. (2000). *Deregulation of Network Industries.* AEI-Brookings Joint Center for Regulatory Studies, Virginia University.

[115] Averch, H., Johnson, J.L. (1962). Behavior of the firm under regulatory constraint. *American Economic Review,* 52, December, 1052-1069. Retrieved from http://pascal.iseg.utl.pt/~carlosfr/ses/averch_johnson.pdf.

[116] Tamonis, M., Kveselis, V., Tutlytė, O. (2002). Kainų reguliavimo pasekmės šilumos tiekimo įmonių veiklos efektyvumui. *Organizacijų vadyba: sisteminiai tyrimai,* 9-21. Retrieved from http://etalpykla.lituanistikadb.lt/fedora/get/LT-LDB-0001:J.04~2002~1367183092694/DS.002.0.01.ARTIC.

[117] Stern, J., Cubbin, J. (2005). *Regulatory effectiveness: the impact of regulation and regulatory governance arrangements on electricity industry outcomes.* Policy Research Working Paper Series 3536, The World Bank. doi: 10.1596/1813-9450-3536.

[118] Vilpišauskas, R. (2004). Tarptautinis konkurencingumas ir Lietuvos eksporto politika. *Pinigų studijos. Vilnius*: Lietuvos bankas, (1), 54-69.

[119] Donahue, J. D. (1989). *The privatization decision: public ends, private means.* USA, Basic Books.

[120] Gomez-Ibanez, J.A., Meyer, J.R. (1993). *Going private: the international experience with transport privatization.* Washington, D.C., USA, Brookings Institution.

[121] Ramamurti, R. (1996). *Privatizing monopolies: lessons from the telecommunications and transport sectors in Latin America.* Baltimore, ML, USA, The Johns Hopkins University Press.

[122] Parker, D. (1998). *Privatisation in the European Union: theory and policy perspectives.* London, UK, Routledge.

[123] Redwood, J., Hatch, J. (1982). *Controlling public industries.* Oxford, Blackwell.

[124] Estache, A., V. Foster, Wodon, Q. (2002). *Accounting for poverty in infrastructure reform: learning from Latin America's experience.* Studies in Development Series, Washington, World Bank Institute. Retrieved from Retrieved from http://www-wds.worldbank.org/external/default/WDSContentServer/WDSP/IB/2002/04/26/000094946_02041304004943/Rendered/PDF/multi0page.pdf.

[125] Growitsch, C., & Wein, T. (2005). Negotiated third party access—an industrial organisation perspective. *European journal of law and economics, 20*(2), 165-183.

[126] Pittman, R. (2003). Reform of the regies autonomes: should Romania follow the new orthodoxy of vertical separation? *Economica* 12, 159-182.

[127] Geradin, D., Kerf, M. (2003) *Controlling market power in telecommunications, antitrust vs sector-specific regulation.* Oxford, Oxford University Press. doi:10.1093/acprof:oso/9780199242436.001.0001.

[128] OECD (1997). *The OECD Report on Regulatory Reform: Synthesis Report.* Retrieved from: http://www.oecd.org/gov/regulaotry-policy/2391768.pdf.

[129] Baumol, W.J.; Sidak, J.G. (1995). *Transmission pricing and stranded costs in the electric power industry.* Washington DC, The AEI Press.

[130] Joskow, P. (2008). *Challenges for creating a comprehensive national electricity policy.* Working Papers 0819, Massachusetts Institute of Technology, Center for Energy and Environmental Policy Research. Retrieved from http://economics.mit.edu/files/3236.

[131] Borenstein, S., Bushnell, J. (2000). *Electricity restructuring: deregulation or reregulation?* Working Paper Series, Competition Policy Center, Institute for Business and Economic Research, UC Berkeley. Retrieved from http://www.ucei.berkeley.edu/ucei/bushnell/cato.pdf.

[132] Haney, A.B., Pollitt, M.G. (2011). Exploring the determinants of "best practice" benchmarking in electricity network regulation. *Energy Policy*, Elsevier, vol. 39(12), 7739-7746. doi: 10.1016/j.enpol.2011.09.018

[133] Joskow, P. (2006). *Vertical integration.* Retrieved October 15, 2011, from Retrieved from http://www.quickmba.com/strategy/vertical-integration/.

[134] Joskow, P. L., Schmalensee, R. (1986). Incentive regulation for electric utilities. *Yale Journal on Regulation*, 4, 1–49.

[135] Haney, A.B., Pollitt, M.G. (2009). Efficiency analysis of energy networks: An international survey of regulators. *Energy Policy*, Elsevier, vol. 37(12), 5814-5830. doi: 10.1016/j.enpol.2009.08.047.

[136] Kopsakangas-Savolainen, M., & Svento, R. (2010). Comparing welfare effects of different regulation schemes: an application to the electricity distribution industry. *Energy Policy,* 38(11), 7370-7377.

[137] Laffont, J.J., Tirole, J. (1986). Using cost observation to regulate firms. *Journal of Political Economy*, vol. 94, no. 3, part 1, 614-641. Retrieved from http://www.jstor.org/stable/1833051.

[138] Rogerson, W. P. (2003). Simple menus of contracts in cost-based procurement and regulation. American Economic Review, 919-926.

[139] Littlechild, S. C. (1983). *Regulation of British Telecommunications' profitability: report to the Secretary of State, February 1983.* Department of Industry.

[140] Jamasb, T., & Pollitt, M. (2003). International benchmarking and regulation: an application to European electricity distribution utilities. *Energy Policy,* 31(15), 1609-1622. doi: 10.1016/S0301-4215(02)00226-4.

[141] Armstrong, M., Sappington, D. (2006) Regulation, competition and liberalization. *Journal of Economic Literature,* 44, 325-366. doi: 10.1257/jel.44.2.325.

[142] Becker, G.S. (1976, August). Comment. *Journal of Law and Economics*, 19 (2), pp. 245-48.

[143] Becker, G.S. (1983). A theory of competition among pressure groups for political influence. *Quarterly Journal of Economics*, 98 (3), 371-400. doi: 10.2307/1886017.

[144] Stigler, G., Friedland, C. (1962). What can regulators regulate? The case of electricity. *Journal of Law and Economics*, 5 (October), 1-16. Retrieved from http://www.jstor.org/stable/725003.

[145] Peltzman, S. (1993). George Stigler's contribution to the economic analysis of regulation. *Journal of Political Economy,* 818-832. Retrieved from http://www.jstor.org/stablc/2138597.

[146] Peltzman, S., Levine, M. E., & Noll, R. G. (1989). The economic theory of regulation after a decade of deregulation. *Brookings Papers on Economic Activity. Microeconomics,* 1-59. doi: 10.1093/acprof:oso/9780198765295.003.0003

[147] Levy, B., Spiller, P.T. (1994). The institutional foundations of regulatory commitment: a comparative analysis of telecommunications regulation. *Journal of Law, Economics, Organization*, vol. 10, no. 2, 201-246.

[148] Joskow, P. L. (1974). Inflation and environmental concern: structural change in the process of public utility price regulation. *Journal of Law and Economics*, University of Chicago Press, vol. 17(2), 291-327. doi: 10.1086/466794.

[149] Simon, H. (1959). Theories of decision-makinig in economis and behavioral science. *American Economic Review* 49 (June), 253-283. doi: 10.2307/1809901

[150] Cyert, R., March, J. (1963). *A behavioral theory of the firm*. Englewood Cliffs, NJ: Prentice Hall.

[151] Nelson, E., Winter, S. (1973). *An evolutionary theory of economic change*. Cambridge, MA, Harvard University Press.

[152] IHT (France), 27 September 2007.

[153] Guasch, J. L. (2004). *Granting and renegotiating infrastructure concessions: doing it right*. World Bank Publications.

[154] Guasch, J. L., Laffont, J. J., & Straub, S. (2007). Concessions of infrastructure in Latin America: Government-led renegotiation. *Journal of Applied Econometrics*, 22(7), 1267-1294.

[155] Acemoglu, D., & Ozdaglar, A. (2007). Competition and efficiency in congested markets. *Mathematics of Operations Research*, 32(1), 1-31. doi: 10.3386/w11201.

[156] Zakem, A.J. (1991). Competition and survival in the electric generation market. *Public Utilities Fortnightly*, December 1, 128(11), 23-26.

[157] Stevenson, R.E., Penn, D. W. (1995). Restructuring the electric utility industry. *Land Economics*, August 71(3), 354-367.

[158] Bushnell J., Mansur, E., Saraavia, T. (2008). Vertical arrangements, market structure and competition: an analysis of restructured US electricity markets. *American Economic Review* 98(1), 237-266. doi: 10.3386/w13507.

[159] Bradley, S., Hausman, J., Nolan, R. (1993). Global competition and technology. Bradley, S., Hausman, J., Nolan, R. (Eds.), *Globalization, technology, and competition: the fusion of computers and telecommunications in the 1990's*. 1993.3-32. Boston, Harvard Business School Press.

[160] Ohmae, K. (1991). *The Borderless World*. New York, HarperCollins.

[161] Thierer, A.D. (1994). Unnatural monopoly: critical moments in the development of the Bell System monopoly. *Cato Journal*, vol. 14, no.2, 267-285. Retrieved from http://object.cato.org/sites/cato.org/files/serials/files/cato-journal/1994/11/cj14n2-6.pdf

[162] Rioja, F.K. (2003). The penalties of inefficient infrastructure. *Review of Development Economics*, 7(1), 127-137. Retrieved from http://www1.worldbank.org/publicsector/pe/pfma06/rioja-penalties.pdf

[163] Metraštis, L. S. (2004). Statistical yearbook Lithuania 2005/Lietuvos Statistikos departamentas. *Vilnius: Lietuvos Statistikos deparatmentas.*

[164] Metraštis, L. S. (2007). Statistical yearbook Lithuania 2005/Lietuvos Statistikos departamentas. *Vilnius: Lietuvos Statistikos deparatmentas.*

[165] Metraštis, L. S. (2010). Statistical yearbook Lithuania 2005/Lietuvos Statistikos departamentas. *Vilnius: Lietuvos Statistikos deparatmentas.*

[166] Metraštis, L. S. (2013). Statistical yearbook Lithuania 2005/Lietuvos Statistikos departamentas. *Vilnius: Lietuvos Statistikos deparatmentas.*

[167] Kuodis, R. (2010). *Energetinės nepriklausomybės ir energetikos reguliavimo ekonomika*. LPK konferencija, 2010 11 25.

[168] Official Statistics Portal (2014). Retrieved from: http://osp.stat.gov.lt/en/rodikliai56.

[169] Cibinskiene, A. (2010). Empirical study of infrastructure natural monopolies prices impact to country's competitiveness. *Economics and management*, no. 15, 55-61.

[170] Porter, M.E. (1990). *The competitive advantage of nations*. Reprinted in 1998 by Palgrave.

[171] Lengyel, I. (2003). *Economic growth and competitiveness of Hungarian regions*. Paper prepared for "Reinventing Regions in the Global Economy" RSA Conference, 12th – 15th April 2003, Pisa, Italy, p. 18. Retrieved from http://www2.eco.u-szeged.hu/region_gazdfejl_szcs/pdf/Economic_growth_and_competitiveness_of_Hungarian_regions.pdf

[172] de Vet, J. M., Baker, P., Dalgleish, K., Pollock, R., Healy, A. (2004). *The competitiveness of places and spaces*: A Position Paper. Rotterdam/Leeds/ Birmingham/Brussels.

[173] Gardiner, B., Martin, R., Tyler, P. (2004). *Competitiveness, productivity and economic growth across the European Regions*. ERSA conference papers from European Regional Science Association, 36. Retrieved from http://www.camecon.com/ economic_intelligence_services/eu_regional/downloadable_files/Regional%20Comp12 FEb%20copy.pdf 10.1080/0034340042000292638

[174] Atkočiūnienė, V. (2009). Kaimo vietovių konkurencingumą lemiantys veiksniai. *Ekonomika ir vadyba: aktualijos ir perspektyvos*, 3 (16). 49–59, Retrieved from http://vddb.library.lt/fedora/get/LT-eLABa-0001:J.04~2010~ISSN_1648-9098.N_3_16.PG_49-59/DS.002.0.01.ARTIC

[175] Jatuliavičienė, G., & Kučinskienė, M. (2010). Competitiveness and innovation synthesis in the integrated global economy. Ekonomika*: mokslo darbai. Vilniaus universitetas, Vilnius,* 89(2), 76-94.

[176] World Economic Forum (2013). The Global Competitiveness Report (2012–2013). Retrieved from http://www3.weforum.org/docs/WEF_GlobalCompetitiveness Report_2012-13.pdf

[177] World Economic Forum (2014). The Global Competitiveness Report (2013–2014). Retrieved from http://www3.weforum.org/docs/WEF_GlobalCompetitiveness Report_2013-14.pdf.

[178] World Economic Forum (2015). The Global Competitiveness Report (2014–2015). Retrieved from http://www.weforum.org/reports/global-competitiveness-report-2014-2015.

[179] IMD electronic source. (2014). Retrieved February 5, 2014, from: https://www.worldcompetitiveness.com/OnLine/App/Index.htm

[180] Statistics Lithuania (2012). *Energy Balance 2011*. Retrieved from: http://osp.stat.gov.lt/services-portlet/pub-edition-file?id=2148

[181] NCCPE (2010). Regulations of National Commission for Energy Control and Prices. Retrieved from: http://www.regula.lt.

[182] EUROSTAT (2010). Retrieved from: http://ec.europa.eu/eurostat/data/database.

[183] Statistics Lithuania (2013). Sustainable development indicators 2013. Retrieved from: http://osp.stat.gov.lt/services-portlet/pub-edition-file?id=2868.

[184] Statistics Lithuania (2016). *Energy Balances 2001-2005.* Retrieved http://osp.stat.gov.lt/services-portlet/pub-edition-file?id=10501.

[185] Statistics Lithuania (2008). *Energy Balance 2007.* http://osp.stat.gov.lt/services-portlet/pub-edition-file?id=12709.

[186] Statistics Lithuania (2010). *Energy Balance 2009.* http://osp.stat.gov.lt/services-portlet/pub-edition-file?id=14289.

[187] Newbery, D. (2002). *Issues and options for restructuring electricity supply industries.* Cambridge Working Papers in Economics 0210. CMI Working Paper CMI EP 01, Department of Applied Economics, University of Cambridge. Retrieved from https://www.repository.cam.ac.uk/bitstream/handle/1810/308/EP01.pdf?sequence=1.

[188] Lovei, L. (2000). *The single buyer model: a dangerous path toward competitive market.* The World Bank Group, Public Policy for the Private Sector, Note number 225.

[189] Nagayama, H. (2007). Effects of regulatory reforms in the electricity supply industry on electricity prices in developing countries. *Energy Policy.* no. 35, 3440–3462. Doi: 10.1016/j.enpol.2006.12.018.

[190] Garen, J., Jepsen, C., & Saunoris, J. (2011). The Relationship between Electricity Prices and Electricity Demand, Economic Growth, and Employment.

[191] Gil, J., and L. V. de Souza. "The Flight of the European Bumblebee." *Project Syndicate* (7 February) (2013).

[192] Bernanke, B. Gertler, M., Watson,M. (1997). *Systematic monetary policy and the effects of oil price shocks.* Presented at the Brookings Panel on Economic Activity, March 27-28, Washington, DC. Retrieved from http://econ.as.nyu.edu/docs/IO/9382/RR97-25.PDF.

[193] OECD (2001). *Report on Experiences with Structural Separation.* Retrieved from: http://www.oecd.org/daf/competition/50056685.pdf.

[194] Hattori, T., & Tsutsui, M. (2004). Economic impact of regulatory reforms in the electricity supply industry: a panel data analysis for OECD countries. *Energy Policy,* 32(6), 823-832.

[195] Zhang, Y. F., Parker, D., & Kirkpatrick, C. (2008). Electricity sector reform in developing countries: an econometric assessment of the effects of privatization, competition and regulation. *Journal of Regulatory Economics,* 33(2), 159-178.

[196] Fiorio, C. V., Florio, M., & Doronzo, R. (2007, June). The electricity industry reform paradigm in the European Union: testing the impact on consumers. In *Consumers and Utility Reforms in the European Union Conference.*

[197] Joskow, P.L. (2006). Markets for power in the U.S.: an interim assessment. *The Energy Journal,* 27(1): 1-36. doi: 10.2139/ssrn.845785.

[198] Kadoya, T., Sasaki, T., Ihara, S., Larose, E., Sanford, M., Graham, A. K., ... & Eubanks, C. K. (2005). Utilizing system dynamics modeling to examine impact of deregulation on generation capacity growth. *Proceedings of the IEEE, 93(11),* 2060-2069.

[199] Sweeney, J. L. (2002). The California Energy Crisis. *Journal of Energy Literature,* 8, 100-103.

[200] Roques, F. A., Newbery, D. M., & Nuttall, W. J. (2005). Investment incentives and electricity market design: the British experience. *Review of Network Economics, 4*(2).

[201] Sioshansi, F. P. (2008). Introduction: Electricity market reform—Progress and remaining challenges. *Competitive electricity markets: Design, implementation, performance.*

[202] Arango, S., & Larsen, E. (2011). Cycles in deregulated electricity markets: Empirical evidence from two decades. Energy Policy, 39(5), 2457-2466.Sweeney, 2002.

[203] Roques, F. A. (2008). Market design for generation adequacy: Healing causes rather than symptoms. *Utilities Policy, 16(3),* 171-183.

[204] Yarrow, G. (2008). *Report on the impact of maintaining price regulation.* Regulatory policy institute, Oxford, UK. Retrieved from http://www.aemc.gov.au/Media/docs/Prof%20Yarrow%20Report-80834941-a50a-4bcd-8b0c-184b30791b18-0.pdf

[205] UNECE (2012). The Impact of Liberalization of Natural Gas Markets in the UNECE region-Efficiency and Security. Retrieved from: http://www.unece.org/fileadmin/DAM/energy/se/pdfs/wpgas/pub/ImpactLibNGM_UNECE_EffSec.pdf.

[206] Westin, P., & Lagergren, F. (2002). Re-regulating district heating in Sweden. *Energy Policy, 30*(7), 583-596.

[207] Varian, H. R. (1996). Differential pricing and efficiency. *First Monday*, 1(2).

[208] Aronsson, B., & Hellmer, S. (2009). An international comparison of district heating markets. *Fjärrsyn Rapport*, 27.

[209] Söderholm, P., & Wårell, L. (2011). Market opening and third party access in district heating networks. *Energy Policy, 39*(2), 742-752.

[210] Grohnheit, P. E., & Mortensen, B. O. G. (2003). Competition in the market for space heating. District heating as the infrastructure for competition among fuels and technologies. *Energy policy, 31*(9), 817-826.

[211] Tennbakk, B. (2000). Power trade and competition in Northern Europe. *Energy policy*, 28(12), 857-866.

[212] Fridolfsson, S. O., & Tangerås, T. P. (2009). Market power in the Nordic electricity wholesale market: A survey of the empirical evidence. *Energy Policy, 37*(9), 3681-3692.

[213] Spanjer, A. (2007). Russian gas price reform and the EU–Russia gas relationship: Incentives, consequences and European security of supply. *Energy Policy,* 35(5), 2889-2898.

[214] Palm, J., & Magnusson, D. (2009). Medias rapportering om fjärrvärme: framställning och budskap nationellt och lokalt.

[215] Littlechild, S. C. (2001). *Electricity: regulatory developments around the world.* The Beesley Lectures on Regulation Series XI IEA/LBS, London 9 October. (Revised version 12 November 2001) Retrieved from http://www.hks.harvard.edu/hepg/Papers/Littlechild%2012-01%20Beesley%20lect.pdf.

[216] Newbery, D. M. (2001). Privatization, restructuring and regulation of network utilities. Cambridge, MA, MIT press.

[217] Roggenkamp, M. M., Boisseleau, F. (2005). The liberalization of the EU electricity market and the role of power exchanges, p. 1-28, in Roggenkamp M. M., Boisseleau F. (Eds), *The regulation of power exchanges in Europe.*

[218] Bergman, L.G., Brunekreeft, C., Doyle, von der Fehr, N-H., Newbery, D.M., Pollitt, M., Regibeau, P. (1999). *A European Market for Electricity?* London, Centre for Economic Policy Research.

[219] Glachant, J.M. (2001). Attractiveness and accessibility of 16 electricity markets in Western Europe, in E. Hope, L. Melamed and M. Lychagin (Eds.), *Electricity economics,* policies, Russion academy of sciences, 187-208.

[220] WEF (2012). The global energy architecture performance index report 2013. Retrieved February 15, 2014 from Retrieved from http://www.weforum.org/reports/global-energy-architecture-performance-index-report-2013.

[221] OXERA (2001). *Electricity liberalization indicators in Europe.* Retrieved from Retrieved from http://ec.europa.eu/energy/electricity/publications/doc/oxera_summary.pdf.

[222] Streimikienė, D., Bruneckienė, J., Čibinskienė, A. (2013). The review of electricity market liberalization impacts on electricity prices. *Transformations in business and economics*, 12 (3); 40-60.

[223] Streimikienė, D., Čibinskienė, A. (2015). Assessment of electricity market liberalization impact on success in avhieving EU energy policy targets in Lithuania, *Economic Computatution & Economic Cybernetics Studies & Research* 49(1); 1-20.

AUTHORS' CONTACT INFORMATION

Dr. Dalia Streimikiene,
Professor,
Mykolas Romeris University
Email: dalia@mail.lei.it

Dr. Akvile Cibinskiene,
Assoc. Professor,
Kaunas University of Technology
Email: akvile.cibinskiene@ktu.lt

INDEX